Praise for *Witness* and ⸻⸻ otkin

"Eric Sirotkin does what only the very best lawyers can do—transform combat into co-creation, aggression into appreciation, and ultimately fear into love. In *Witness*, he creates new and positive possibilities for his clients, their attorneys, and the world."

–Gary Zukav, author of *The Seat of the Soul*
and *The Dancing Wu Li Masters*

"Justice has always been a constant struggle and Eric Sirotkin exemplifies the type of lawyer activist that impacts hearts and minds and our world at large. *Witness* is a personal journey but one that reminds us all that we can make a difference."

–Paul Bardacke, former New Mexico Attorney General and mediator

"In a world driven by crass consumerism and conspicuous consumption, with an exaggerated emphasis on self indulgence and self fulfillment, Eric Sirotkin is that rarest of creatures: an internationalist in every best sense of that word; a champion of selfless service to others, performing great feats/deeds of self sacrifice. Eric is a grassroots intellectual, with a brilliant intellect and rare intellectual acuity and excellence, a great analytical mind and impeccable integrity. He is that rarest of lawyers, always being humble yet caring, placing his clients cause foremost; imbued by a great work ethic, and by always being the consummate professional. Eric epitomizes what I regard as the perfect progressive lawyer, by: firstly, regarding himself as a human being and humanitarian; secondly, as an activist (both socially and politically); and only, thirdly, as a lawyer."

–Johnny Delange member of Parliament South Africa 1996–
2016 and Chair of the Parliament Justice Committee

"The interest and support of your project has been a great encouragement to us at the Truth and Reconciliation Commission."

–Archbishop Desmond Tutu

"Your contribution and suggestions for the new constitution for South Africa have been very useful. I must say that your warmth and comradeship here in Cape Town was very much appreciated and has added to our faith in the struggle of the poor and the exploited."

–Dullah Omar South Africa Minister of Justice (1994 - 2005)

"The depth and sincerity of Eric Sirotkin's commitment to equality and human rights never ceases to amaze me. His capacity to communicate this knowledge in such a spell binding, down-to-earth and -easy-to-comprehend way is refreshing—a master in the art of reaching out and truly educating others."

–Frank Miranda, former SNCC activist and Director of the New Mexico Human Rights Office

"Eric Sirotkin is a leading attorney in the human rights arena. I have worked closely with him in recent years in the area of human rights and he has demonstrated to me the knowledge, insight and ability to relate to younger people."

–Prof. Arthur Kinoy, author of *Rights of Trial*

"Eric Sirotkin has delivered a powerful account of his extraordinary life of social advocacy. *Witness* will take its place amongst those rare stories that inspire us to take our own stand and join the heroes of the world who have always relied on the power of love and the justice of integrity to finally prevail against the forces that seek to divide us."

–Will Wilkinson, co-founder The Academy of Natural Wisdom, author of *Now or Never*

Witness

ERIC SIROTKIN

Witness

A Lawyer's Journey from Litigation to Liberation

White Cloud Press
Ashland, Oregon

White Cloud Press books may be purchased for educational, business, or sales promotional use. For information, please write: Special Market Department
White Cloud Press
PO Box 3400
Ashland, OR 97520
Website: www.whitecloudpress.com

Cover and Interior Design by Christy Collins, Constellation Book Services

First edition: 2017

Printed in the United States of America

17 18 17 18 19 20   10 9 8 7 6 5 4 3 2 1

Library of Congress Cataloging-in-Publication Data
Names: Sirotkin, Eric, author.
Title: Witness : a lawyer's journey from litigation to liberation / by Eric
 Sirotkin, with a little help from Nelson Mandela, Archbishop Desmond Tutu,
 the Dalai Lama, and the people of Cuba and North Korea.
Description: Ashland, Oregon : White Cloud Press, [2017]
Identifiers: LCCN 2017010443 | ISBN 9781940468488 (pbk.)
Subjects: LCSH: Sirotkin, Eric. | Lawyers--United States--Biography. | Civil
 rights lawyers--United States--Biography. | Mandela, Nelson, 1918-2013. |
 Tutu, Desmond. | Bstan-ídzin-rgya-mtsho, Dalai Lama XIV, 1935- | South
 Africa. Truth and Reconciliation Commission. | South Africa--Politics and
 government.
Classification: LCC KF373.S5695 A3 2017 | DDC 340.092 [B] --dc23
LC record available at https://lccn.loc.gov/2017010443

MIX
Paper from
responsible sources
FSC® C011935
www.fsc.org

Table of Contents

Introduction

*What is demanded is a change in our
imaginative picture of the world.*
—Bertrand Russell

Soweto, South Africa—February 17, 1991

A storm is brewing as South African Airways flight number 237 touches down at Jan Smuts International Airport. The armed struggle has been suspended and exiles are returning. Prisoner #46664, Nelson Mandela, is now free and thousands more have been granted indemnity, but most still await release. Descending from the plane it feels as if I'm stepping into the pages of history and witnessing the last gasp of apartheid.

I'm only thirty-four-years old, but have practiced civil rights law for nearly a decade. It's my first trip to South Africa and our group of American lawyers are set to meet Bheki Mlangeni, a human rights lawyer, as part of our work with the African National Congress (ANC) to create a Constitution for this fractured nation. Days before our arrival, Bheki receives a package containing a Walkman with a tape labeled, "Evidence of Death Squads." He dons his headset and pushes play. The immediate explosion kills him instantly, blows out one wall and every window of his home.

I learn of Bheki's death as we drive past his shattered home in Soweto. Pausing at the boarded-up windows, a chill runs through me as the violent death of a colleague brings the threat of violence closer to home. I feel shocked and on edge. Getting out of the van we're surrounded by dozens of children, and I notice our guides' tense faces as they anxiously watch in every direction looking for any signs of trouble. "If I say it's time to leave," Dumisa tells us, "you should move without haste back into the vans." This only deepens my fear and concern, but the children's wide eyes, laughter, and smiling faces are my saving grace, reminding me why I've come to South Africa.

Safely back at the hotel my shock and sadness at Bheki's death soon turns to anger. These enemies of freedom would stop at nothing to hold on to power. The white government has yet to agree to elections or reining in the secret police and I'm sure our presence is viewed by them as a threat. Am I safe? Bheki's murder was further brazen proof that apartheid's institutionalized separation feeds on blood and heartache. These people must not only be stopped but pay for their crimes. That's what my upbringing and legal training taught me, that to achieve justice you fight back. It was all I knew.

▼ ▼ ▼

Bophuthatswana, South Africa—April 27, 1994

Three years later freedom came at midnight to South Africa. I've returned as an International Election Monitor and I'm shivering as a cold wind gusts across my face and through the Mmbatho Plaza. Two soldiers, one black and one white, march toward the flag posts. The gathering of mostly black homeland residents watches transfixed as the two flags of the formerly fragmented South Africa are lowered, and the new united flag rises toward the sky. The words Seamus Heaney wrote to celebrate Mandela's release from prison run through my head: "once in a lifetime, the longed-for tidal wave of justice can rise up, and hope and history rhyme."

With fists raised to the sky we sing the new unified national anthem that includes *Nkosi Sikelel' iAfrika* (God Bless Africa) with its century-old motto of *Wisdom, unity and peace.* At that very moment the all-white Parliament and the all-black homeland are dissolved. As the last note of the new anthem sounds, bursts of shouts and whistles accompany spontaneous dancing. People orchestrate their own rhythmic celebration of freedom. Strangers embrace and we dance with each other. Individuals coalesce into a community. It's an explosion of joy.

The pain that so many endured made this transformation possible. It justifies the struggle against seemingly insurmountable odds, and if the walls of separation in South Africa could be brought down, I'm feeling anything is possible. Apartheid's chains had been wrapped around everyone's spirit, whether black or white, but tonight the people's spirits are soaring together. We're celebrating the end of apartheid, but it feels like a regeneration of my own heart. We all feel linked to one another and to the star-drenched sky above. Here at the tip of Africa a palpable feeling of unity rose like the harvest moon, illuminating new possibilities and hope for our fractured world.

Apartheid had separated more than racial differences. It suppressed something innate, a connection with one another. What I experienced in South Africa was an entirely new way of being and it felt contagious, exhilarating and frightening. I felt like I was undergoing an emotional transfusion. What was happening to me, and what would it mean? I realized I would have to change my life, my work, and relationships forever.

Years later, I learned that this had a name: *Ubuntu.*

▼ ▼ ▼

Witness is my story of discovering a world of new possibilities and finding a new skill set for living and working in the twenty-first century.

I'd been a warrior for justice. Success came from winning, exposing wrongdoing in corporations or challenging governmental malfeasance. Bringing generals, archbishops and CEOs to their knees made me feel powerful, like I was "doing something." It had become my drug of choice: like Kissinger —"the ultimate aphrodisiac."

Even before my sojourn to South Africa I had grown increasingly detached and restless. I knew something was missing. Were we as human beings destined to be combatants, finding satisfaction in vanquishing and defeating our enemies? Was I fueling a system that put us at odds with one another and the rest of the world? Having won the "battle," glancing back at the casualties along the way, I could not escape the feeling I'd lost my self along the way. Something deep inside me was whispering, we *all go to sleep dreaming of something greater.*

As a young teenager defying US foreign policy and later in the rough and tumble of New Mexico courtrooms, I'd felt passionate about changing the world. But later this craving for a more connected and humane story for my law practice, my own children, and the planet became my anchors. Through a remarkable web of human relationships, sages, and spiritual teachers, a new story—an era of *ubuntu*, wherein we understand our innate connection to one another—was unfolding for me.

Archbishop Desmond Tutu described it to me as the "essence of being human," and I took to applying it in the courtroom and in places of historic separation and heartache. From Washington to Havana, Soweto to Pyongyang, from the Punjab to the Navajo Nation, I learned that seeds of hope can bloom even against great odds. When I adopted *ubuntu* consciousness, conflict became constructive rather than destructive, hopeful rather than helpless—an opportunity for healing and my own transformation as a lawyer and as a human being.

Holding onto the dream of something greater can be challenging; my prayer is that my experiences will inspire you to create a new story for yourself and believe in your power to transform the world around you. It is the ultimate journey of the heart. Indigenous Grandmother Agnes Baker Pilgrim says: "The greatest distance in the world is the fourteen inches from our minds to our hearts." Here's how I learned to close the gap.

▾ ▾ ▾

PART I

The Art of War

Oh you masters of war

▾ ▾ ▾

I just want you to know
that I see through your masks
—Bob Dylan

CHAPTER 1

The Battle Begins

Because law, my boy, puts us into everything.
It's the ultimate backstage pass.
—Al Pacino in *The Devil's Advocate*

Albuquerque, New Mexico, Metropolitan Court—June 20, 1983
The arraignment courtroom began to shake. Deep in the basement of the Metropolitan Court I brace myself against the courtroom wall thinking earthquake or riot. Judge Smith is already on the bench when the door opens and in march my thirty-three clients singing loudly: *Going to lay down my sword and shield, down by the riverside. . . . Ain't going to study war no more.* A fearless choir saying to the system "We shall not be moved."

Before being dragged away by the police, my clients, ages eight to sixty, had laid down their bodies to blockade Albuquerque's Kirtland Air Force Base, where Sandia National Labs was housed, as part of a national Disarmament Day. The goal was to prevent workers, even for a few hours, from engaging in the research and development of first-strike nuclear weapons. President Reagan had just announced his Strategic Defense Initiative, or Star Wars plan, to counter the Soviet's "evil empire" and, as in my childhood, we were heading toward another missile crisis. So after they laid down, I stood up to represent them.

Law became my "backstage pass" to actively raise great questions before our institutions and question the powers that be. I'd been out of law school two years when I counseled the demonstrators on their rights to protest and now stood by them in court, flexing my new power as a lawyer, seeking to expose the madness, relishing every opportunity to fight the masters of war.

Judge Woody Smith, an eclectic slightly balding pony-tailed judge, appeared more at home in his band Woody and the Woodpeckers than in a judge's robe in Metropolitan Court. He sits with his robe half open as my clients enter the courtroom with such bravado after blockading the Air Force base. Unlike most judges, who would have gone ballistic, Woody, the consummate musician, perhaps tapping his foot under the bench, allows the demonstrators to at least finish the chorus before banging his gavel and calling the courtroom to order. It's electric.

On this hot summer evening, I can make out the blurry silhouettes of dozens of supporters outside the thick oblique glass of the visitor galley in the underground arraignment courtroom. Coming together with others to express solidarity of purpose is touching something deep within me. Across the country more than 1,500 protesters have been arrested for civil disobedience today at weapons plants, defense contractor facilities, and submarine bases. At Livermore Laboratories in California, as each row of demonstrators was arrested, another took their places, and they, too, were arrested. The process continued for more than six hours. It's a historic struggle to save the planet, energized by the force, power, and courage of the protesters and I'm proud to be their lawyer.

War with the Soviet Union is looming ominously as President Reagan's "first strike" strategy recklessly pretends that our country could actually win a nuclear war. At the push of a button the US and the U.S.S.R. are poised to destroy Earth many times over with their more than twenty thousand nuclear weapons of mass destruction ready to be launched from dozens of countries around the world. It's institutionalized insanity, with most Americans suffering from denial, succumbing to fear and helplessness, either adopting a duck-and-cover mentality or collectively ignoring reality like monkey figurines: see no evil, hear no evil.

Yet perhaps the tide is turning. Just last year on June 12, 1982 more than a million people marched in New York City in a call for nuclear nonproliferation and an end to these stockpiles of weapons. I felt inspired by the turnout and ready to support, encourage, and conspire with them in their battle for peace even if it meant the next step is to break the law. I can't help but wonder what would have happened if all one million of them sat down and refused to move until the madness ended.

Having participated for more than a decade in your run-of-the-mill peace marches, with singing, chants, slogans, and speeches, I've seen how easy it is for the government to ignore that one day of action, write it off as "fringe" elements, or even use it to praise our great democracy, while quietly firebombing a village on the other side of the planet. Villagers fleeing their home or losing a child likely coined the popular protest slogan: "This is what democracy looks like?"

The need for civil disobedience is rising and these arrests around the country today could be a reminder to people that we must take direct action to stop those who have been building the bombs in our name. Courage is contagious.

I'd organized a group of twenty local lawyers to be on hand for a show of legal force at the arraignment. Some of us had a history of protesting, but for most the closest experience with our nuclear madness was ducking and covering under their desks in grade school. As I watch them counsel their clients in all corners of the courtroom, the atmosphere is pulsating with power and intention.

In preparatory meetings and trainings weeks before Disarmament Day I'd discussed with the protestors the option of pleading not guilty and going to trial with a strategy of putting nuclear weapons and the system on trial. After all, the law provides a full defense if you're acting "to avert a greater evil." It's aptly called the "necessity defense." Laying down and blocking the production of nuclear weapons intended to be used in a first-strike war seemed not only justified but under international law a civic duty. I was chomping at the bit to publicly reveal the real criminals—the government and military industrial complex.

But taking such a risk is a highly personal choice. Charges carry possible jail time and fines, and officers often confuse noncooperation with resisting arrest. Courts have sometimes ruled disingenuously that a necessity defense applies to all criminal cases except protests. Many of our clients feel that their point has been made in the street and in the resulting media attention. Most have other jobs besides stopping nuclear war. As dozens start entering their "no contest pleas," I'm left wondering if I'll be able to extend the protest to the courtroom.

Judge Smith gives the thirty-one clients who didn't challenge the charges a deferred sentence, meaning "don't be blockading any Air

Force bases for ninety days or I'm goin' be really pissed." If the clients stay out of the street the charges go away. Other than a full dismissal of all charges, this type of deal on criminal charges stemming from civil disobedience is a blessing. But as we near the end of the group two very different defendants, a young, rebellious, lanky Dan Enright, and a greying portly minister, Les Dohner, take the leap, standing and boldly declaring, "Not guilty, your honor." My thirst for battle explodes and I'm smiling ear to ear. A glance from Judge Smith makes me think he heard me whisper: "Let the fun begin."

▾ ▾ ▾

Albuquerque, New Mexico, Metropolitan Court, State of New Mexico v. Dohner and Enright—October 1983
In the legal business we call these "show trials"—it's a forum to bring the message of the demonstration to the broader public. Sometimes there is more press or debate about the issues from the trial than the from demonstration itself. One cannot exist without the other and the courtroom becomes an extension of the people's action on the street. Yet, we also know that we are in an uphill battle, as issues on international law, treaty obligations, and Nuremberg defenses aren't your usual misdemeanor trial fare for the judges. Some charges even make the defendant's motivation irrelevant and inadmissible. If the defendant crossed the line: guilty.

Judge Ross Sanchez was the Metropolitan Court trial judge assigned to oversee the trial. Not the best draw, but his brother was the Archbishop of Santa Fe and we hoped some of that compassion might spill over into his ruling. We convinced him in a pretrial conference to move the case to the larger district courthouse to accommodate the expected overflow crowd of observers. Stacking the courtroom is one of the goals of political show trials. Judges aren't always swayed by public opinion, though in New Mexico at that time judges had to face regular elections. But a crowd brings out the press and it's healthy that courts know they are being scrutinized. We can forget they work for us. As I arrive that morning the local TV news stations are fixing cameras in the courtroom to provide live footage.

Petty misdemeanors, like this case's "obstruction of movement" charges, had a penalty of up to ninety days in jail and a three hundred-dollar fine. Such cases do not provide for jury trials, so we are left trying to convince an elected judge to do the right thing. Having just turned twenty-seven years old and fresh out of law school, I felt the pressure and great responsibility of holding the liberty and freedom of my clients in my hands. Both clients knew we were putting the government on trial, but each understood they could go to jail. I felt equipped on the politics, but concerned about making a simple mistake in procedure, so I sought out a trial co-counsel. The ideal candidate was New Mexico criminal attorney Nancy Hollander, one of the original founders of Students for a Democratic Society (SDS). She had gone on to become a partner in a major Albuquerque law firm. Nancy listened to my pitch and as I was leaving she was smiling broadly and I heard her from down the hall shout: "Game on."

I prepared Les and Dan to testify about why they had blocked the Air Force base. While the defense of "necessity" justifies breaking a law to avert a greater evil, your actions must be deemed by the judge or jury to be "reasonable." The example always given is when your neighbor's house is on fire and you trespass without permission to rescue someone, the law states you are not guilty of trespassing "by reason of necessity." In our case the state of mind and motives of the defendants were essential to show why they blocked entry to the Air Force Base and it returned the message of the protest front and center. Surely stopping nuclear annihilation was a reasonable justification to simply lie down on the street and obstruct movement.

Another defense was based on International Law, alleging that all citizens, as declared at Nuremberg after World War II, have an affirmative duty to challenge our government if it is breaking International Law or engaging in war crimes. The entire nation of Germany was charged with "failing to act" against Hitler. The UN Charter, a treaty overwhelmingly ratified by the US Senate, making it under our Constitution "the supreme law of the land," prohibits nations from threatening to use force unless they have been attacked or they receive formal approval of the UN Security Council. First-strike weapons pointed at Moscow were by their very existence such a threat, and barred by our Constitution. Of course, our government's track record with following our treaties has not been very good—ask any Native American you meet.

I stressed to Nancy and our team of law student volunteers that we needed to go after the larger powerbrokers. "We need these witnesses to prove there actually *are* first-strike weapons on the base and that they are working on them," I said. "Without it we can't prove the house is on fire." Nancy agreed. Of course I added that I didn't mind "fucking with them" a little too or helping the public wake up and recover from its mad sheep disease.

The law students gleefully served the subpoenas to George Dacey, the president of Sandia National Laboratories, a private national lab, and to the director of the entire Western Nuclear Defense Agency, both housed at Kirtland Air Force Base. The jaw-dropping looks on their faces when they were served to be witnesses in a Metro court petty misdemeanor case for "obstructing movement," and the empowerment of our students, was priceless. For me it fit perfectly as we were out to show that *they* were the ones obstructing . . . obstructing peace.

On the morning of trial, US Attorney William Lutz, a recent conservative Reagan Republican appointee, strolls into the judge's office with a gaggle of attorneys demanding that the subpoenas be "quashed."

"Why are we wasting our time," he quips with the arrogance of those who think they run the world. "This is a traffic case, not some circus."

To his credit Judge Sanchez listened to him and then to us without saying a word, appearing more overwhelmed rather than simply respectful. I'm certain he had never seen such a federal show of force in his magistrate city courtroom.

"They want to strip us of our defense," I argued. "What do they have to hide? We have to prove the threat on the base and behind their weapons systems in order to justify our clients' actions."

Then to the surprise of all he interrupted saying he'd heard enough and denied their motion. The witnesses would have to testify. He would allow our defense to go forward. We were elated. Lutz left with his tail between his legs.

The local county assistant district attorney, likely out of law school for just a few months, also never expected so much firepower. We put on a strong case. I examined Sandia Labs president, Dacey, about nuclear weapons technology and the weapons at the base. You could feel the growing empowerment of the supporters in the packed courtroom when he was forced by the judge to answer our questions. A physician talked about the medical consequences of nuclear war. Our defendants spoke from their hearts.

But I could not read Judge Sanchez. He sat there with a blank stare for much of the trial, seemingly disinterested. The cameras were rolling and the courtroom was packed. When we finished our case he didn't even exit for a few moments to reflect or to prepare his opinion. He simply said, "I find the defendants guilty. Sentence will be thirty days in jail and a two hundred-dollar fine. Court will stand in recess."

We were stunned. Jail time for a first offense petty misdemeanor was unheard of in City court. I now realized that the US Attorney's visit had sent a message and that old Judge Sanchez had an agenda. Fortunately for us, Metro court criminal cases are like practice rounds, and anyone convicted can request a new trial in state District Court before, what we used to call for these very reasons, a "real judge." We immediately filed our appeal and the verdict was wiped out. But you can never wipe it out in the minds of those who come to protests or who want to engage in courageous civil disobedience. The message was clear. If you step over the line, you will do time.

Bernalillo County District Court—January 1984

Even if the verdict had been negligible, our clients were prepared to do a second trial to seek an acquittal. They truly believed they were acting for a higher purpose. In the months between the two trials my mind was racing with taking it to another level. I'd attended law school believing lawyers have the power to change the world and expand social justice through the courts. *Brown v. Board of Education* helped shift racial inequality in education, Clarence Darrow took on creationism and religion in the Scopes Monkey Trial, and the Supreme Court unanimously put the brakes on Nixon's claim of an imperial presidency in *United States v. United States District Court.* I wanted to further bend Dr. Martin Luther King's "moral arc of the universe" toward justice.

It had taken a conscious effort to keep my eye on the prize during law school to hold onto my commitment to the disempowered at every turn. Many students arrived with lofty objectives, only to have them systematically shredded by a pile of debt, limited employment opportunities, and a training devoid of heart and soul—praising the law and ignoring the impact on community and everyday people as collateral damage.

To counter this, I joined the National Lawyers Guild, an organization that stood since 1937 for the notion that "human rights are more sacred than property interests." The Guild remains the only national legal organization looking at corporate power abuses and standing for economic justice.

Through the Guild, I met committed people, including Ernie Goodman, a Detroit lawyer and Guild founder who had fought for civil and labor rights for decades. As the Kirtland trial ante was being upped to District Court I remembered a conversation with Ernie on organizing and the practice of law. One evening I asked Ernie, "How do you mix your politics and your legal work?" He smiled and told the story of being asked to defend an African American woman named Ruth who in the early 1960s had stabbed a white sheriff who was beating down her door in a western Michigan town.

"I told her family I would come and defend her if they called a meeting to discuss setting up a defense committee," Ernie said. He didn't have to tell them that the issues were broader than this one murder charge—they lived it daily.

"A meeting was called, and then another, and when the case was over that group became a champion for civil rights in the area long after the lawyers had moved on to the next case." Empowerment became the road to social change. Ernie was changing the world by bringing people together.

I quickly convened a group of local activists and lawyers and we formed the *Defense Committee for Non-Violent Peace Activists.* We needed an ongoing archive of material and resources so we wouldn't have to continue reinventing the wheel. That October on UN Day another group of demonstrators, including some of our clients whose ninety-day prohibition had just expired, again blocked the base as part of an international protest against nuclear weapons. On another front people in our community were being threatened with prosecution for assisting refugees fleeing death and oppression from Central American dictators and death squads. The war against Reagan's agenda was just heating up. The committee researched first-strike weapons, developed media campaigns, and ran something we used to call, in the pre-internet stone age of organizing, the "phone tree." And that's land lines, folks!

The Defense Committee, with the support of the local ACLU, raised out-of-pocket-cost funds. Seeing ourselves as part of the movement, our time was pro bono. We did everything we could to keep the community and media interested in the trial. In the course of the appeal to District Court, we secured a permit for a rally and mock trial during the lunch break outside the courthouse. I watched the "puppets for peace" and the evil general with his chest full of medals and found it not so different from what was going on inside the courtroom. After the trial our defense committee continued to meet regularly, did training workshops, and became the legal arm of the local peace and justice movement for years to come. I could see Ernie smiling.

It was not lost on us that the appeal trial would begin in the first month of the infamous year of 1984. Orwell wrote in his classic:

> Do you begin to see, then, what kind of world we are creating? . . . A world of fear and treachery and torment, a world of trampling and being trampled upon, a world which will grow not less but more merciless as it refines itself. Progress in our world will be progress toward more pain . . . there will be the intoxication of power, constantly increasing and constantly growing subtler. Always, at every moment, there will be the thrill of victory, the sensation of trampling on an enemy who is helpless. If you want a picture of the future, imagine a boot stamping on a human face—forever.

And in walked a cocky Chief District Attorney Robert Schwartz to try an appeal of a petty misdemeanor. This was becoming high-profile and he wanted in on the action.

"Hi Bob," Nancy said smiling. "What occasion graces us with your presence today?"

"Just doing the people's work," he said. "And someone's gotta see that you all don't get out of hand again."

The DA was followed by a return appearance of US Attorney Lutz, this time challenging on the day of trial our calling Admiral Aut of the Base's Nuclear Defense Agency as a witness. Déjà vu.

"All rise," the bailiff cried, and emerging from behind the curtain came Judge Patsy Madrid, a recently elected Hispanic woman who Nancy considered a personal friend. As she settled her small frame into the bench, she smiled at the packed courtroom. We were certain we'd get a better shake from her than Judge Sanchez.

"I understand the US Attorney is here on a matter, Mr. Lutz."

"Yes your honor. The Defense is at its old tricks again. This Admiral knows nothing about the facts of this case or what happened at the Air Force gate back in June. He was not even on base at that time. Furthermore, we have not had enough time to brief the Admiral on what is classified material."

"Your honor," I countered, "We are not interested in raising classified material and I intend to only base my questions on material derived from non-classified sources. Does Mr. Lutz really contend that this head of an important government agency does not know what is classified material? This trial is about first-strike nuclear weapons and what our brave clients tried to do to stop a nuclear holocaust, and this witness is highly relevant for establishing the facts. Otherwise we are left to guess about what is going on at the base and we have a right to claim necessity as a defense."

Smiling I added, "Without him, how do we prove what they were trying to stop by laying down in the road is . . . ," pausing I turned and looked right at the Admiral, "a greater evil?"

My heart was doing somersaults. This is why I went to law school, endured courses in tax, property, and contract law, and the months of bar exam preparation. I was relishing this front-row seat to power.

I reveled in being able to school the powerbrokers about the impact of their choices and hopefully incite them, even from a self-preservation Pavlovian reaction, to choose a different path in the future. Many had never been deposed or forced to explain their conduct publicly. A trial forces them to sit and hear how their action or inaction hurt my clients, and all too often changed the trajectory of their lives and dreams. If I could crack their hearts or minds open, even for a few seconds, perhaps they could get a glimpse of something greater and in turn do the right thing. As a lawyer, I could force them to listen, but it was the exhilaration of slowing their power train and holding them accountable that got me off. If they feel the electric shock, rats tend to seek a new path. I plowed forward, my legal taser in hand.

Judge Madrid offered to either exclude the witness or postpone the trial to another date until the testimony could be cleared through Washington. We knew this would tie the case up for months and with a packed courtroom, the press watching, and a noon rally planned outside, we chose not to press for his testimony. We still had Dacey, the president of Sandia, and many times we call witnesses to not only have them present facts but to infuse a dose of community account-ability for their actions.

We missed that opportunity to shred and expose Admiral Aut before the community. At least he'd been ordered to appear by the people and knew we were watching. I'm confident he'd never heard directly his work and "evil" uttered in the same line. I'd been ready to examine him on the history of nuclear weapons at Kirtland including the famous incident in 1957 where a nuclear bomb fell through the bomb bay doors of a B-36 bomber near the base. The bomb fell 1,700 feet to the ground and its high explosives detonated, showering frag-ments as far as one mile from the impact point. They "reported" no radiation released outside the lip of the crater. And if you believe that I have some swampland in Florida you can buy . . . .

As Aut left the courtroom D.A. Schwartz wasted no time. He moved to exclude all our defenses on international law and necessity. "If they can't show that the harm they sought was immediate, then all evidence about base activities should be struck," he argued. He then had the au-dacity to allege that we, and he mentioned me by name, "were using the trial as a general forum on nuclear war." Imagine that! The judge held firm and told Schwartz to save that argument for his closing.

The prosecution only put on the arresting officers, but we were able to reveal that they were not skilled or trained in handling dem-onstrators, that our clients were cooperative and nonviolent and that the Albuquerque Police Surveillance Unit had been spying on the local peace movement and had advance information on the demon-stration.

Dan and Reverend Les testified about their involvement in the peace movement and their fear of nuclear war. They had tried writing letters to Congress, phone calls, and peace marches, but none had worked. "Our government was acting illegally and it put all of us in harm's way," the minister, decked out in his finest church attire, testified. "I could not be silent."

Our first expert witness was Dr. Gordon McClure, a physicist who had worked for twenty-seven years at Sandia National Labs. His eyes had been opened when he saw the weapons he helped produce and their danger. He joined the nuclear freeze campaign a few years prior and Judge Madrid certified him as an expert in physics and nuclear weapons. He described how the current "launch on warning" policy made nuclear war a greater risk. "Those working in the industry never discuss the dangers and spend only 3 percent of their efforts on verification issues."

There could be false warnings of nuclear attack, and our weapons systems actually make us less stable because of the possibility of an erroneous response. Confronting D.A. Schwartz's questions of a lack of "imminent danger," Dr. McClure said, "Nuclear war could begin within twenty minutes." The courtroom gasped.

Next was Dr. Dan Kerlinsky, a psychiatrist, who had written and lectured on the arms race, but whose young face made him look just out of high school. He was certified, over objection from the D.A., of course, as an expert in the field of psychiatry and the psychology of the arms race. He testified that if an individual felt in fear of great bodily harm from a series of threats of nuclear war over a period of time that it would be "eminently rational" for them to break a city criminal code violation to attempt to avert the danger. He made it clear that most people attempt to suppress the severity of the danger through a psychiatric coping mechanism called "denial." Having been raised my whole life with the lingering threat of nuclear annihilation, these words rang true.

Judge Madrid listened intently. When Dr. Kerlinsky finished and rose to leave the stand she said, "Just a moment, Doctor." Judges rarely ask questions but she glanced down, paused and looking back up asked, "What do you advise parents to discuss with their children in this area?"

Yes, I thought, she gets it. Kerlinsky, in an eloquent manner, said parents should "take whatever steps that they feel are rational that might contribute to a lesser risk of nuclear war as a way of helping their children feel more comfortable and assured that the authority they are giving their parents is well placed." I smiled proudly. How perfect. The same challenge was being presented to the judge to courageously assure us that our faith in her was also well placed.

Finally, I called Dr. Michael Heisler, a medical doctor from Physicians for Social Responsibility (PSR) and member of the Governor's Civil Defense Planning Board. It was this board's recommendation that led to New Mexico becoming only the fourth state to reject federal funds for defense planning in the event of nuclear war. It was amazing that a state as vested in the nuclear bomb as New Mexico, home of Los Alamos Labs and the Manhattan Project, would take such a bold stance, basically stating, "Get real. There is no defense after nuclear war." Planning for nuclear holocaust implied that we could survive nuclear war and that the use of such weapons was possible and defendable.

Kudos to the amazing Governor Toney Anaya, who supported this position and in four years as Governor also opposed the death penalty by commuting the death sentences of all death row inmates and declaring New Mexico a sanctuary for Central American refugees fleeing oppression. He was hounded from office the following year by the media, and the shifting conservative sands of Reaganism, but I am still today astounded by his courage.

Dr. Heisler had extensive experience with burn and trauma victims and was qualified by Judge Madrid as an expert in the medical consequences of nuclear war and Civil Defense Planning. His vivid recitation of a bomb blast over Albuquerque, complete with charts of the medical consequences in concentric circles in and around the city, left a score of pallid faces in the courtroom. Even after preparing him for trial and knowing the answers I still felt a chill through my body as he brought it home before the court and the media.

The laws of the State of New Mexico require that once a case for necessity has been established, the "burden" shifts to the State to establish beyond a reasonable doubt that the defendants were not acting under such reasonable fear. It was clear to us, and we argued in closing, that because the State presented no witnesses on the issue, the defendants should be adjudged not guilty. D.A. Schwartz's flippant stroll over to the courtroom window to declare that he heard no sirens blaring was not evidence. Nancy's closing was brilliant. We had come up with an analogy to a group of German citizens possibly sitting down at the gates of a concentration camp to tell the employees that they were not going to work on this gas chamber today.

She asked, "Would we have thought it unreasonable, or would we thought it courageous?"

Schwartz countered by stating that the "duress" type defense requires "a gun be at the head to take away your volition and will." He apparently had not read the decision in the Court of Appeals in the case of my client Rose Torres, where the court ruled that a victim of ongoing domestic violence could still raise duress when their partner forced them to participate in a crime. No gun to the head needed. Today with nuclear war twenty minutes away and thousands of warheads pointed in our direction, if we wait for sirens we'd be in deep shit.

Judge Madrid thanked us and retired to her chambers to prepare her decision. We were feeling great. What could she do but acquit? She allowed the defense, we proved it beyond a reasonable doubt and they offered no rebuttal to it. But we knew it would take guts and backbone as Patsy Madrid, who later served as Attorney General and ran for Congress, had her eyes on higher office. After an hour Judge Madrid returned with her decision.

After clearing her throat, she told the packed courtroom that it had been her "privilege" to hear this case and called it "the debate of the great principles of law and probably the most important topic that has ever faced this nation." She then spoke of her own experiences in visiting Hiroshima and the Memorial War Museum, and a few tears filled her eyes. She gets it, I said to myself. That trip had convinced her that nuclear war "is more horrible than our minds can imagine." In addition, she stated "The people in our country do not have a clear understanding of what these issues are, of what is really at stake here." The courtroom was fixated on the bench. Okay, keep going.

She then spoke of our country's founding being based on civil disobedience against the Crown. In reference to our clients she declared "I respect their courage. However . . ." She paused. (Oh god. I knew it was too good to be true.) "These defendants have had their day in court and since they voluntarily chose to commit civil disobedience they accepted the responsibilities and consequences of their actions." She then "rejected" the defenses of necessity and international law and sentenced the defendants to two days in jail (which they had already served) and to fifty hours of community service at a school assisting with the care of abused children. She rose and the bailiff bellowed, "The court is in recess." As was justice it seemed.

I felt shell-shocked, amazed, and bewildered. Judge Madrid found, as politicians so often do, the middle way. "No backbone to go the distance," I told Nancy. The defendants chose to accept the punishment and not appeal their case. It would have made for an interesting appeal as the evidence of the case was so one-sided. However, in light of there being no appellate case law on the applicability of this defense to anti-nuclear weapons demonstrators, it was probably in the best interest of the movement not to appeal. No law is sometimes better than making bad law and we did not want to foreclose others that followed from raising these defenses. The words of my law school torts professor were echoing in my mind: "Law is simply what judges do."

Judge Madrid told the packed courtroom that the nuclear stand-off needed debate, but I needed more action than simply nice words. Albert Einstein said, "The unleashed power of the atom has changed everything except our ways of thinking. Thus we are drifting toward a catastrophe beyond comparison. We shall require a substantially new manner of thinking if mankind is to survive." For me, at this time, new thinking simply meant stopping them and the madness. I was angry at anything and anyone who supported the military-industrial complex feeling they were no "brothers or sisters" of mine. It took many years of making contact and opening of my heart to take Einstein's words to a deeper meaning.

Through years of litigating against the National Laboratories over weapons, health and safety, and free speech, even representing the guards union at Los Alamos, I came to feel compassion for those working in the labs and the nuclear weapons field. The "enemy" label that I and many of my activist friends used was far too simple. A schoolyard taunt of who's more evil serves no one. As Dr. McClure testified, the people he worked with were good people but they needed to shut down their hearts and their minds to cope with the results of their efforts. It was a guilt borne by J. Robert Oppenheimer when he wrote in his diary on the eve of Hiroshima and Nagasaki:

"Now I become Death, destroyer of worlds." –Bhagavad Gita . . . Those poor little people. Those poor little people. They are to be killed by "Fat Man" and "Little Boy," either from the blast or the radiation. The multitude of the bodies, all laid out will carve deep wounds inside me. And the hundreds of hungry children will feed upon my soul until nothing is left. I am so sorry I let this project carry on for so long. It would have been so easy to end this project when the Germans surrendered, but I had to take it this far. It is entirely my fault.

Years later I would learn that *ubuntu* places no blame. In the end we are all Oppenheimer. We are those workers at the National Labs. Looking back I realized even I had stood in such shoes and faced difficult choices. But in those earlier days my compassion was not driving the ship. I felt we were in a life and death struggle for planetary survival, and *we* had to stop *them* by any means.

▾ ▾ ▾

CHAPTER 2
Baby Blue

The world is a dangerous place to live,
not because of the people who are evil,
but because of the people who don't do anything about it.
–Albert Einstein

Protest had been in my blood from an early age. I was a "red-diaper baby," the term given to the children of socialists, though perhaps it was more pink, as my parents weren't party members. They'd met as young progressives in 1947 and their first date was to a play aptly titled *Waiting for Lefty* by Clifford Odets. My early years included folk concerts and peace rallies, and my parents taught me the value of working for social and racial equality. Despite touting universal brotherhood, to most of their generation it was still a battle between *us versus them* and our stereo console rang out with scratchy Woody Guthrie records: "Which side are you on, boy, which side are you on?"

I knew my side. It was proudly with the underdogs: unions, working people, demonstrators for peace and justice, and those disenfranchised by the system. Despite this upbringing and some early efforts to fight for peace, my own path was anything but linear. Like most, I had to confront my own contradictions and unresolved heartache, frustration, and separation before trusting in new possibilities.

Vietnam Antiwar March on Washington D.C.—April 15, 1971
The battle for peace and civil rights was exhilarating for a lefty teenager. In April 1971, after an all-night charter bus ride from Detroit to Washington, chaperoned only by my sixteen-year-old stoner friend Mark, we cheered wildly as Country Joe McDonald took to the stage

during our antiwar demonstration on the lawn of the US capitol. What better release and feeling of power for me, a fourteen-year-old kid from Motown, surrounded by priests, grandmothers, and hippies, and a half million people yelling "Fuck . . . Fuck . . . Fuck," as I sought to do something more than simply survive in this crazy divided world.

The force of people in the street made me believe we could change the world. Most of us returned home feeling less alone or released from our guilt for the sins of our government, but looking back, the "movement" felt unfocused and ill equipped to sustain the struggle needed to achieve any deeper systemic change. Peace was being narrowly defined as merely the absence of war and Dr. King's message that it was intrinsically linked to social justice at home and abroad had been muffled when he was gunned down on that balcony in Memphis.

We were being marginalized by *them* as hippies and radicals and, sometimes in dramatic fashion, and no uncertain terms told to shut our mouths. Within two weeks of returning from the massive gathering in Washington, six student protestors were shot and killed at both Kent State and Jackson State universities. One of the students killed was James Earl Green, who was, like myself, still in high school. I shuddered, realizing that any of those dead students could have been me. I felt scared, but mostly I simply felt angry and a deep resentment toward the police and our politicians. The battle trenches between *us and them* were growing wider.

A deeper change was needed beyond merely ending the war in Vietnam, but what it was remained an enigma. The next year I listened intently to George McGovern, who had just been crushed by Richard Nixon in the 1972 presidential campaign, as he said, "Change does not rush in like a river."

"No shit," I said, seeing how Nixon was reelected to the White House despite the cloud of Watergate, secret bombing campaigns in Cambodia, and a Vietnam war still raging.

But McGovern had taken courageous and sometimes unpopular stances and his reminder about the power of taking action hit deeply: "You have to keep your eye on the prize against great odds and not sit back passively." That I could understand, but what concerned me most was his reflection upon his presidential campaign, where he was trounced by Richard Nixon's "dirty tricks" forty-nine states to one, concluding: "If you stir up the hornet's nest, you better be ready to be stung."

Detroit, Michigan—Summer 1974

After high school, I sweltered in the summer heat for fifty-plus hours a week as a laborer at Arcade Machine and Tool, which not only made auto parts for the waning Detroit car industry, but machines that built bombshell casings. My father knew the owner and had gone out on a limb to get me the job, so feeling some obligation to my dad, I took the job. I remember the chill I felt seeing the tiers of wood pallets filled with sample bombshells stacked high along the shop wall. My job became painting the bomb-building machines a bright baby blue. So this is where bombs come from, I thought. As my heart sank I numbed out, never sharing my politics or discomfort with others, and silently continued to paint.

I could not shake the feeling of seeing these bombs falling on villages and destroying lives. Here I was, a young peacemaker, who'd been raised to question war, caught in the machine. Four dollars and fifty cents an hour and tons of overtime was a lot of money in those days, and college was around the corner. I came home covered in grease, paint, and heartache; an early lesson in what many people do when it comes to war—paint over in our minds the war machines in a pretty shade of blue and blind patriotism, to cover their true identity as weapons of death and despair.

Day in and day out my heart was breaking as it felt like I too was now quietly burying the dead. I was not alone. With the end of the war it felt as if the bottom of the movement for change had fallen through the floor and people returned to their quiet lives, detached and tired from the years of war protests.

As I painted away, memories of the past many years of unresolved traumas returned to haunt and confuse me. In 1967, the Detroit riots had brought snipers, burnt buildings, and bodies to streets already dripping with fear and despair. I was eleven year years old when I watched Army troops and tanks patrolling in my own neighborhood, making me feel afraid, as if the war had been brought home. My city became more polarized, increasingly split down Eight Mile Road by race and class.

The next year the assassinations of Martin Luther King and Bobby Kennedy, who'd given their lives standing up to these divisions and the war, shocked me and my family. I was a young campaigner for Kennedy, whose long bangs and shy demeanor reminded me of myself. The night he fell it felt like a dagger to my hope and young heart.

During dinner we'd watch the news on television with its nightly scenes from the distant war—stretchers, the sound of gunfire, bomb blasts. My parents would quietly simmer and shake their heads, but no one ever asked me through all of these events how I was feeling. I detached and closed down my heart. It was too painful and disappointing to feel much of anything else. Now my summer silence with the bomb machines felt like a personal betrayal to myself and the values I'd been raised with and brought this familiar pain back front and center, leaving me adrift in loneliness.

Like many, I felt traumatized by the tragedies, and the triumphs were too few and far between. I was now an adult, able to drink, vote, and die for my country, but confronting my own heart or expecting anything greater seemed more dangerous. I quietly left for college to lick my wounds, feeling increasingly numb, and burying the guilty feeling that I had just contributed to the evil I abhorred.

Michigan State University, 1974—1977

Experts say that the purpose of a college education is to empower the student with life skills that enable her or him to contribute positively to society, a place that bestows wisdom and enlightenment. For many it's about experimentation and exploration, but often in unexpected ways. I'm not sure where I learned the most—memorizing the various states of the Soviet Union (How do you spell Kyrgyzstan?) or tripping on acid down Grand Avenue watching the sidewalk buckle.

Michigan State was a renowned party school—especially in comparison to its big academic brother the University of Michigan in Ann Arbor—and it certainly lived up to its reputation. With the drinking age at eighteen, on any given night our recently co-ed dorms became havens to raucous keggers where beer flowed swifter than the Red Cedar River, which had recently flooded the campus. Bongs and Turkish water pipes served as bookends, and in those days before the "war on drugs" we smoked marijuana in dorm rooms and hallways as if an odorless hybrid had been invented to cover our folly. I was living what Nietzsche meant when he said, "I would only believe in a God that knows how to dance." How I escaped with grades to get into law school and Phi Beta Kappa became one of life's great mysteries.

In my sophomore year the whole nation felt numb and apathetic in the midst of the nation's bicentennial celebrations. But all patriotic hype wasn't about recapturing the dream of the founders of equal rights, but a plea to purchase every conceivable bit of consumer crap dressed up in the red, white, and blue bicentennial dress.

Despite my past couple of years devoid of activism, my anger with my country was palpable. "I mean what's to celebrate?" I told my dorm floor mates. Knowing I was just getting started, they scampered to their rooms for cover as I shouted down the hall after them, "Vietnam, Hiroshima, slavery . . . tribal genocide across the west." I sighed. "A trail of tears, not of triumph." And as the last door slammed I said to myself: "And if I see one more commercial featuring a portly, balding actor flying a kite in an electrical storm I'm outta here."

Yet there were moments that kept my heart afloat. Tucked in our dorm's stairwell late into the night, I found solace reading Nietzsche: "One must have chaos within oneself, to give birth to a dancing star." I was learning from philosophers that we should build a life more akin to that dancing star than one caught up in the drama and traumas of life. Through the words emanating from the depths of Plato's cave, Marx's "workers of the world unite," or Hegel's "everything has its time," I began to release the guilt brought on by my past years of silence and the pain I'd been carrying for our world's indifference to suffering.

Meanwhile, there was little happening on the home front to give me much faith in humanity, as we'd just elected a born-again Christian peanut farmer named Jimmy as President of the United States. "What's next?" I quipped, "An actor?" But my studies in political philosophy and courses in the Mexican and Cuban Revolutions were stirring up something familiar, and at age twenty I defied the US travel ban and landed in Havana, home of Fidel, sugar, and leftist brigades, knowing something was waiting for me, but not realizing that it would alter my worldview and re-ignite my thirst for justice.

▾ ▾ ▾

CHAPTER 3

Dancing with the Enemy

The philosophers have only interpreted the world, in various ways.
The point, however, is to change it.
–Inscription on Karl Marx's tomb, London, England

Merida, Mexico—March 1977

"Please don't go to Cuba," she begged. The phone line in the old Merida motel was scratchy but I could make out the voice of my old high school girlfriend who had opened, and then three years later, shuttered my tender heart. I'd shed many tears and swore not to let myself get so connected or feel that much again. I'd spent the past two years trying to forget her, shifting my focus onto a series of detached relationships, often checking my heart at the door.

It was 1977, the age before internet, faxes, or cell phones, and her finding me in Mexico felt mind-boggling and surreal. "It's dangerous," she said as I glanced around imagining I'd fallen into a dream or entered the Twilight Zone. It didn't help that Humberto, who ran the motel that housed myself and twenty other visiting Michigan State students had already led us in a post dinner "cafe" session—his buzz word for smoking a joint.

"It's safe, Margie," I assured her. "People from around the world go all the time," purposely not mentioning that most were Soviets. I explained that five of us, including a professor, were hitching a ride with a Mexican travel tour, as Mexico had long-standing relations and historical connections with Cuba. "For many Mexicans," I said, "It's like a trip to Disneyland, only tropical."

She seemed more at ease, though I sensed she'd consumed a few mojitos before she called. "I miss you and want to see you when you're back," she said, words I'd only dreamed of hearing, and as I hung up the phone shaking my head, my heart was ecstatic. "What was that all about?" But her warning stopped me in my tracks. Dangerous? My first nervous thoughts about the trip surfaced. I hadn't thought of it as anything other than an adventure—the ripe mix of challenge and recklessness so common to a nineteen-year-old. While most American college students were contemplating Daytona Beach or Fort Lauderdale, I was off for "spring break in Cuba," an ironic choice between excessive self-indulgence and revolution. Could it be that the pull to change the world had returned? Of course being a lush tropical island didn't hurt either.

While signing forms from CubaMex Tours releasing them from liability and reminding me that the US government bans travel to Cuba, I'm drawn to the clause at the bottom where I'm asked to certify that I'm not a spy for any foreign country. Margie's warning is starting to sink in as I've chosen to defy my government and cross the great divide to this embargoed nation. As I told my parents when I called them to borrow the two hundred dollars needed for the trip, "I have to go. I'm not sure why but something is waiting for me there."

In the 1970s we were a world divided wherein a nation was given two choices: the road to socialism through communist control and conformity aligned with the Soviet Union or China, or a US-sponsored democracy with its capitalist "free" market system. Europe was divided, the city of Berlin split in two by its infamous wall, and millions were killed in Korea and Vietnam in ill-fated attempts to win them over to our side. Clearly the trip was my personal challenge to our nation's policy of isolation and separation, long before I knew of ubuntu or ever met a Cuban or Soviet.

It was the height of the Cold War and no one I knew had ever met anyone currently living in the Soviet Union—the evil empire—or for that matter anyone from one of their "satellite" nations. My grandparents left Russia between 1907 and 1910, and over several years worked their way to the United States. How quickly most Americans forget that they, too, are immigrants.

For my entire life the media, teachers, and our government had all told us that Russians were the "enemies" bent on burying us. When people asked me about my name—Sirotkin comes from Sirota, and means "orphan" in Russian—I'd usually change the subject rather than endure their suspicious stares or discomfort. If I did say "It's Russian," the awkward silence that followed was painful.

After the 1962 Cuban Missile Crisis, the Soviets replaced their missiles in Cuba with rubles. This had reached nearly a hundred billion dollars in annual subsidies and credit. Soviet ships were able to dock freely in Cuba, only 90 miles from Florida, and the tropical island became a place for chalky white Russians to escape the harsh Moscow winters. I wanted to bridge the gap and break through on a human level—hoping to reach out past the Cuban embargo to the Cuban people. But in the back of my mind it was the chance to talk freely with Russians about peace, and release my guilt about my heritage, that caused me to ignore the risks and board Mexicana Flight #616 to Havana.

Havana, Cuba—March 11, 1977

Arriving at Jose Marti Airport I notice my hands shaking. Lloyd, who'd taken the name Paco, clears customs ahead of me. I watch them carefully examining his book *Cuba: The Making of a Revolution*. My agent is a woman whose bright blue eye shadow surprises me, thinking it would be seen as counter-revolutionary. She meticulously examines my visa and my socks. We then surrender our passports to "Companero" Rafael, our CubaMex tour guide. Leaving the airport, I feel I'm in the belly of the beast with no escape, but on the way downtown an electronic sign flashes my new motto: "We will confront difficulties and we will conquer them."

Cuba feels like another planet or a throwback in time. Ancient cars fill the streets—old Packards and Oldsmobiles from the 1930s and 40s. Billboard images of guerrilla fighters with automatic weapons are juxtaposed with smiling babies. Someone has the bright idea that the same marketing techniques used to sell laundry soap could sell revolution.

I'm caught in a web of paranoia and intrigue. Who's watching? I was in enemy territory and distrust feels natural and prophylactic. I turn to my schoolmate Cindy and whisper, "Do you think there are bugs in the room?"

"Not sure," She deadpans "but I expect they'll be quite clean. They probably spray."

"No," I say, not appreciating her humor, "recording bugs."

She looks at our motley crew and laughs, "Why would they bother?"

I expect to see pictures of Fidel but surprisingly never see photos or statues of the infamous El Comandante. Entering my room, I find it clean, basic, and sterile. The clock radio is playing Russian music, as if they'd been expecting someone else, and with a quick glance under the lampshade for any listening devices, I find only a bulb oddly stamped in English "Made in the U.S.S.R." I sing a refrain of the Beatles: "You don't know how lucky you are boy, back in the US, back in the U.S.S.R . . ." If anyone's bugged the room they've learned one not so tightly held secret about myself—absolutely tone deaf.

The hotel bar is right out of the 1940s with puffy red booths and black and white prints dotting the walls. We're the only customers. It's humming with live Cuban salsa rhythms and we order a round of rum and cokes and Cuban cigars. I'm puffing away when a group of Soviets suddenly waltz in and take their place on the other side of the lounge. My first impulse is to go over and greet them but their grandiose demeanor feels intimidating. They're laughing and shouting over the music and as the song ends one nearly bald, stocky Soviet with puffy eyes approaches the band and whispers something to the band leader. Before this waddling bureaucrat makes it back to his table, the band strikes up a Russian march. We groan and the Soviets start pounding their table. Band member faces betray their agony. Energy drains from the room and for a full half an hour we endure the jarring transition from salsa to a full parade on Red Square.

I'm pissed. It appears to be the Soviet version of the Ugly American. I had held the naive opinion that people raised with a collective consciousness would extend it to others. It was my first taste of superpower imperialism—something that has no ideological borders. It was as if they didn't even see the musicians or have respect for their culture. My vision of meeting them had been quite different. Big bear hugs and toasts to world peace. Was this a Cold War game to demonstrate to the newly arrived Americans who rules this playground? If so, Round One had gone to the Soviets. What a world!

Having come under the cover of a Mexican tour group, we took full advantage of freely wandering about at night. Cuba is at its peak period of mega-state control and the formal rationing of goods, as people stand in line at stores to secure numbers that would give them the chance to buy kitchen items at noon the next day. "To each according to his needs," or more likely, "to each when we have it on the shelf."

On our first night we walk for hours talking with a few Cuban students, one in fatigues who is in his compulsory military service. We all are thirsty to learn about each others' lives. This is what happens when people, as opposed to governments, meet—something that would hold true on my journeys from Soweto to Pyongyang. There is a natural curiosity and a desire to connect when you let go of the battle—the political us versus them scenario.

"You can get food without rationing coupons?" they ask, surprised as they can't understand how everyone would get what they need. "They don't," I say, struggling to explain and justify free enterprise to someone who has only known centralized distribution their entire life. The concept of homelessness is just as foreign, as everyone in Cuba is given a place to live. I think of the thousands who weather winter on the street in the US and feel embarrassed for my country. On a compassionate human scale we aren't making the grade.

"Have you seen *The Godfather, Parts 1 and 2*?" asks Ariel, a Cuban student with a long black braid and serious eyes. Apparently they all have and she wants to know if we have many problems with the Mafia in East Lansing, Michigan. I laugh, realizing that most people in the world learn about the US from the silver screen . . . or the barrel of a gun. They have as many stereotypes of us as we have of them.

Many questions are about racial problems in the states and class struggle, or, most often: "How much do your jeans cost in America?" Miguel, a tall lanky Cuban, tells me about his fighting in Angola and a visit he took to the U.S.S.R. I ask him about China and he quickly gives the party line "Oh . . . they are not important." Boy, did they bet on the wrong horse!

While traveling the next day around the Plaza de las Armas we're mobbed by a pack of boys who ask not for money but for for *plumas* or *chicle* (pens or gum). We ask them about school, life, and chewing gum. Our guide, Rafael, embarrassed by the youngsters, pulls some of them aside and gives them a dose of revolution: "How are you going to learn? If you get one piece of gum then you will want two, three, then four. Your exam scores will drop and you will be held back." Yet, he smiles and says, "Quit now and there's still hope for you." Most of the boys still linger, thinking, I suspect, more about four or five pieces of gum than the revolution or their lesson plans. Kids are kids every-where. Later we see Rafael chewing gum and ask him if he would soon want more. He smiles, catching our counter-revolutionary humor, and quickly says, "It's for my sore throat that's so parched from talking to you and answering so many questions."

There are more than one hundred Russians staying in our hotel. They seem to know little Spanish and are perpetually dour. Perhaps they're a workers group rewarded with a trip for making a quota. Does being a member of the Communist Party come with a vacation benefit package? One morning in the hotel "boutique" Professor Bailey and I share a good laugh at Paco's hand language skills as he tries to communicate with a Soviet man who apparently speaks no English. A breakthrough comes as the professor asks him "Sprechen Sie Deutsch?" and the two of them light up as they begin to communicate in rudimentary German. It's as if a dam has been broken. We ask him to dinner, but he says, looking over his shoulder, "Nyet—I cannot," but he agrees to meet us at seven PM in the hotel bar. That evening we wait, excited, but he doesn't show. I picture a KGB officer deciding a rendezvous with Americans was not on the agenda. We only have a couple more days and I worry we'll not get another chance.

The next morning a light rain is falling as we board the tour bus for a trip to lavish cemeteries and revolutionary battle sites. A voice asks us in English, "Are you American?"

"I'm Mike, and I'm from California," he says.

"What brings you to Havana?" I ask him, surprised to discover another gringo.

"I've lived here for over sixteen years. I'm a journalist and I work with CBC and ABC News," he says, seemingly excited that he has found some fellow Americans.

"Congratulations on being legal tomorrow," he says smiling broadly. Apparently President Carter had just announced he would not renew the travel ban (renewable every six months) on travel by US citizens to Cuba, Vietnam, Cambodia, and North Korea.

"Can I get a shot of you getting on the bus?" he asks.

"Why not," I say, feeling more proud of our trip than fearful of government reprisal. We disembark and he films us re-boarding as a scoop for the news on the lifting of the travel ban. "Free at last" I say to him, flashing a peace sign.

The tour group scene begins to feel orchestrated and constrictive, so Paco and I leave the bus to wander more freely and snap photos. Alone for some time, my paranoia returns. What if we're suddenly picked up and swept away? As Americans we are not here officially, have no diplomatic relations, and we hail from the "enemy" that has inflicted such harm on this island. Just two years ago, during the US Senate Investigation into the CIA, Senator Frank Church had concluded: "We have found concrete evidence of at least eight plots involving the CIA to assassinate Fidel Castro, from 1960 to 1965 . . . the proposed assassination devices ran the gamut from high-powered rifles, to poison pills, poisoned pens, deadly bacterial powders, and other devices which strain the imagination." One that always stuck with me involved an exploding cigar. I picture us never being seen or heard from again, found guilty for the sins of our fathers or at least being fed a jimmy-rigged cigar and told to "puff."

Instead I open my eyes past my fear and I'm caught in the infectious smiles of the Cuban people. They are clearly not the "enemy." I'd imagined a cold, icy, authoritarian atmosphere with curfews and downtrodden people, but walking back in silence through the beautiful old colonial city of Havana, whose architecture feels majestic and proud like Paris, we pass children laughing and racing past their mothers, and men sunning themselves in the park or napping along the tree-lined promenades. I feel my whole body relax. This mysterious city ninety miles from America is grabbing me and not letting go. Night falls, traffic melts away and the side streets become giant sidewalks filled with people strolling past fountains and flower-draped balconies that beckon toward a simpler time. It's in these still human moments that borders and differences dissolve and I deeply feel our common humanity, that it sinks into my heart and reminds me that we as a world can be so much more.

▼ ▼ ▼

After a day in the countryside, we run into our Soviet "friend" in the lobby. We exchange small tokens, but these are big gestures when your countries are poised to kill each other. As I'm dozing off after a day of sun and socialism, I surprisingly hear my clock radio picking up a US radio station. Here I am in the "Communist Gulag" ninety miles off our shores and listening to a radio station from Arkansas. I listen past midnight when it turns country—contradictions seeping through airwaves. If we truly want to end the Cuban experiment, we should normalize relations and flood the island with a tidal wave of blue-jeaned tourists with dollars and attitude. Simple solution, but instead we chose isolation and separation—an early lesson for me that having an "enemy" to demonize must serve the interests of powerful people at home.

Sleep continues to be a luxury we can't afford as we want to connect with as many people as possible. Paco and Cindy knock on the door and drag me from bed. Turning the corner from our hotel we're joined by Jose, a Cubano who enjoys walking with us at night and sharing perspectives on our crazy world, and tonight he has two friends with him, a mechanic named Enrique and his wife. Enrique and I walk ahead and he invites me to his home for lunch the next day. As the night winds down he has me follow him to see where he lives. From the outside it looks huge with steps going up from a courtyard.

"Good. I'll see you tomorrow," I said.

"But I have to show you where my home is," he replies. We mount the steps and each room around an open courtyard has a makeshift wooden gate with a lock. One family per room. He said there is not very rich or very poor in Cuba, "but I am on the lower end." The room has a bed, tabletop stove, standing closet, and small table for his entire family.

When I arrive the next morning, word is out and the meeting attracts several more curious Cubans squeezed into the small room. His family graciously shares with me their beefsteak, a highly prized commodity for Cubans in this time of embargo and shortages. They show me their rationing book and give me an expired one to take home in my pants after we tear out any names or identifying information. It's feeling like "Spy versus Spy." Enrique is not very political, but one visitor asks to speak to me in English, outside the understanding of those in attendance.

He leans in and says, "We can eat, but we can't think. Do you see this silk shirt?" he explains, pointing at his multi-colored long sleeve shirt. "I had to get this from Puerto Rico on the black market."

I notice that to "think" for himself seemed more about "shopping" than a desire to debate great ideas of the day.

As night begins to fall I walk back with Jose, who notices the colored lights on our hotel rooftop and asks what was happening.

"I heard it's a party," I tell him.

"Are you going?" he asks with excitement.

"No. I can't afford it, it's like twenty dollars," I say, a little embarrassed. But this trip had stretched me to the edge.

"Here," he says, taking the equivalent out of his wallet in Cuban pesos. "I can help."

I'm shocked by his heartfelt gesture toward me—a near stranger—while they face shortages and rationing. In the years ahead I would remember this and similar gestures by the Cubans when given food and great hospitality by those with seemingly little in South African shanties or small huts in Mexico or India. The rich connection fostered by unselfish giving is unparalleled. Like most gifts from the heart, this gesture had a ripple effect in both the long- and short-term: it contributed to my paying it forward with countless hours of peace-building, but on that night this selfless act of giving finally brought me together with the Russians.

▼ ▼ ▼

As the band plays on, I pile my plate with food, say a quiet thanks to Jose, but even more, think of Enrique's tiny family quarters. Each bite of food feels like a blessing and a curse. I see Paco and Nancy have finally infiltrated the Russian circle. After days of struggling to communicate with the Soviets in our Havana hotel, our new Russian friend, Viktor, has found one of his female comrades, Galina, who speaks a little English. Between her, Viktor's creative sign language, a touch of German and a Russian dictionary, I finally get what I'd been seeking: a chance to connect and bridge the great divide between our people. Viktor is a Moscow engineer and teaches workers at night, while Galina is also an engineer and lives in the Uriel Mountains. We move seamlessly from Cuban cigars to Russian cigarettes, from rum to vodka, and the world gets smaller with each laugh.

Galina means "shining brightly, calm or serene" in Russian. I understand it as I'm lost in her blue eyes. We talk into the night and we're no longer Soviets or Americans, just people sharing laughter and a love of rock and roll.

"Do you want to visit the United States someday?" I ask.

"Yes," Galina says cautiously, as if saying something subversive.

"But he *really* would like to visit," she adds, smiling at Viktor, which might explain his many approaches to us over the past several days and his efforts to engage us on John Lennon and the "bee-tells." We exchange stories, photos, Russian pins, addresses, and hopes for world peace.

Galina and I dance closely until midnight. As I hold her in my arms I'm tearing up, feeling the weight of the Cold War on my heart; wondering how we can end this madness that says we're enemies. I feel like the Germans and English in World War I who across the battlefield during a Christmas Eve cease-fire shared Christmas carols and then partied together like brothers till dawn before returning to the bloody business at hand.

Someone at the hotel throws a switch, and the rooftop turns from gala to darkness, ending the party. Detente is over and we feel our way off the roof, down the darkened steps, and back into our separate lives of quiet desperation in a nuclear world. The encounter has had a profound effect on me. In the months and years later when I hear the words "Soviet Union" my mind goes not to Lenin, Stalin, or gulags, but to Galina and her blue eyes. Peace had become personal. Who could think of attacking and bombing someone after dancing cheek to cheek?

▼ ▼ ▼

The next day we board the plane to Mexico City and connect back to the States. In Dallas at customs we spread out in various lines, occasionally exchanging conspiratorial glances sneaking through with our keepsakes: caches of Cuban memorabilia, Russian cigarettes, and Havana cigars. I picture Galina in line in Moscow customs coveting the Michigan State sweatshirt I gave her that morning, hoping she doesn't have to explain its source. I feel freer, both personally and politically, less a victim of our governments' efforts to keep people apart than when we'd left for Cuba. In part it's due to the expiring travel ban, but mostly a result of reaching out rather than demonizing the "enemy."

Beyond feeling smaller, the world feels more humane and the possibilities greater. While the system in Cuba has its challenges, inconsistencies, and its dark side, for the most part it was a nation working hard, against great odds, to do things for its people. By taking peace into my own hands, outside of the rhetoric or the anger of protests, it makes images of the future feel hopeful. Clearly there was something powerful beyond words about connecting on a human level, but what to do with that energy? How can I move from words to action and bring home what I'd witnessed and experienced? What is it asking me to do?

Fidel Castro, himself a lawyer, described a revolution "as struggle between the future and the past." Until now I'd never understood that such a battle goes on inside us as well. While my activism had ground to a halt in the bomb machine factory, I was choosing to let go of the past and move forward. Something was coming alive within me and I'm feeling pulled to follow Fidel's path. Not to the jungle or backwoods with a handful of rag-tag fighters, but to law school to acquire the weapons I need to defeat injustices and the exploitative divisions running the show—the essence of what could be called revolutionary law. The week after returning to the states I sent off my first application and after a dozen rejections from around the country found myself full circle with the chance to be born again where it all began. The letter began simply "Welcome to The University of Detroit School of Law." The past was giving me the tools to confront the future.

▾ ▾ ▾

CHAPTER 4
A Silver Tongue

Even a dead fish can go with the flow.
–Jim Hightower

Santa Fe, New Mexico—October 1981
"All rise," boomed the clerk for Chief Justice Mack Easley of the New Mexico Supreme Court. A longtime rancher and judge, Easley glanced down at the few dozen of us who had passed the bar and were ready to serve as torchbearers for justice. With several other justices present, he told us, "Raise your right hand. If you leave with anything from today let me leave you with one thing." How exciting, I thought. Pearls of wisdom from the Supreme Court—insights into the uncertain road ahead. He cleared his throat and began. "I was down at Tibo Chavez's ranch and Tibo's son told me this joke. What's the difference between the Ku Klux Klan and the Supreme Court?" He paused as if waiting for one of us to chime in, "The difference," he paused again, smiling, "is that the Supreme Court wears black robes and scares the hell out of white folks. Now repeat after me . . . ."

A few polite chuckles rose up around me. I was shocked. It was like a cold shower. I never expected to hear "abide by the law" and a joke about the Klan uttered in the same breath as I took my oath as a lawyer. Months before, a jury acquitted Klan members who had shot and killed African Americans engaged in a protest march in Greensboro, North Carolina, so the comment was particularly insensitive. Was the Chief Justice telling us that the line between the Klan and the Court was that thin? Or was Justice Easley so detached from the world around him that he just didn't care? A little of both I suspected.

What did I expect? After all, I'd spent three years in law school being taught what they called "detached objectivity" and reducing a case down to its most narrow holding, rather than considering broader social consequences. Such an education breeds lawyers who separate from their hearts—and conversely are in need of a good laugh. But the Chief Justice's joke was anything but funny and it became for me a sign that justice, even in the court system, would be a constant struggle.

The irony was that I too was ready to take *white folks* off their high horses and start "scaring the hell" out of corporations and our government. In the years that followed, I continued my assault on the military-industrial complex. I challenged major defense industry contractors on behalf of whistleblowers who questioned their fraudulent charging practices, represented a Los Alamos Lab employee who complained that he was ill-equipped and not trained to be cleaning up internal radiation spills—they actually donned the scary suits and used Windex—and defended thousands of demonstrators as they challenged US bombing, ecological destruction, and intervention in both covert and overt wars.

During my work with demonstrators, prosecutors would shy away from pursuing charges knowing we would push to put the government on trial, and I gained a reputation as an unpredictable opponent with an agenda. One opponent even made me agree, as a term in the settlement agreement, not to make a documentary film about them or the case.

I wore these badges of power proudly and used them to my advantage whenever possible. If they believe you operate "outside the box," then they have no way to control the situation—an irritant to those who believe they hold the power and have a God-given right to set the agenda. My goal became to seize back the power for "us," the workers, students, and the disenfranchised, while helping bring the powerbrokers to their knees. I was angry at the world they'd created or allowed to fester. If I'd had the power to put them behind bars I would not have hesitated. But with each time I held their feet to the fire, something was stalking me and challenging me to go a little deeper. Along the way it was a series of unexpected clients that surprised and helped me let go of a few of my prejudicial attitudes and limitations.

Guarding the Bomb

Los Alamos, New Mexico—1982–1984

My moral arc was taken right to the edge with my first opportunity to represent a labor union—the recently privatized security guards union from the weapons facility at Los Alamos National Laboratory. At first I wanted nothing to do with representing them. It felt like I would be supporting the very people who secure our weapons industry on behalf of the masters of war. To me the system needed to be dismantled, not protected. The last thing I needed was to be part of the bomb-making process again. But I needed the work and at least it was battling the Reagan policy of privatization, so I made the leap in early 1982, becoming counsel for the International Guards Union of America Local 69.

Negotiating a collective bargaining agreement was a challenge. First, I was a young, inexperienced twenty-seven-year-old lawyer who didn't look the part. Second, I didn't want to focus only on the economics, because the guards often end up around radioactive spill cleanup and accidents, and so confront serious health and safety issues. While most of the workers put wages and job security on the top of their list, I'd use any meeting with them to increase dialogue on issues that reminded them of the deadly work of their employer. It was at times a delicate dance, but an early lesson in dealing with politically diverse communities and becoming a more empathetic listener.

It took us close to a year to negotiate a contract. Delay empowers employers because the workers, often worn down by time, usually capitulate on sticking points. Employers know this and take full advantage. The negotiating sessions between *us and them* were arduous and hostile, but I refused to be crippled by the fight. I was confronting Los Alamos National Labs, the birthplace of the atomic bomb, and dealing with the guarding of our nuclear weapons programs, but damn if I'd let anyone steal my sense of humor. In one session when we had backed them in a corner at the bargaining table, the company lawyer John Nivela angrily shouted at me that I was a "silver-tongued devil." In response I promptly stuck out my tongue and twirled it back and forth. Local 69 rules! Nivela just shook his head and lowered his face toward the floor, lest his clients would see that their hard ass counsel was about to smile.

Litigation, unfair labor practices, and handling grievances for the union gave me great experience, and even led me to be asked to teach labor law at the law school, but it was the personal relationships that impacted me the most. As I ate and drank with the guards and came to know them and their families, it became an early lesson that there is more that unites us than separates us as workers and as human beings on this planet. My projections about the employees in the "evil" defense industry came from my own prejudices. We all make difficult choices. My own experience shutting down my heart when working on the bomb machines helped me to better understand their choices and to further forgive my own. I was learning that each client was an opportunity to stretch my boundaries and grow on a personal level— all steps on my journey.

Albuquerque, New Mexico—1986

"You can choose to break the law," I said to the church congregation, citing scripture and ancient Greek and Roman history to support their giving of sanctuary. "It's written in Isaiah 14:32 that 'the Lord has fixed Zion in her place, and the afflicted among God's people shall take refuge there.'" It's not often that a sworn atheist gets to give a sermon from the pulpit, let alone one that supports the parishioners defying the federal government.

I used my voice as an attorney to "aid and abet" the Sanctuary Movement—an underground railroad that began in the United States in 1981 to help Central Americans fleeing repression, persecution, and the violence of their governments. Our government was ignoring international and domestic law by rejecting their claims as political refugees, as the US Government was often funding the dictators oppressing them, so we the people had to act.

Unlike the protesters at the Air Force base, the individuals involved with sanctuary work were not facing petty misdemeanor obstructing movement or trespass charges, but federal felonies for aiding and abetting illegal aliens. The penalty was five or more years imprisonment, and a fine of about $2,000 per refugee assisted. Helping a family of four could get you twenty years.

I knew the safe houses and would get phone calls at all hours of the night asking me to be on call if something happened to a particular sanctuary worker. It would be a generic message that meant that someone I knew from Albuquerque was moving refugees. At times I wondered who was listening in on our phone line and it was scary, especially with two young kids of my own, knowing I, too, could be indicted. At the same time I had a sense of empowerment born of defying the most powerful government in the world in the name of justice.

I felt proud and powerful to be part of the largest grassroots civil disobedience movement in the United States since the civil rights protests of the 1960s. Remarkably, some 70,000 Americans had signed a "Pledge of Resistance" promising to respond with peaceful sit-ins of government buildings in the event of a US invasion or major military escalation anywhere in Central America. The people were becoming the buffer to all-out war, keeping US troops out of Central America— one of the most courageous and little known acts of civil resistance in our history.

The refugees I met were so grateful, but always nervous and looking over their shoulders. The children, usually silent, clung to their parents like a life saver thrown to them in a turbulent sea. I represented a lay nun, Pat Malcolm, identified as a co-conspirator in an indictment, and assisted as a legal spokesman for the trial of a journalist and minister charged with multiple felonies.

Fortunately, Pat was never brought to trial, as the Justice Department's interest in putting nuns and priests in prison was waning. It didn't hurt that in the case of journalist Demetria Martinez and a Lutheran minister, an Albuquerque jury found them not guilty of aiding and abetting refugees fleeing oppression, a major victory for the movement.

After the dust settled I met with Pat and she gave me an etching she'd made of a wide-eyed Salvadorian child, one of the children she had transported to safety, keeping his family from harm's way. Every time I look into those eyes it reminds me why I chose this path. Pat's courage taught me that we have a responsibility to the world's children to use our power to work for peace. I'd stood with proud religious activists who showed me the power of compassion and taking a higher road. They broke through the prejudice I'd held about religious people as dogmatic or rigid, as I found them simply so deeply loving and committed to justice. Sister Pat would quote to me St. Thomas Aquinas: "Three things are necessary for the salvation of what he ought to believe; to know what he ought to know what he ought to do."

Conscience

New Mexico Air National Guard—1990
Steve Schiff, our new local district attorney and future Congressman, trades his suit for his reservist uniform whenever he is called upon to provide legal advice to the New Mexico Air National Guard. Today I'm with him and a panel of officers hearing my client Maria's request to be released from the National Guard because she had evolved into a conscientious objector (CO). Even the monthly training weekends filled with weapons and war games is turning her stomach and her conscience.

To claim CO status one must demonstrate that you refuse to bear arms or participate in military service on the basis of religious or moral principles. The Supreme Court had described it as being based on the "depth and fervency" of one's beliefs, even if they were not religious in character. My case was going to put the morality of war front and center. It was another chance to take on the establishment and put the military on trial.

Once again our case turns on our psychology expert, Dr. Dan Kerlinsky, who has met with Maria and can attest to the emotional trauma of her training with the tools of war and identify when her conscience had evolved to opposing war in any form. Maria describes what it felt like going for the military exercises or supporting them in any way. Her sadness was palpable and her genuine words were mostly met by a mix of scorn and embarrassment by the panel.

Shakespeare said it is the artist's job to hold a mirror to society. I think the same applies to lawyers. Looking into the eyes of the officers hearing the case I could see that I was making them feel uncomfortable as the reflection required them to examine their own conscience—a place they did not want to go. By choosing peace, I told them, Maria had taken an honorable position, and in closing told the panel about the power and courage behind such a choice. Of course, at every turn I mentioned the media and the publicity this case would generate if they ruled against conscience and a soldier's morality.

After two days of testimony Col. Schiff emerged and said, "They're granting her an honorable discharge . . . but it's not because they

agree with you. They just don't want to see *you* again." We had antici-
pated that they would simply administratively discharge her, but they
apparently felt that we would be relentless in our appeal and publicity. The honorable discharge showed that soldiers could move toward
peace without sacrificing those benefits of their service. I'd argued to
the judges that when our conscience speaks we must listen. Yet in the
end it was not the law or a change in their hearts that swayed them,
but my reputation as a rabid peacenik lawyer who represents demonstrators, and the way I relished turning a simple military discipline
case into a political issue.

I felt proud that in some small way a peacemaker could scare the
military machine enough to get an honorable discharge for a courageous soldier for peace. For me it was a powerful dual victory. A
small step to remove one less soldier from the battlefield—because,
in Buffy Sainte-Marie's words, "without them all this killing can't go
on"—and an opportunity to put a case of conscience before those in
charge. And rather than march away, they had to sit there and listen!

▼ ▼ ▼

These victories were intoxicating. Throughout my first decade of
practice I used my power as a lawyer to address human rights and
justice issues not only within the defense and nuclear weapons in-
dustries, but within the Catholic Church, the Albuquerque Police
Department, the University Board of Regents, and most major corporations across the state.

Despite these small victories over the power structure, I was growing frustrated that the world didn't appear to change. When it came
to war as an acceptable method to resolve conflict, my country rolled
ahead blindly, never learning from our past. Martin Luther King, Jr.
warned us in 1967 that "our very survival depends on our ability to stay
awake, to adjust to new ideas, to remain vigilant . . . to learn to live as
brothers or together or be forced to perish as fools." Most Americans
remained silent to the out-of-control military-industrial complex, a
war in the Gulf in Kuwait was brewing, and I could not escape the feeling that *we the people* had granted *them* a license to "perish as fools."

▼ ▼ ▼

CHAPTER 5

Gazing into the Abyss

*He who fights with monsters might take care lest he thereby
become a monster. And if you gaze for long into an abyss,
the abyss gazes also into you.*
–Friedrich Nietzsche

Albuquerque, New Mexico—1991
"Linda's dead, Mr. Sirotkin." Words can permanently burn into your
mind. She hadn't called that morning, nor gone to work. Her sisters
found her in her apartment, lying next to the pills, and immediately
called me. I was stunned. Just the day before I had assured her that
she would not have to return to work in the federal agency where she
had faced daily harassment. We'd prepared a letter she could hand
over if they were forcing her back to that environment. "You're protected," I told her. "Don't worry. Call me if there is any problem." I felt
confident we had our bases covered, but her fear and anguish were
too great.

The new director of the agency ordered her back to her old unit
"for the efficiency of the service." Linda pled with her new boss not
to move her, as she'd become suicidal working under that supervisor's harassment. I angrily imagined a bean counter in a tiny federal
cubicle performing the cost/benefit analysis: "She might not commit
suicide if she returned, many just threaten but don't follow through,
but by our figures if she doesn't return surely the efficiency of the department would suffer." But mostly I thought of her young daughter
and what they would say to her.

Challenging injustice, discrimination, and abuse at work should
have made Linda a hero. Instead, she was labeled a troublemaker and
made to feel isolated and alone. A complaint by an employee is not

seen as a sign for expanding dialogue, growth, or communication, but a threat and a declaration of war against the employer. In the eyes of her employer she was a GS-12, a numerical classification, to be seen and not heard. The "efficiency of the service" too often excludes its "human" resources.

"The machine, yes the machine," wrote Carl Sandburg, "Never wastes anybody's time / never watches the foreman / never talks back." Instead of standing by her in court, I was standing at her graveside.

Linda did not need a warrior preparing for battle, she needed an intervention. I could not escape the feeling that I should have done more. I was working detached, behind the scenes, like a general on the hillside running the strategy of the battle below as troops fell. Perhaps if I'd marched into the office with her therapist and sat with the employer to concretely work out solutions, rather than drafting a letter, or assuring her we had the ammunition stockpiled to win, she'd still be alive. But I'd not yet heard of ubuntu, or understood seeing conflict as a shared problem. I was working with the methodical combative toolbox most of us were given, lying in wait until it was time to pounce.

Over the years it's become clear in the world of work, still researched by lawyers as *Master and Servant* law, that violence to oneself or others was becoming all too often the answer for desperate workers who felt ignored or disrespected. At the time of Linda's death, workplace homicides occurred at a rate of four per day in the US More than half of these stemmed from layoffs or terminations. Workplace violence was the second leading cause of occupational injury. I listened with my heart racing as Mike, a short, slightly graying client, detailed his plan to kill his supervisor: "I drove by the house, staked it out, planned it, had the gun in the car," he says, rocking back and forth on my office sofa in a soft matter-of-fact voice devoid of any obvious anger. "Thank God I drove to the hospital instead and admitted myself rather than kill the son of a bitch."

I found my niche in bringing claims for wrongful discharge or discrimination against employers—an effort to rebalance the scales of justice in the workplace or corporation. It was clear that the stress of being treated as a replaceable part, working isolated, or feeling combative at work, could be deadly. With more heart attacks occurring between 8 and 9 AM on Monday mornings than at any other time during the week, causing that hour to become known as "Black Monday Syndrome," it is clear that work needs to be seen as not simply a means to earning a living but key to making and maintaining a life.

Glancing back in the mirror one morning I could see in my face that long hours and battle fatigue were taking their toll. I'd hit the ten-year skid mark as a lawyer and my discontent and disillusionment with my profession were showing. I worked hard to improve the work environment for my clients, but was now seeing that something would have to shift for me as well. The reflection in the mirror was all too familiar. There's a look of helplessness that I've seen a hundred times in the painful and vacant faces of employees confronting an insensitive or hostile work environment. Was I seeing it in mine?

Tools of the Trade

Linda's death had a profound effect on me. I'd become a junkie for shredding adverse witnesses, blackmailing someone into a settlement, making a perpetrator squirm, or taking down an opponent before a jury, while telling myself that the ends justified the means. But when Linda died I could feel more acutely the bodies left in my wake; no longer could they be simply written off as acceptable collateral damage. "They" were not merely "defendants" but people who like Linda had struggled with their own challenges and demons. I'd justified the harm I could inflict as a type of instant karma or retribution for the opponent's role in my client's injury, but suddenly I couldn't shake the feeling that the line between me and the federal bean counter who ordered Linda back to work was growing thin.

Was litigation destined to be war? Having entered the courtroom arena for years like a Roman warrior arriving at the Coliseum, pumped by the roar of the crowd, I had prided myself on how well I'd learned to play the game—seeking to punish, humiliate, and take down the oppressor. Few I knew ever questioned the brutal and exploitative manner in which we solved conflict, charging forward to "fight" the "good" fight. Arthur Kinoy, both a friend and mentor, who took on the Nixon White House and the House Committee on Un-American Activities (HUAC), used to throw his fist in the air and shout "Power to the People" while driving his audience of young law students and lawyers into a frenzy as he added: "And *we're* going to win." But was winning everything?

The pursuit of truth in our current model of lawyering felt less about fairness and more a tug of war until one side drags the other into the mud, or surrenders into a bottle of pills. Lord Henry Brougham captured this attitude perfectly in his 1820 defense of Queen Caroline against King George IV's charge of adultery, declaring that a lawyer "in performing this duty to his client must not regard the alarm, the torments, the destruction which he may bring upon others. He must go on regardless of consequences." Little had changed over the centuries. My profession felt more destructive than constructive. As with Linda, it became all about ruthless "efficiency" rather than human need. In the end, was this justice?

Violence Begets Violence

I have always abhorred violence. The first time I saw my father break down sobbing was while recounting his brother Marvin's last days, before being killed near Normandy at the end of World War II. Even thirty years after this violent death, it still haunted him and the tragic loss and anguish from war felt somehow passed down to me as if embedded in my genes.

As I turned eighteen, tragedy came closer to home as I received the call that my Uncle George had rolled down his car window as his mistress' enraged husband, a soft-spoken man who had been kind to me, blasted him in the face with a sawed-off shotgun. The numbness and silence the murder brought to our family never fully dissipated.

Watching the fiasco in Vietnam and our folly in Central America I never understood how violence could do anything but beget more pain. Now I was becoming consumed with the question of why I'd chosen a profession so fraught with violence, where aggression was rewarded over compassion or understanding.

All around were the casualties of the legal system: victims who had come for aid or justice, only to be belittled or humiliated by war-like tactics of their opponents' lawyers or judges who launched ego-driven diatribes laced with hostility toward the clients, or more often, toward even the most conscientious lawyer. Abusive, violent, or angry outbursts became a legal strategy many used to scare away an adversary. "If you file the case against my client we'll go nuclear," one lawyer threatened, meaning he would inflict pain beyond one's imagination. Lawyers I met asked me to share some "war stories," the trophies earned in courtroom battles, where the mercenary attorney hired for the fight finds solace and memorabilia in the extent of pain inflicted on the other side.

I began to notice how I'd been feeding this frenzy with violent language, going to a hearing to "kick some butt" or "tear apart the witness." We'd celebrate "killer" cross examinations where we "went for the jugular," "destroyed" the witness, or "took his head off." Supporting evidence was "ammunition" we could use to be the first to "draw blood." A prospective client once leaned into me and said they had come to see me because they'd heard "I was a real ball-breaker." I didn't totally dissuade him of the perception, but after he'd left the office I stared out the window asking myself: "Ball-breaker? Funny I thought I was a lawyer."

This combative system had taken its toll on me. I felt ragged and disillusioned. It was a cold winter morning when the phone rang and I recognized the voice of a colleague from New York. Her words could not have come at a better time as they shook me from my trance and gave me an offer I could not refuse.

"Come to South Africa" she said. "Mandela is free. A transformation is brewing."

▼ ▼ ▼

PART II

Ubuntu Rising

Camay (Quechuan word): the act of breathing unity into something.

CHAPTER 6
Embracing the Unknown

Trust thyself: every heart vibrates to that iron string.
–Ralph Waldo Emerson

US Federal District Court—Albuquerque, New Mexico—
February 1991

As the Walkman explosion took the life of Bheki Mlangeni, I was battling race discrimination on safer ground before a jury in the US Federal District Court. Despite it being just days before my first trip to South Africa, no one had sent word of Bheki's death. For the past weeks my days and nights were consumed in a surreal battle wherein my client, Sandy, an African-American news journalist and anchor, was challenging her treatment at and firing from Channel 13. Sandy had faced an offensive work environment from the moment her plane touched down in Albuquerque to start her new job. Andrew Hebenstreit, the white station manager and son of the station's owner, picked her up at the airport. He was dressed in farm garb and his face was painted with black shoe polish.

"I'm Andy," he said, holding out his hand. "Come along. We're having a Halloween party." He spoke in a feigned southern black sharecropper voice, as if expecting her to play his sidekick "Amos" for the evening. Her shock and humiliation upon arrival in the Land of Enchantment was clear in her voice and through her tears. My job was to link Andy's attitude to her treatment and help a jury understand racism in America.

The CBS-affiliated station was struggling to lift its anemic ratings, and Sandy was a shot of fresh air. But Hebenstreit's bizarre behavior continued with racially and sexually charged jokes in the workplace.

After several years of enduring his patronizing and offensive comments Sandy began objecting. Soon after, he fired her and the newscaster herself became front page news.

The Hebenstreit family was extremely wealthy and had owned the station for a generation. To me this was a case of the rich plantation owner operating as if he ruled the world with impunity. Clearly I was putting them into a box and making my own black and white projections, but I relished the opportunity to play Robin Hood and spread their wealth around in the name of justice. Making the family and their millions pay for their arrogance became the goal. I deposed Hebenstreit's mother, family members, and would have gone after old man Hebenstreit if he hadn't died a few years earlier.

A trial sometimes deters an employer from treating other employees in a similar manner. But I wanted something more. A part of me wanted to see Hebenstreit humiliated and exposed before the public. This was the type of retributive justice I'd been raised on. My goal was clear: Hebenstreit was going down.

The station defended the case relentlessly and was not going to give up without a fight. They hit Sandy hard with clips of several on-air miscues gleaned from hundreds of her broadcasts, and spent tens of thousands of dollars on New York City TV news experts who claimed even though she had anchored for many years she was, in their expert opinion, "incompetent." The federal courts, now stacked with conservative Reagan and Bush I appointments, continually blocked our ability to discover the necessary documents under the guise of streamlining litigation and saving costs.

The battle extended beyond us versus them to us versus the judge. I pushed to have Andy's substance abuse admitted and secure evidence of how others who made similar mistakes had been treated, but the judge excluded most of it as too "prejudicial." I thought giving the control of people's livelihoods to Andy was akin to letting an intoxicated driver take the wheel—someone should pay for the accident they caused. Sandy didn't have the resources to match the experts—terminated employees rarely do—and we relied upon the jury to see through the exaggerations and post hoc justifications.

But the lawyers for the station made it a case of us versus them, implying that it was her race that kept her in the job too long, playing to the fears of the white jury that "they" were a threat to "our" jobs.

With no blacks in the jury pool and New Mexico in 1991 only having a 3 percent African-American population, I knew that a "jury of her peers" wasn't happening.

Divide and conquer often rules the battlefield in the courtroom, and while railing at the inequality I was oblivious to the fact that by turning this workplace and family upside down, I was playing the same game, albeit on the side of good. No one on either side saw the other side as human beings sharing a common humanity. Feelings of anger, outrage, and condemnation ruled. We made the choice to go toe-to-toe and it was getting bloody.

The trial dragged into the third week and onto the doorstep of my much-anticipated trip to South Africa. I'd been asked to have input into the new constitution for the emerging rainbow nation and I felt thrilled and proud to participate in this unique transformation from apartheid, but it also made my upcoming closing argument in a racial bias case particularly poignant. On the last day of trial, just hours before my flight to South Africa, the courtroom was filled with the press and supporters on both sides.

Sandy took me aside when I arrived. "Thank you for believing in me. I know we're going to win," she said. We hugged.

I told her "No, thank you. I'm proud of you for taking on this important struggle."

I knew she felt battered and bruised from the onslaught. "We've won already." I added. "He'll think twice before hurting someone else."

But I knew the verdict was always the great unknown. As we waited for the judge to arrive I couldn't shake the fear that their *blame the victim* strategy had left its mark.

I'd been up all night preparing my closing, and, as I took my place at the podium, I knew I'd also be facing two further days of travel without sleep beginning that afternoon.

"Ladies and gentlemen of the jury," I began. "You have the power to restore fairness to this unfortunate and tragic event. You can send a message to this employer that there is no space in the heart of our nation for inequality."

Closing arguments are the joyful culmination of being a trial lawyer. Part actor, part teacher, after weeks of disjointed testimony we get to finally talk to the jury and make them feel that they are part of a historical continuum for justice. I never talk down to a jury; instead I mix education with a little entertainment.

I continued: "Race discrimination manifests differently today than in the days of Jim Crow. We still research employment law under *Master and Servant* law in the legal books. Racism is not as blatant here as in a place like South Africa," my mind floating out across the sea, "but it can linger in the attitudes and insensitivities of the Master when the Servant steps out of line or speaks her mind."

They listened intently and I was becoming convinced that the nods were genuine.

The most meaningful aspect of this closing argument for me was that Khlari, my seven-year-old son, came to watch his papa in action. After finishing my closing, I looked back and Khlari's smile from the back row told me I'd won at least one vote. The court called a recess and the judge wished me a safe journey. I took my son's hand and rapidly left the courtroom to catch my flight to South Africa, which was leaving in forty-five minutes. My newly minted associate, Becky, stayed to hear the defendants' argument and the court's instructions to the jury.

Heading to Africa was for me like diving into a great unknown. I would bear witness to a country's efforts to break loose from its chains of racial separation and express directly my solidarity with the anti-apartheid movement. In New Mexico years before, I had joined with Governor Anaya to push for state divestment in South Africa, preparing the legal arguments that the state could base its investment decisions on moral and ethical considerations. All around the world the cry of *Free Mandela* and *End Apartheid* created a groundswell for unity and justice—an international call to action. With many nations imposing sanctions on South Africa, the isolation was taking its toll. Today I was stepping out of the storybook, moving beyond the theoretical, and into history in the making.

On a personal level my heart felt as if it were on a parallel track with those in the struggle—yearning to break free, but from what I did not yet know. While the jury began its deliberations on racial equality here at home, I was sprinting to the gate with only minutes to spare. Falling into my seat I let out a huge sigh and suddenly broke out in tears. I needed this trip.

The Soul Snatchers

Johannesburg, South Africa—March 1991

For the first time in a decade of lawyering I was not there when they read the verdict—not there for my client, win or lose—something I will always regret. Two days after landing in Joburg, through a crackling phone line, Becky spoke the words I was not used to hearing: "We lost." I was shocked and disappointed that after years of struggle and the passage of key civil rights laws, racial bias still ran deep and increasingly could not be rectified through the courts. I spoke to Sandy the next day and offered my condolences, but I could feel her pain and anger even from thousands of miles away.

Hanging up, I, too, felt hurt and angry. It must have been the rich Hebenstreit family, or the biased jury, or the judge's rejection of evidence. Clearly the fear-based divisive defense strategy had impacted the deliberations. I needed someone to blame. I suddenly felt so alone and millions of miles away from home. In a world of winners and losers too often the loser cries alone.

I went out into the African twilight and sat on the curb. Dozens of black domestic workers were walking swiftly down the streets after a long workday to begin their two-hour or more journey back to their township homes. Despite it stripping a piece of their dignity daily, each day they'd return to work, take care of the white children, and clean and wash the homes of the minority. No talking or visiting on the street corner after a long day, as they must catch the vans, trains, and buses that ensure that they are out of "white areas" before dark and able to see their own families.

This nightly ritual reminded me of the eerie scenes of mass exodus from the film *Invasion of the Body Snatchers*, but here it more aptly could be called *Invasion of the Soul Snatchers*. Apartheid had invaded the soul and stripped human dignity down to its bare bones in the name of racial superiority. South Africa was the ultimate example of the Age of Separation as race and class divisions were preserved behind high walls and barbed wire and an economic system supported by cheap and highly controlled labor that caused families to be separated for months or years at a time. The wounds ran deep. The contrasts were sharp. I stood at the entrance to a Johannesburg

Mercedes auto dealer and beyond it as far as the eyes could see were shanties, shacks made of rusted tin, scrap wood, and cardboard. More than eight million lived in shacks without running water or electricity. What a mountain to climb.

It was so clear that South Africa had to change its fractured relationships in order to survive, but the trial in Albuquerque had me wondering whether, in America, we had really come so far. Laws do not automatically result in a change of attitudes and the way people live their everyday lives. Why was I here? Was it to be part of history or to feel part of something outside my tiny world? As the tired workers passed me in the street I realized I too was tired, marching disconnectedly and mechanically from case to case, blindly accepting the flawed, impersonal legal system as a way to resolve human disputes. In litigation the parties go back to their separate lives and learn little about each other. Something was missing.

Clarence Darrow said, "Justice has nothing to do with what goes on in a courtroom; Justice is what comes out of a courtroom." The lesson for me was getting clearer each day. I needed to get out of the courtroom battles and resulting heartache. There had to be a better way to resolve conflict. No surprise that the township I visited the next week was called Crossroads.

When I arrived in South Africa its future was also anything but certain. Just months before, Nelson Mandela had been released after twenty-six years in prison. The white South African government was refusing to discuss a transfer of power or free elections. Fifty-five people were killed by state-sponsored sectarian violence in the township of Alexandria days before my arrival. Everywhere our diverse group of lawyers went, people shared personal stories of great sacrifice and triumph that exemplified courage and perseverance. Nearly everyone I met had lost friends or family in the struggle.

An Unsophisticated Minority

Crossing blood-stained pavement, where a week prior a battle of ANC supporters and government-sponsored Zulu members of the Inkatha Freedom Party took place, I'm reminded that we are in a war zone. My eyes follow the dried streak of blood as I nervously enter the downtown Joburg high rise that now houses the African National Congress (ANC). Moving from a revolutionary underground organization to a political party is clearly an historic step forward and a work in progress.

The furnishings are quite simple and its walls, while sporting a few posters of the anti-apartheid movement, remain empty and in need of paint. I'm reminded that less than a year ago they were a banned organization forced to work on the run, at war with the government that remarkably still remains just down the block in more regal quarters. As I'm seated around the long conference table where Mandela and the ANC national executive committee map out their hopes for the future, in walk Walter Sisulu and Joe Slovo.

Sisulu, a short man with squinting eyes and a soft smile, was Mandela's closest confidant for decades in prison on Robben Island. He reminds us that very little has changed at that point as they have the same parliament, police, army, judiciary, and civil service as before. Slovo, whose white skin matches his mane of white hair, is an ANC leader from the Communist party. While cleaning his pipe he says, "We had always hoped to avoid violence but we didn't choose an armed struggle, it was chosen for us." Slovo remarks that justice is a constant struggle, adding, "You can repeal all the race statutes tomorrow but Apartheid will still be here in effect." They both indicate that they are prepared to return to armed struggle if the government will not step aside and let democracy rule. I sense their resolve but also their deep yearning to write a different story.

Cyril Ramaphosa, the secretary general of the ANC and future parliamentarian arrives and quips that the white government's Minister of Constitutional Affairs is still warning against a disposition "that will give power to an unsophisticated majority." They all smile at each other. They know, as I have seen, that they have hundreds of brilliant ANC comrades who, like Mandela, have demonstrated amazing patience and wisdom.

These brave freedom fighters stand in great contrast to much of the white population, which is only ten percent of the country, that is clutching to its power and wealth through the police thugs and military. As we're leaving I say to my group, "Being 'sophisticated' in the oppression of millions should qualify you for prosecution, not parliament." I'm embarrassed for my skin color, as if a white stain connected me in some way to these apartheid criminals.

South Africa's ruling National Party seeks to hold onto the spoils of the apartheid system it created in 1948, so they spout this warning of "unpreparedness to rule" to raise fears and delay the inevitable. Fear, as a strategy, has always had an impact. If you say something often enough, people start to believe it (think "weapons of mass destruction"). I recalled the flight from London to South Africa where a woman of Indian origin sat in the seat next to me and parroted the government line perfectly. She said, "They are like children and you can't give them power because as it now stands as they would not know how to use it"—as if the current administration, which classified her as "colored," had done such a bang-up job.

Most of us are children when it comes to understanding the dynamics of human relationships or our connection to something greater. A glance at the twentieth century reveals that those in power ran international relations more like schoolyard bullies than like adults engaged in active listening, problem-solving, and nation building. "My bomb is bigger than yours," or "Give it back or I'll beat you up," reflect bullying more than efforts to build a more peaceful world. Yet, my experiences in South Africa are pointing to something mysterious and powerful, but unknown, that changes us and the world if only we open our eyes to it. It's a sparkle, a hope against great odds and a feeling that we all share a common humanity. It's a hope and dream of something greater that lives within us all: ubuntu.

Cape Town, South Africa—March 1991

One evening I arrive at an ANC *braai*, the Afrikaans word for barbecue, in the yard of a stately Cape Town home. It's filled with dozens of people of all races—a gathering that a year prior would have been illegal. A group of political prisoners had been released from prison that afternoon and such moments are cause for celebration.

When the newly released prisoners arrive fresh from the boat from Robben Island, they literally fall into the arms of their loved ones and comrades. Tears and smiles are flowing everywhere. Dullah Omar, the future Minister of Justice, stands up on a chair and raises his fist and the yard falls quiet as they all sing the revolutionary anthem that fueled their hope for peace, *Nkosi Sikelel iAfrika*. He then declares that it's not the time for their usual long-winded speeches, but to rejoice. People turn and embrace everyone around them and the party melts into music and dancing. In a nation that had suffered too many funerals, freedom is to be savored, and we all dance as if there is no tomorrow.

Over the next few weeks the large hearts of the South Africans continued to touch me as we work closely with people who had only dreamed of this moment. There is a directness here between people that pierces right through barriers and speaks to something innate in us all. After our meetings on the ANC-proposed Bill of Rights and a conference on a new constitution, Pius Langa, the future Chief Justice of the Constitutional Court, summed it up best when he told us, "This gathering has been not just an encounter of minds, but the encounter of souls—a homecoming." Zola Skweylya, an ANC constitutional scholar and future Minister of Social Development, appreciated the solidarity, and said "We've missed talking and touching through the years because of the curse of apartheid." While there's a nervous energy about the unknown days ahead, all concluded that what South Africa needed was peace.

In the morning, as groups of children surround our delegation, a small girl, no more than five years old, barefoot in a rumpled pink dress, takes my hand and leads us through the dusty streets of the shanty town outside Cape Town. With boycotts and a lack of facilities or supplies, few are in school. I thought of my young boys at home. Sasha was only four years old, and how much we take for granted: a home, breakfast, safety, a peaceful moment. All around me I see abject poverty, but also, despite such painful conditions, the brightest and most hopeful eyes I've ever seen. People invite us into their makeshift homes, often bound together with wire, rope, and deferred dreams, offering us tea with such a sense of respect and welcoming. I can feel my life shifting.

Bringing It All Back Home

On the last night in Cape Town, after days of discussing a potential bill of rights replete with workers' and women's right, and a right to education and human dignity, I lay watching the ceiling fan turn above my bed. I too must stop mechanically moving in circles and cleanse the war within me. I have no idea what that will look like, but I know I need to reframe my whole approach to conflict and ground myself in something deeper than my legal training. My choice is to either continue as a gladiator warrior "fighting back" and playing to the roar of the crowd, or learn more about humanity and the power of passive resistance to injustice.

Albuquerque, New Mexico—April 1991

Returning from South Africa I call together the six employees in my law office and announce that I am taking the practice in a different direction. We're phasing out of our trial cases and only taking cases to represent people to negotiate a peaceful and fair resolution with their previous employer. If we're not successful I'll simply pass it on to other lawyers who can take it to court, but that I must take a new and more direct approach to helping people without them having to go to war. My officemates are upset, as they knew most of their jobs were focused on extensive trial preparation that would become unnecessary, but they can see that this trip has changed me and that I am determined.

It was a great unknown. I felt the great courage exemplified by the ANC comrades and their battle against apartheid and I knew it was time to change the way I did business in my community. There's something unnatural about the way we operate and I want to be more in sync with the natural rhythms and relationships around me. But can I earn a living? Will employers respond to a letter that invites dialogue rather than threatens battle, or accept that it's a shared problem that warrants working together on solutions?

The pulse running through me while in South Africa was driving me forward. The camaraderie of the ANC activists and deep craving for peace came from something in their hearts and in their relationships. Bringing home the messages and integrating them into my own life was calling me. It was time to take the leap.

▾ ▾ ▾

CHAPTER 7

Hope and History

Hope is a state of mind, not a state of the world.
–Vaclav Havel

Bophuthatswana, South Africa—April 1994
A cold wind rippled through the Mmbatho Plaza. Two soldiers, one black and one white, marched toward the flag posts. The gathering of mostly black homeland residents watched transfixed as the dual flags of the formerly fragmented South Africa were lowered, and the new united flag rose toward the sky. Freedom came at midnight to South Africa on that historic night as the words Seamus Heaney wrote to celebrate Mandela's release from prison ran through my mind:

> . . . once in a lifetime
> The longed-for tidal wave
> Of justice can rise up,
> And hope and history rhyme.

With fists raised to the sky we sang the new unified national anthem that included *Nkosi Sikelel' iAfrika—God Bless Africa—*with its century-old motto of "Wisdom, unity and peace." At that very moment the all-white Parliament and the all-black homeland were dissolved. The last note was greeted with bursts of shouts, whistles, and dancing. On that amazing night the people orchestrated their own rhythmic celebration of freedom. Strangers embraced and danced with one another. Individuals coalesced into a community. It was an explosion of joy.

South Africa's liberty had been bottled up for so long that when the cork popped at midnight on April 27, something more elemental than new law and political prisoners were liberated. Apartheid's chains had been wrapped around everyone's spirit, black and white, and tonight the people's spirits soared together. Dancing along with everyone else, I realized that we were celebrating not only the end of apartheid but a regeneration of the heart. Apartheid had separated more than bodies. It had suppressed something innate—a connection with one another, the essence of being human. Here at the tip of Africa a palpable feeling of unity rose like the harvest moon, illuminating new possibilities and hope for our fractured world. It was contagious, exhilarating, and frightening.

Much of the world viewed South Africa's pending election and transition to democracy as nothing short of a miracle. Gandhi's early struggles against apartheid taught him that "The spirit of democracy is not a mechanical thing to be adjusted by the abolition of forms. It requires change of heart."

My heart needed this trip back to South Africa badly. The year after my first trip I'd gone to India seeking something on a spiritual level, but after three weeks of questions and answers with a guru and then moving among the ancient history of Rajasthan, it left me more confused than enlightened. While freedom and liberation were the hallmark of the South African struggle, I was seeking my own personal liberation of the heart. But my struggles were challenging me at every turn.

I'd made the decision to change my practice from trials to conciliation, but such an approach was still new and uncertain and my life seemed anything but peaceful. Weeks after returning from my first South Africa trip, my wife had a horrific car accident that left her on her back for years, and we struggled to connect on a deeper level between the pain and the tears. Khlari had become a budding teenager and our relationship became more combative. In order to cope with everything spinning around me I'd closed off a part of me that was too painful to face. I needed to feel hopeful and to witness the triumph of healing over great adversity. Where better than in the country that just three years earlier had shaken my world and opened me up to new possibilities?

As an international election observer, I was charged with reporting to South Africa and the United Nations whether the election appeared "free and fair." The whole world watched as a former political prisoner, Nelson Mandela, was expected to become president of South Africa. An international mediation between the Mandela-led African National Congress and the Zulu led Inkatha Freedom Party (IFP) had collapsed, and the IFP leader Chief Buthelezi was still calling for a boycott of the elections. Hundreds of people had died in sectarian violence in the weeks prior to our arrival. As my plane touched down in Johannesburg, the ability to avoid a bloodbath at this late stage was in doubt. Some, including South African singer extraordinaire Miriam Makeba, told me I was brave and "slightly crazy" to be heading into such a firestorm, but something inside me was trusting on a deep level that peace would prevail.

Bop

The formation of several nominally independent homelands was a method of separation and control instituted under apartheid. South African blacks were over 85 percent of the population but lived on only 13 percent of the land, and millions had been forcibly relocated from their homes because of the color of their skin. When the South African government cleared out a particularly rebellious township or neighborhood they would bulldoze people's homes and ship them off to a homeland. In 1986 more than 70,000 relocations took place in one township alone in order to break up dissent and advance the economic objectives of apartheid.

The Afrikaner Weerstandsbeweging (AWB), known as the Afrikaner Resistance Movement, was a right-wing racist paramilitary force bent on disrupting the elections. A month before our arrival more than 700 armed AWB men drove into the South African black homeland of Bophuthatswana (Bop), shooting random blacks along the way. They were fighting to preserve the homeland system of racial separation but also dubbed it *"Ons is op 'n kafferskiet piekniek"*—"a kaffir-shooting picnic."

News channels around the world and within South Africa covered little of their rampage. But on March 11 the AWB was cornered near the Mafikeng airport, and a Black Bop policeman became the buzz of the international media as he executed at point-blank range three wounded AWB members as they pled for their lives. The policeman said simply,

"What are you doing in my country?" and fired. The shooting was captured by journalists and broadcast worldwide. Pundits questioned whether South Africans were ready for freedom, reporting that the country was bracing for a civil war. I was assigned to monitor in Bop.

Days after the AWB shooting spree, Louis Mangope, the homeland leader aligned with the apartheid government, went too far. About forty people were shot and wounded, three critically, when police opened fire on demonstrators in the Bophuthatswana capital of Mmbatho. The dictator Mangope fired the staff of the Bophuthatswana Broadcasting Corporation for reporting on the deaths and closed down television and radio stations. That week hundreds were wounded and sixty more people killed as the people took to the streets and demanded their right to vote. The strike brought public services to a halt. The people would not be denied.

To conservatives, Bop was a key last stand to save the Age of Separation in South Africa against the horrors of a multi-racial state. But the majority of people welcomed elections, wanted reincorporation, and wanted to vote. They rose up in such numbers that Mangope and the AWB were forced to flee.

As I connected to Bop Air from the Johannesburg airport and flew north the outcome was anything but certain. The AWB had turned their attention to building bombs, while the Zulu Inkatha Freedom Party, still boycotting the elections, continued its bloody clashes with ANC supporters, leaving scores dead and more heartbroken across the fractured country. Would people be too afraid to vote? Perhaps I was crazy to head into such a battle with no apparent skin in the game, but I never doubted retuning to South Africa. Yet, the first thought that I might die thousands of miles from home surfaced. I thought of my boys, my wife, friends and how they, despite the dangers, supported my trip. One of the side effects of not really being in touch with my feelings was that I didn't have to do "scared shitless."

An Atmosphere for Freedom

Staring out at the rolling hills below, I'm reflecting on our anemic voter turnout in the States where the majority do not even bother to vote. In 1992, US voter turnout had risen 5 percent—to a whopping 55 percent. Nearly 100 million did not vote while in a small homeland South Africans were dying simply to get that right. During my lifetime people in the US had also died to protect and secure the right to vote. I'm haunted by the photos of Chaney, Goodman, and Schermer, who had gone in the 1960 Freedom Summer to Mississippi only to be murdered by whites who resented their efforts to help register black voters—our own deadly battle with apartheid. I now understood their courage and determination on an entirely different level.

As we land in Bop my heart is racing as I wonder if I too would be ready to die to stand up for freedom. Looking back I see how frightening it was, but at the time, "feelings" were to me more dangerous than what lay before me. Driving from the airport into the Bop capital of Mmbatho, I'm struck by some of the modern facilities juxtaposed with the shanties. The tiny office of the Independent Electoral Commission (IEC) in neighboring Mafikeng was buzzing like a beehive as workers rushed about frantically answering calls and moving out with voter pamphlets and election materials. The IEC was independent from the government but was given the task of administering the election, deciding disputes, and pronouncing, along with international observers, whether the election was free and fair.

The IEC was barred from setting up shop in Bop until after Mangope was run out of office. They had less than a month to move from chaos to an infrastructure for a free and fair election for millions of people in the homeland. Apart from handling complaints and engaging in voter education, they had to set up and staff 167 polling stations. It was in the IEC office that I first met Felicia Roberts.

Felicia was a lawyer and sub-regional director of the northwest region of the IEC. She was a courageous fighter for justice, making great efforts to pull her white community along kicking and screaming into the twentieth century. Though she was young, a neurological condition made it necessary for her to use a cane, but she was tall of stature and filled the room with confidence when she entered. I could not have possibly known then that only two years later I would dine with her and my friend and mentor Haywood in Cape Town at the last meal before their untimely deaths.

Felicia suggested that we accompany as many IEC officials as possible as they conducted their investigations, adjudications, and mediations in support of the election.

"The goal of the IEC," she told us, "is not to merely strive for a free and fair election, but to create an atmosphere for one."

"How do you create a healthy atmosphere with so much turmoil and so little time?" I asked.

She smiled and said, "It involves reaching into the hearts of the people, finding potential flashpoints of conflict and resolving those clashes or calming fires before they arise."

A government's goal of "reaching into hearts" was a refreshing notion. I knew why I'd come.

My pre-election days were filled meeting with police, political party representatives, and poll workers. But late into the night I would share my observations by writing my notes into short articles and reading them over the phone to a bleary-eyed editor at the *Albuquerque Tribune* who was running them in the local newspaper.

Sharing my words and experiences contributed to this new world we were all seeking to create. Congressman Dennis Kucinich spoke with me once about the power of words, inspiring me to change the dialogue whenever possible: "We can have the world any way we want it," he said. "But if our world is constructed of words of hate, violence, and admonishment, it's very painful. On the other hand, if our world is made of words of love, hope, or joy, we create that too." I wrote an editorial in the *Tribune* before leaving for South Africa to share the hope I was experiencing:

> On the eve of these elections, as I fly to bear witness to true democracy in action, I urge the world to not focus on the violent acts of those bent on delaying democracy. We should be celebrating the liberation of millions of people and praising the courageous South Africans who struggled in prison, in exile and in pain for the right to live free.

Having viewed the press coverage of the violence over the past months I wanted an avenue to refocus the dialogue. The international press focused more on the execution by the policeman than on the heroic uprising of the masses in Bop. Too often we feel victimized by the media's bias, silence, or limited vision. I did not want to silently witness the change in South Africa, but share as I could what I was seeing on the ground. Active witnessing requires more than simply showing up. The *Tribune* graciously printed my articles verbatim, allowing me to connect with thousands back home on this historic long walk to freedom. The nightly collect calls with my editor also gave me a connection to my hometown and reminded me that I was there on behalf of my friends and neighbors.

Common Dreams

Our small group of observers are traveling to the countryside to observe the IEC investigation of complaints related to violence and police abuse. The police play a key role in guarding polling stations from acts of terror, but have often been the tool of the people's oppression. Conflicts in villages and at polling stations needed to be defused so people could feel free to come out and vote. We're heading to the Dinokana tribal village to investigate a claim of assault by a police officer and questionable arrests of ANC supporters. Our IEC workers are armed with a radio to connect with the defense forces in the event of a conflict. The last time the IEC was here, the two tribes brandished weapons and the South African Defense Forces had to be called by radio, arriving in helicopters to secure the site and separate the factions. As we approach the town Sechele, our IEC monitor tells us, "The radio's gone dead. I can't reach the base."

A discussion ensues and we decide to continue on to the village. There is little time before the election and these issues cannot wait. I admire their courage and determination, but their nervous joking tells me they're worried. Like us, their backgrounds are in the law, mediation, or social work. They had seen themselves running an election, or arguing for justice, not defusing a war zone. Adventure has never been my strong suit either. At that moment a hot bath at the hotel sounded really good.

When we arrive, a group of children gather around us and one boy, no more than twelve years old, brandishes a large knife—though more like a toy or trophy than a threat. Our presence in Bop as international observers has generated some news coverage and it pays off as the clerk at the Trading Post approaches us with a broad grin. Waving the children away he suddenly takes my hand and says, "I saw you on Bop Television. So pleased to meet you!" The police we are investigating seem less enthralled as they approach in a green pickup flashing their automatic weapons and slowly passing our van. They make their presence known several times as the IEC's interviews occur, and one can't tell if they are guarding us or trying to guard their secrets.

Yet the witnesses bravely tell their tales of police abuse, armament caches, and a thrown hand grenade that may have been a tear gas canister. The IEC can do little at this point about the allegations except to promise further investigation into the police misconduct. Still, the mere presence of someone affiliated with the government who shows concern and listens deeply to their issues is something new, and it teaches the villagers a lot about what to expect in a more inclusive democracy.

Standing out above the conflicts is the wonderment of it all. Everywhere we go we find serious bouts of election fever. A woman tells how her nine-year-old nephew, who has heard so much about voting, came in crying and told her, "My heart is so sore. I want to vote." The Voter Education Campaign was astounding. Comic books and ads and posters on voting are everywhere, and a local NGO, Lawyers for Human Rights, held seventy-six workshops on voting over a ten-day period, including within prisons. *Vote Africa* materials were distributed widely in the cities in both the English and Tswana languages. Even a sign in the washroom seems to point to a new world: "Peace cannot be so long as you've got a gun. If you have it, take it to the police station. Please, now. Not another death later." The stations have large drop boxes for weapons—no questions asked.

But in the countryside it is more difficult to reach people and the IEC teams often must rely upon local white farmers to "assist" their workers. At times we would learn of a campaign by some farmers to provide misinformation by telling their workers to put an X next to the names of the candidates they were voting against. Others receive threats of losing their jobs if they do not vote for the National Party. We visit ANC headquarters and are told that some people have been told that if they go to vote they will be shot by the Bop police. With the police having just weeks before been standing by the dictator Mangope, the people distrust them immensely. Much of the voter education is aimed at reducing such fears. These misinformation campaigns are investigated and whenever possible appropriate voter training is provided.

"Whenever possible" is the relative term as the resources for the unit are stretched and we are in a dramatic countdown to the election days. Fortunately, South Africa had decided to hold three days of voting. The first day is reserved for elderly people, those with disabilities, pregnant women, police and military, prisoners, and IEC employees. It also serves as a dry-run to deal with ballot shortages, staffing needs, and the inevitable long lines. Communication with stations is also complicated because radio contact can be sketchy in rural areas.

Reaching into Hearts

Turning out the vote is seen as the key to success and essential for universal acceptance of the results. People can register to vote at any time, even on election day. But the more lofty goals of crafting a long-term culture of peace after years of institutionalized divisiveness is what truly motivates these workers. The week before the election we are heading with an IEC mediator and two monitors to help settle a dispute. I call them "smokechasers," like those firefighters in the hills of New Mexico near my home who locate fires after lightning has hit and struggle to bring them under control.

Two villages side by side, mostly populated by people who were relocated under apartheid, are in a dispute that threatens the local election process. The village of Bakolobeng is led by a chief whose entire tribe was relocated against its will in 1976 from lands their fore-fathers had owned for decades. Under apartheid whole areas were declared "white zones," and the blacks on the land would be forci-bly relocated. It is one of the great tragedies and evils of the system. In an effort to weaken families and separate people from their roots, thousands of men were forced to work hundreds of miles from their homes and live in bunkhouse dormitories called hostels in newly cre-ated townships. With forced relocations happening often in the dead of night without any notice to the families, many men were unable to locate their families when they returned home after months at work. As we approach this election dispute I realize we are about to dive into this deep pain of separation and unresolved anger.

The conflict arose because the adjacent township of Lakgoabi had spilled over into a no-man's-land that lay between them and the more established village of Bakolobeng The township residents are composed of a patchwork of people relocated from various areas and they are constantly jealous of the village. The Bakolobeng chief has had a more formal and favored status with government officials, who over the years have put more modern facilities into the village. The people from Lakgoabi township deeply distrust the police and feel they have been more responsive to tribal needs than those of the township.

This conflict came to a head when a few days earlier one of the township members had been shot by the police and the IEC, who knew nothing of these tensions, placed the polling station in the more modern Bakolobeng tribal offices. The Lakgoadi were upset, felt further marginalized, and were afraid to come into the village to vote. We head to Bakolobeng to observe the IEC as it tries to mediate the tension.

As we drive north we pass hundreds of acres of corn on "white farms" where black workers have lived for decades in a form of indentured servitude. Stopping at a crossroad, I make eye contact with a black worker in the field next to our van. He has no shoes and flashes me a toothless grin, but does not stop working. What will freedom mean to him? In South Africa there are over seven million people living in shanties, most with no running water or electricity. Unemployment hovers around 40 percent. Thirty percent or more are illiterate. The tasks facing this new government are daunting and people will want to see the results they believe go hand-in-hand with freedom. I smile back, but my heart aches at the task that lies ahead after the ballots are counted and the real work begins. I imagine some of the peacemaking efforts are meant to build patience in people for the long road ahead.

Understanding a little of the complaint at hand, the IEC officials look for a suitable place to set up a second polling place in Lakgoadi so that the township people can feel more safe and empowered. The shanties of cardboard, paper, and scrap lumber seem to roll on for miles. We stop at a local store that could be a possibility, but it looks no different than most of the homes, except for the rusted Fanta soda sign over the door. Such last minute stations and the truncated time-table to prepare for the election in Bop pose quite a challenge.

As we enter the tribal offices for the mediation we are met by a small delegation and the chief. The ninety-two-year-old chief, who doubles as the local minister, sports a long gray beard, soft eyes, and wears a slightly rumpled suit. One of the township representatives takes my hand and says, "We hope that in your presence we can reach a peaceful resolution." Peacemaking out in the open seems much more effective than behind closed doors. We are led into a room which is just large enough for the mammoth conference table as representatives from each side, including four local policemen, clan leaders, and Lakgoadi council members and youth leaders, squeeze in and silently face off.

Our IEC mediator, Vivienne, is the only woman in the room. She is tiny but full-bodied, and the men listen to her with great respect. All are allowed to speak. Sometimes the chief, in deference to us, speaks in English. "We are honored to have you here," he tells us. "Many of us have only heard of the US, but to have you come to our village is very important." But it is Vivienne who commands the most attention as she massages the dialogue to common ground. Remembering that they all share a common story is essential: All have been relocated or forced to the homeland by pressure or circumstance. Listeners on both sides nod in agreement as one township youth leader says, "I'm so sorry in my heart that one man can bring another man to such a sorry state of affairs."

After three hours of speaking about fears, upsets, and justice, the parties agree that there will be no new settlements added to the disputed land and that, after the election, the new government and courts will address the dispute. All agree that a peaceful and fair election process is essential as a nation and they all pledge to put aside their differences and make this happen. A second polling station is set up in Lakgoadi. As the mediation ends, we all rise and a soft prayer is sung in beautiful harmonies, as if they had been singing together forever. Its sounds echo through me. I am witnessing the power of true peacemaking in action—as Felicia said, "reaching into hearts."

Throw Them into the Sea

That night we attend a barbecue at Vivienne's home. After a hard day of working, the IEC workers take to joyous drinking and dancing. These people work and play equally hard. Many of the women from the IEC have changed from their slacks and western work clothes and are decked out in dramatic colors and head wraps. They dance with such power and their tongue-twirling yelps send the room into a frenzy. I spy Vincent, an IEC monitor, outside looking at the sky. I wander out and see he is in a reflective mood.

"Vincent? You okay?" I ask.

"Just looking at the stars," he says. "We are so close. This is a day for which we have dreamed, just to put an X on the ballot."

We both watch the moon rise and I am reminded that for many of these IEC workers it is also their first-ever opportunity to vote. Days later, after returning from voting, another IEC worker, Sichele, summed up his feelings of liberation and the resulting responsibility: "I now understand why people were trembling." I am not alone in feeling the magnitude of the moment.

The next morning I awake to good news. Inkatha Freedom Party President Mangosuthu Buthelezi said Inkatha had agreed to accept the results of next week's elections, if we, the international community, endorse the process as free and fair. This is huge. The Zulu/ANC clash resulted in over twenty thousand deaths, including four hundred in the past five weeks, and Mandela worked hard to get them on board.

The IFP story is intrinsically linked to apartheid's efforts to foster separation through divide-and-conquer techniques. Inkatha played straight into the white government's hands, as the military built a strategy to delay freedom by encouraging black-on-black violence. The South African masters of apartheid, along with US conservative groups such as the International Freedom Foundation, secretly gave millions of dollars to the Apartheid government and to Zulu Chief Mangosuthu Buthelezi's Inkatha Freedom Party, ostensibly funding the violent confrontations with members of the African National Congress.[1] The goal was to keep blacks divided and killing each other so that the rest of the world would say, "These Blacks are so tribal that they can't be given political and economic power."

The South African struggle for freedom also became a playing field for the cold-war dynamics of the day. The IFP professed strong anti-communist sentiments and became the darling of conservatives like Senator Jesse Helms and President Ronald Reagan. Mandela was not removed from the US "terrorist" watch list until 2008, and the CIA's role in his capture and subsequent imprisonment is now emerging. On the other hand, Buthelezi opposed sanctions and dined at the White House with Presidents Reagan and George H. W. Bush, and was touted as the alternative to the more radical ANC, which had communist members.

To most of the world it was Mandela who was a hero and he had worked feverishly to bring the IFP into the fold. Shortly after his re-

---

1. Sam Kleiner, "Meet Conservatives Who campaigned for Apartheid South Africa," *The Nation,* July 9, 2013.

lease in 1990, Mandela went to Durban, the heart of Zulu support, and made this plea in a famous speech to a full stadium: "My message to those of you involved in this battle of brother against brother is this. Take your guns, your knives, and your *pangas*, and throw them into the sea. Close down the death factories. End this war now!" It became his mission to stop the bloodshed and reach out to all South Africans.

Arriving at the IEC office I saw how a collective sigh of relief had now replaced the dark cloud of uncertainty. The elections would now go forward without the Inkatha cloud hanging over our heads. Though I was hundreds of miles away from any Zulu stronghold, all felt like this fractured nation was finally coming together. Days later a box arrived with thousands of stickers with Buthelezi's photo and the name Inkatha Freedom Party to be placed in the last spot on the ballot.

Several nights before the elections we head to the giant sports stadium in Mmbatho with our IEC friends for a highly needed distraction. For years, international sports teams boycotted South Africa and we were now going to the first international soccer competition held in the Mmbatho stadium. The Zimbabwe National Team takes on South Africa and the stadium is bursting with new-found pride. When the South Africans score their first goal the place explodes, but when late in the game their second goal goes in and seals the 2-0 victory, the people go into a frenzy. Everyone is hugging and bursting with pride. As we exit into the streets thousands of people are still chanting "South Africa, South Africa, South Africa." We can tell it's not simply about a game, but something larger—they are cheering a new dawn.

▼ ▼ ▼

On the day before the election I awaken to the news that a car bomb exploded in central Johannesburg, killing nine people and wounding more than one hundred. The message is clear. "Don't vote. We can strike anytime." I feel a chill down my back as I remember that just days before I had stood on that very corner. I think about my friends monitoring in Johannesburg and hope they are safe. This election process is a roller coaster of emotion; from the highest highs to fear and mourning in the same day. Sadly, in South Africa this is how they have lived for years.

▼ ▼ ▼

CHAPTER 8

Holding onto the Gift

*I have cherished the ideal of a democratic and free society in
which all persons will live together in harmony and with equal
opportunities. It is an ideal for which I hope to live for and to see
realised. But, My Lord, if it needs be, it is an ideal for which
I am prepared to die.*
–Nelson Mandela at his trial in 1964

The election days are unlike anything I have ever experienced before or since. On the morning of April 27th, the usual hustle-bustle
of the streets is replaced by a hushed, almost reverent silence. Everyone is either in line voting or watching the progress of the election
at home on *Good Morning South Africa*. The image of Mandela voting
that morning is beamed around the nation and the world throughout
the day.

My first stop is the hospital in Mafikeng, an old British colonial
building built in 1898. Glancing down the long corridor I am struck
by the hundreds of people, many in wheelchairs or on crutches, waiting in line to vote. The image is compelling. After so many years of
bombings, violence, and dehumanizing treatment it's as if a nation,
though battered and beaten, has arisen, magnetized by a force greater
than their bodies, across the finish line. Down the street more than
five hundred people are in line for voter IDs. Computerized photo-
graphic equipment allows them to leave almost immediately with
their voter cards.

I enter a polling station just as a group of white South African Defense Force soldiers burst through the door armed to the teeth with
machine guns. The room goes silent. Is the dream over? "We're here
to vote," the captain tells the frightened monitor. A nervous laugh

comes from those in line. The monitor manages to say simply, "Yes, of course. But you'll have to leave your weapons outside." Rules are rules. The captain thinks about it for a moment and then they retreat, lay down "their swords and shields," and join the line. They now stand side-by-side with those they had previously fought and struggled to disenfranchise. Scripture has never been my strong suit, but I can't help but mouth the words "and the lion will lie down with the lamb." It's a miracle brewing.

As we traverse the countryside we pass people walking toward the polling stations. Some stations are one hundred kilometers apart. Arriving at the first rural polling station the lines are wrapped down the road for as far as the eye can see. More people are pouring in on buses and donkey carts. Truck loads of workers are brought in by white farmers. Voters clutch their ID cards, and I ask one elderly woman dressed in her finest multi-colored wrapped skirt and cloak, "How do you feel about the wait?" She smiles infectiously and tells me "We've waited so long. This line is short compared to the road we've traveled."

The ballot itself is a beautiful sight; nineteen political parties are represented, reflecting the diversity of the emerging rainbow nation. There are the familiar parties, like the ANC, Pan-African Congress, the National Party, and Inkatha. But scroll down and you see the Keep it Straight and Simple Party and the Sports Organization for Collective Contributions and Equal Rights—the SOCCER Party. Today as a result of this proportional representation system, more than fifteen parties hold seats in parliament. This is what democracy looks like.

When the goal is to get everyone to vote, you have to get creative. A woman arrives in a vehicle but is unable to walk. There are no wheelchairs or stretchers at this polling place. The presiding officer makes it possible for her to vote through the car window.

As an observer witnessing for peace we are told to not get involved in the actual election process. But sometimes a human need arises and we're called upon to assist, even in small ways. I help a man carry his frail, elderly mother in a chair into the voting booth. After she votes we lift her chair and lean her forward so she can, with her own hands, place the folded ballot into the ballot box. She could not walk or speak a word, but she made the effort to be here on election day. In Mafikeng there is some confusion on how to seal the first ballot box. I'm asked to help and I end up sealing the first ballot box from the region to head out for counting. It's a thrill to get hands on and demonstrate the solidarity I feel so strongly within.

I'm also in the actual voting booth with voters who have either asked for help from the election official or been encouraged to ask for assistance by an overzealous white poll worker. We accompany them into the booth to witness and report back to the IEC if we felt the monitor was being intimidating or simply assisting, a gray line at times.

Prejudice and bigotry will not dissolve merely with an election or the approval of an interim constitution guaranteeing equality. In the United States we abolished slavery and passed the Equal Protection Amendment to the Constitution in the nineteenth century, and the voting rights and civil rights acts in the early 1960s, but it took activism by people in the streets and the courts to make it more of a reality. As a result we purposely choose to focus on voting stations run by whites in the rural areas of Bop as we suspect that these old attitudes might be running the show.

In one station an official representative from the National Party seems eager to talk to me. She tells me that she is fearful of the future and casually asks, "So how is it with the niggers in your country?"

"Pardon?" I ask, as if my mind were playing tricks or I had inadvertently stumbled into one of those movies where people are forced to speak what they're thinking inside.

She repeats herself verbatim. My first instinct is to respond with anger and tell her that it is her type of attitude that still contributes to divisiveness and bigotry in our country. But I remember the lessons from the week before in mediation and listening, and instead I acknowledge her feelings: "Change and the unknown can seem frightening," I say. I tell her of the successes of our civil rights movement and the fact that African Americans, as a minority, have had to struggle against incredible obstacles to achieve more equal opportunities. "We still have a ways to go." I say. "But in the end we are all just people with the same hopes and dreams for our children."

She listens intently and nods. I can't really tell if she takes it in or is thinking, "Oops, I picked the wrong white guy to ask." But later she offers me tea and a biscuit.

Too often we focus on the words that were used and miss the chance for dialogue and communication. This monumental, negotiated process between the oppressor and the oppressed in South Africa has taught me much about winning over your opponent with persistence and heart. Nelson Mandela's former jailer, James Gregory, guarded the ANC leader for more than twenty years, but describes Mandela as "closer than a brother." He admits that he had instructions to do everything he could to demoralize Mandela and all the "terrorists." Mandela refused to treat Gregory with anything but respect and talked with him, not as the enemy, but as a fellow human being, sharing stories of family and asking him about his life. For Gregory, something in Mandela stirred him. "He was different." When we meet another on a human level, labels and fear dissolve. Mandela, even in prison, was living Gandhi's words: "We may have our private opinions but why should they be a bar to the meeting of hearts?" Mandela would invite Gregory to his inauguration and maintained contact with him over the years.

We witnessed a sharp contrast between stations run by the white farmers and those being monitored by black Africans. In white polling stations nearly all blacks are asked if they need help, while in black-run everyone seems to vote smoothly without much assistance. In a town of Ottoshoop I find myself in a booth with a voter who seems confused. She is a domestic servant and our friend from the IEC, Sechele, is in the booth as the monitor. He tells her in Tswana to vote for who she wants, but she explains that her employer told her she had to vote for a particular party. Sechele tells her that the employer will never know about who she voted for and that she should vote for who in her heart she wants to elect. She reaches for the pencil, whispers, "Cosi Mandela," (King Mandela) and makes her mark. The empowerment and confidence that was delivered in that simple moment is immeasurable.

But it's different when the employers are the ones in charge. In one town we are met by a huge white male presiding officer, probably six-foot-five and nearly three hundred pounds. We watched him throw his weight around with voters. He is hostile to our presence and greets us curtly. I go in the booth with him and a poor farm worker.

"Who do you want to vote for?" he snarls in Afrikaans. The voter mumbles something.

"I can't hear you. Louder," the official orders.

In a barely audible voice, as if being squeezed out of him, he says, "DeKlerk."

The official quickly pencils the X for him next to DeKlerk and sends him on his way to deposit it in the box. I watch the voter shuffle out of the booth. He looks as if he'd been punched in the gut, his eyes are vacant and he lacks the joy that seems so endemic these days. It's consistent with what we heard about intimidation in the rural areas. The official boasts that he knows most of the people voting, which of course means he knows where they work. When we confront him with questions about his approach he dismisses it, saying "These people don't even know how to wash their hands."

This, however, is the exception and not the rule. The story remains one of hope and determination. Even after standing in line for eight hours voters remain ready to make their mark on history. Most times I witness them sliding their finger down the brightly colored page and see them pause by the smiling face next to the African National Congress flag. As if infectious, a long overdue smile in turn blossoms on their face and they say one word: Mandela.

One woman with a woolen cap and cane takes the ballot and just stands there as if in a trance looking at Mandela's face on the ballot and beaming. She has to be taken by the arm to move behind the voting stand. I hear some giddy laughter coming from the booth. Most first-time voters actually appear taller when they leave the booth, with a different gait in their stride, as if a great weight had been lifted. Some shout, or physically leap into the air. Others solemnly move out, their smiles following them out into the street and into the new South Africa. Their craving for respect and dignity had been granted. One elderly man looks right at me as he exits the booth and says, "Now I can die."

A wellspring of inspiration arises when freedom rings. One black African IEC worker told me that he had started classes toward his doctorate some years before but abandoned them because he felt it was useless as most jobs at that level were reserved for whites. Now he explained, "With freedom I am going to go back and get my degree. There will be opportunities and I feel a deep desire to contribute. I am finally truly free."

Free and Fair

The day people got to vote for Nelson Mandela as their president it changed the game. I felt their joy through my bones and in the years ahead would draw upon those moments in darker hours of doubt or despair. It felt like they were casting a ballot for all of us. Voting for the belief in a world of possibility. On those election days my understanding of our common humanity deepened. Langston Hughes danced in my head: "I've known rivers: / Ancient, dusky rivers. / My soul has grown deep like the rivers."

The number of eligible voters in 1994 was estimated to be 21.7 million—about 16 million of whom had never voted before—and the IEC reported an astonishing 90 percent turnout. On election eve a 220-pound bomb ripped through a taxi stand killing ten people and the next day, as if targeting those of us in the international community, a bomb went off at the International Terminal of Jan Smuts Airport in Johannesburg. To me it was their "fuck you" statement to those of us in the world community who had fought apartheid for so long and came to stand up for change. News of the explosions made me realize that as the elections proceeded, we too might become targets of their anger, reminding me to be vigilant and to keep my eyes open for anything suspicious. But the airport bomb turned out to be a last hurrah as they could not overcome the craving for peace and equality sweeping the land.

During the three days of voting and for the next week the news, usually thirsty for violent stories and conflict, reported an unusual peaceful calmness blanketing most of the nation. Astonishingly few acts of violence occurred anywhere in a country that for weeks had suffered from violent clashes and uncertainty. In the week following the election all reported crime had dropped by over 50 percent, incidents of violence between rival political groups disappeared, and the election period was, according to the *Star* newspaper on the second of May, "the quietest in years."

Incoming President Mandela would say in claiming victory, "The calm and tolerant atmosphere that prevailed during the election depicts the type of South Africa we can build. It sets the tone for the future. We might have our differences, but we are all one people with a common destiny." The conscious decision to methodically craft an atmosphere for a free and fair election, along with the hard work of thousands in the IEC and NGOs, was a living example of the power of people over fear.

No election is perfect, especially under such pressures and circumstances. We reported and recorded minor irregularities surrounding placement of election materials, delays in opening stations, lack of Tswana speaking interpreters, and overbearing "assistance" by some white monitors working with first-time voters. Despite what may have looked like intimidation by the monitor, we frequently observed the voter still proudly declare his or her choice: "Mandela." It evoked the old African-American spiritual popularized during the US civil rights movement:

> Ain't gonna let nobody turn me around
> Turn me around, turn me around
> Ain't gonna let nobody turn me around
> I'm gonna keep on a-walkin', keep on a-talkin'
> Marchin' down to freedom land

Full Circle

On the eve of the election I had dropped by the IEC office. I turned the corner and literally ran into a force majeure. When I looked up I heard a familiar voice boom, "Eric!" There was Haywood with his wild hair and beard and beautiful smile and I was the immediate recipient of one of his patented bear hugs. I hadn't known he was in South Africa but it made sense, as he had been such a strong anti-apartheid activist. I treasured the photo of him getting arrested at the South African consulate office in the US, as he was a lawyer always willing to lay it on the line for justice. A brilliant scholar and peacemaker, Haywood Burns had just been appointed the Dean at CUNY law school and I was sure that those students were in for the ride of their life.

I'd just returned from a contentious meeting with the police where they threatened to "shut it down" if the elections became marred by violence. Haywood was a sight for sore eyes, as he always had this way of lighting up your world and making you feel larger than life. He was also a legal observer, so we swapped stories.

"An experience of a lifetime," he said, his eyes shining ever so brightly. "This is where it's happening."

Haywood personally knew many of the South African freedom fighters. He told me, "There is so much potential for this multiracial democracy to become one of the great nations in history." Haywood had championed civil rights in the United States as a young activist with Martin Luther King, Jr. His experience in South Africa, he said, "was like coming again full circle back to Mississippi." We met again that night at the plaza for the new-birth-of-a-nation flag ceremony. I'll always remember how proudly and powerfully he danced as the flag of the new South Africa crackled above us in the cold wind.

Lost in the Wilderness

Deep in the cavernous Mmbatho Civic Center auditorium, now the regional ballot counting station, IEC workers are unfolding ballots throughout the hall and the sounds are like fluttering leaves in autumn. In the euphoria surrounding the actual voting I'd forgotten how crucial the counting process is in making an election is free and fair. If there are substantial discrepancies in the accounting reconciliation of each coded ballot, or boxes are open or missing, it will be fuel for one of the parties to contest the process.

The nation had come so far, and had so many minor miracles and victories, that no one wants to have the election fail now. Seven agents from the top political parties are here, positioned around the many counting tables. Each will have to declare "satisfied" after ballots are read aloud and recorded, which precludes them challenging it later.

Kelepile was the lead monitor for the Mmbatho counting station. She was no more than twenty-four years old. She is one of the few South African women I've seen wearing jeans. I ask her about the day and the counting process, but then, catching my accent she asks me, "Where are you from?"

"The US" I say. "In a state called New Mexico."

"I know America. I went to school for a year in Chicago," she tells me.

"How was it?" I say, thinking it explains the jeans.

Never taking her eyes off the voting tables, she waits, then says: "It was like being lost in the wilderness. One never knew who your true friends were."

I understand what she is saying. Sometimes I too have felt alone and lost in the isolated and apathetic consumer culture of my country.

"What are the main differences you experienced between South Africans and Americans?"

She smiles, and I can sense that she is grateful to be home.

"When you give Americans something, they look at it—sometimes touch it—and then they quickly discard it. But here," she says, turning to face me and looking deep into my eyes, "in South Africa when someone gives something to someone else, they take it," she says softly, pulling her clipboard tightly to her chest, "and they hold it close and it is with us forever."

Her words shake my heart. This was what I've been trying to understand about my experiences in South Africa. The people live with so much passion, a sense of presence and a deep connection to one another. It's what I'd later learn from Archbishop Tutu to be ubuntu. It explained why despite struggle they can still laugh or cry. Tears well up in my eyes. I know it's time for me also to live ever deeper. What a precious gift.

As the actual counting begins, the IEC monitor at the table calls out their counts as they hold up each ballot. All around me, like a choir, I hear dozens of counters almost singing: "ANC, ANC, ANC."

▾ ▾ ▾

The count continues through the day and the following morning. My legs grow tired and I find a seat in the corner of the room to rest. Beginning to doze off, I find myself thinking about my wife, Shady, and how I long to hold her again, to even weep in her arms and show her my emerging heart. I have learned so much about love and life on this trip that I can't wait to share it with her. Like the voters here, she has been so very patient, waiting for my heart to show up. Suddenly she comes to me in the darkness. I sense her eyes running toward me, so brown, like the eyes of a tiger. Her hair brushes my face. Our hearts melt together in a rhythmic dance. I reach out for her just as an empty ballot box drops near me and I'm back in the auditorium, realizing the beating of our hearts has been the sound of the ballots unfolding. But the taste in my mouth is that of our first kiss . . . and I know she is with me. I also know it's time to go home.

After the election Archbishop Tutu graciously said, "The international observers were there to do much more than verify the elections as free and fair, but were like midwives helping to bring to birth this new delicate infant—free, democratic, nonracial, nonsexist South Africa." All of us actively witnessing this change, too, experienced something profound. Like any midwife or mother will tell you, it's the magic that lingers after the birth that makes the struggle all worthwhile.

The IEC and other organizations from around the world declared that the election was substantially free and fair. We filed our report with the United Nations, the IEC, and with the new South African Government. The standard was whether the results "reflected the will of the electorate." When Mandela took the oath of office days later the world ground to a halt to share that moment of hope and joy.

I will never forget watching the millions who had been humiliated, imprisoned, beaten, tortured, and resettled against their will stand patiently for hours across barren scraps of land in rain or hot sun to vote. Archbishop Tutu spoke for all of us after casting the first ballot in his lifetime: "It's like falling in love."

I have learned so much in South Africa that transcends politics and elections. It is a place where men can warmly embrace and a handshake, even between men, will linger into holding hands as they talk, as if to maintain a connection on another level. While speaking, people look deeply into your eyes and listen intently. Such human skills will help them to leap the huge hurdles that lay ahead. But what I've witnessed will serve as lessons of the heart for me to carry forward in my own life, for which I am forever grateful. Today humanity feels less like an endangered species.

The counting is over. As I stroll back to my hotel through the streets of the new South Africa a young black man approaches me quickly from across the street. I kept walking, but he was coming right toward me. Does he have a weapon? Do I know him? Suddenly he sticks out his hand and takes mine in his and breaks into a smile and says: "Peace." He quickly disappears down the street. I'm speechless and embarrassed by my initial reaction. But the message is clear: slow down, take the hand of a stranger, and remember we all crave the same thing—peace.

Waiting for my ride to the airport, I'm startled by the sound of gunfire coming from the alley. The usually peaceful Tswana people in the street start to panic—the murderous AWB invasion was just a month ago. Is it a revolt? Have the white extremists returned? One gunman appears in the street and runs past me, followed by a second. They fire the guns in the air as they pass. It's not the AWB, but turns out to be two overly zealous celebrants who must have just seen Mandela's declaration of victory on the television. They shout, "Madiba," and fire again into the sky.

As Pele drives me to the airport we pass a barren field with a single tree, the *Acacia tortilis*, or umbrella thorn, silhouetted in the distance by the setting sun against an orange sky. It is a moment right "out of Africa" and I am reminded again that despite all the struggles and the horrors of this world, there is beauty all around. I have witnessed an unparalleled historical moment and know that I want to take the gift that has been given to me, actively share it, and hold onto it forever. But somehow I know that there are still mountains to climb. Like Mandela said in 1953, more than forty years before he was sworn in as president, "There is no easy walk to freedom anywhere, and many of us will have to pass through the valley of the shadow of death before we reach the mountaintops of our desires."

▾ ▾ ▾

CHAPTER 9

Going to the Edge

Behold breathlessly the sight
How a raging river of tears
Is cutting a Grand Canyon of light.
–Ani DeFranco

The stone fireplace illuminates more than the room. Cedar pops and sizzles in the warming inferno. I've come by train to the edge of the Grand Canyon, to slow down in the waning days of 1995, and as educator and poet Parker Palmer says in his poem about the Grand Canyon, "Redeem in beauty all my life has been." Soon I will be forty years old and my reflection gene is on high alert. The snow falls, glistening like fine mica crystals, as I walk back after dinner from the stone lodge at the south rim; the soft moist flakes feel alive on my face. Excessive work breeds a disconnection with the body and the world around me and since returning from Africa the glow from the elections gave way to the stress and uncertainty of my career path.

I'm grateful for this trip. A federal judge recently stripped me of a multi-million dollar verdict and another case, one of my last trials since my decision to change my practice, was crumbling under the weight of my client's shifting version of the truth. What was the purpose of spending hundreds of hours over the past months if not to win? What makes one side feel righteous and the other defeated when issues are so rarely black and white, or good and evil? So many questions about the nature of conflict resolution and my role. I lay in the window seat near a crackling fire reading the grand Chilean poet Pablo Neruda: "That time was like never, and like always," he writes. "So we go there, where nothing is waiting; we find everything waiting there."

I'm looking for answers—wanting to hold onto things with a depth and richness like I had experienced in South Africa. Mandela's patient victory and magnanimity had me again questioning the objective of vanquishing the enemy in court. While I was fighting inequality, discriminatory attitudes, and hostile workplaces, I knew that many times my effort to prove motivation for what someone did to my client was at best an educated guess. Even our Supreme Court in *USPS BD. of Governors v. Aikens* has said that direct evidence of a "man's state of mind" is as difficult to ascertain as his "the state of his digestion."

As a result, each case became a canvas on which to paint a story and hopefully help lift our world to a higher place: dispelling stereotypes surrounding race, sex, or age, or opening up a company to scrutiny of its illegal practices. Because of the draconian principle of employment law that most employees may be fired "at will" for no cause, I was often left pigeonholing each case into a narrow legal theory (discrimination, whistleblowing, retaliation) and running with it. The problem is, it's not always a comfortable fit.

Most cases are proven, not through any absolutes or even beyond a reasonable doubt, but by weighing the evidence on the scales of justice—and side to which the scale tips is the "winner." Whether it "more likely than not" that they discriminated became the standard. I'd tell the jury: "If you weigh their evidence and ours and find that it leans 51 percent in our favor then you must find it was discrimination"

But a part of me felt sad with the realization that justice in the courtroom was so far from clear and absolute. It was an elaborate game, an imperfect science, sometimes no more than a biblical split of a baby; not what I'd imagined fundamental fairness or equity to be.

In fact, through the harshness of litigation I found the defendant rarely feeling moved to reexamine their conduct, at least on a conscious level. No surprise really, for when you call someone a bigot or point a finger, a defensive reaction is natural. Even after a jury of their peers would find them to be biased or retaliatory, they'd still blame me, saying I'd twisted the truth. In part they we right. I had bent the story toward my version, but that is what I understood to be my role as a lawyer. Justice was to emerge from such a "contest."

Litigation did little to achieve a peaceful resolution, as it often bred more resentment and anger. One morning in a local cafe, after one particularly hard-fought case in which the City of Albuquerque and

Parents, Jack and Shirley circa 1948. Shared a vision of equality, activism and a love or human rights.

Eric with his Stella 1966.

Tenth grade was a chance to let my hair down. Photo taken in Tangiers, Morocco, 1972, dodging hash dealers.

Washington, DC, November 1969, Moratorium March on Washington against the Vietnam war. Photo through the eyes of a thirteen-year-old.

My sons, Khlari and Sasha. Already starting to rock the music world, circa 1994.

My first law office across from University of New Mexico. I traded environmental law work for office space.

Fidel Castro came to give a greeting to our gathering of lawyers in Havana and then spoke for three-and-a-half hours, 2000.

Rallying and organizing years against President Reagan's cuts to domestic programs. Albuquerque, NM, 1982.

Havana, Cuba, 2000. Climbed a monument with a group of lawyers during a million-person march along the Malecon in Havana, protesting the embargo and the failure of the US government to return Elian Gonzales to his father in Cuba.

Havana, 1977. Had never met anyone from our arch enemy the Soviet Union until then. Pictured here with fellow Michigan State student Paco (L) myself (3rd from L) and two Soviet friends.

Meeting with Bishop Desmond Tutu in East London, Eastern Cape South Africa to record a greeting to our International Monitors of the Truth and Reconciliation Commission and to learn about Ubuntu.

Co-Writer and executive producer on the slam poetry free speech poetic documentary *Committing Poetry in Times of War,* based on a case I had litigated and a police riot in the streets of Albuquerque, 2007.

South Africa, 1997. With my friend Dullah Omar, former lawyer for Winnie Mandela, fellow labor lawyer and the Minister of Justice of South Africa after the ANC won the elections.

First Hearings of the Truth and Reconciliation Commission. Eric (far right) and group of lawyers from the National Lawyers Guild and the National Conference of Black Lawyers with Archbishop Desmond Tutu, 1996.

My mentor and freedom fighting lawyer Haywood Burns just before his death when we were together in CapeTown, South Africa. Photo courtesy of his surviving wife Jennifer Dohrn.

At a barbecue in South Africa as prisoners were released from Robben Island. Future Constitutional Court Justice and ANC activist Albie Sachs raising his fist and leading the welcome home and the singing of Nkosi Sikelel' iAfrika—God Bless Africa.

Eric (far right) with Bishop Desmond Tutu and group of lawyers a arriving at the Cape of Good Hope and to South Africa to work with the ANC on a proposed constitution, 1991.

Citizens listen to the testimony at the Truth and Reconciliation Commission hearings through translation headsets. Nine official languages in the new South Africa makes for creative nation-building, 1997.

its mayor were found to be racially biased and retaliatory, the now-former mayor threatened to assault me. In another case I brought against the Archbishop of Santa Fe for fraud, the opposing counsel, upset at our daring to question his client's ethics, challenged me to a fight in the parking lot. I returned to my office and threw a phone against the wall rather than break his jaw.

When I'd start to question my career choice, a case would arise with enough overt evidence to keep me in the game: the company that wanted to "mitigate the retirement curve" by getting rid of older employees, or as its vice president called them, "dead wood;" the electrical lineman who for more than a decade would pull the pants off the new recruits and spray paint their genitals; the female State Highway Department employees threatened, raped, and forced to endure naked women pinups in the workplace; the police pepper spraying a blind Christian talking about Jesus on the street corner; or the jokes about the Klan from the bellman's white supervisor at the local Marriott hotel.

These cases would force the employer to defend the indefensible and it was pleasurable to watch the rich cats squirm. I couldn't imagine how the defense lawyers were able to sleep, let alone present their cases with a straight face.

Around this time, I received the first-ever City of Albuquerque Human Rights Award. The plaque said, "In recognition of his long-standing commitment, contribution and concern as an advocate and moving force for human rights and human dignity and promoting human rights and equality through the legal profession to the community at large."

I'd never received nor expected awards for my work so it was humbling and a bit embarrassing. I always thought awards go to people with more of a "lifetime" behind them. Besides, while I felt I'd contributed, it seemed so little in comparison with what was needed. I simply was doing what I thought all active citizens in a democracy should do: expose injustice and leave the world a little better for our children.

I should have felt proud and accomplished, but inside I felt unfulfilled. I'd been a warrior for justice and human rights, but still felt part of an elite system characterized by competition, aggression, and a winner-take-all ideal. Somewhere along the way I'd lost a part of myself in this surreal system of quantitative justice. I hopped on a train west with a deep yearning to at least try and change something in my control: the way I lived my daily life. Whitman was speaking to me my deepest desire: "I am mad for it to be in contact with me."

▾   ▾   ▾

I arrive at the Grand Canyon as the federal government shuts down. President Clinton rejected the Republican budget that expanded the military while slashing programs of compassion. Such things make me want to angrily shout across the planet "It's humanity, stupid," but I actually find myself also closing down as if to protect the wounds it sends to the heart. Though the feds grind to a halt, the park is kept open . . . for me, it seems. We tend to label such governmental squabbles as apocalyptic events like the "fiscal cliff," but shuttering the government feels empowering, reminding me that life is much larger than the Beltway and its trickle-down compassion. Life keeps on rolling.

On arrival, the man at the front desk tells me there are no rooms available, but his coworker steps up from nowhere and says he has a room that he holds for special occasions and I end up with a glorious stone cabin with a fireplace fifty feet from the canyon's rim.

I got on the train on a hunch, trusting that by leaving the details to the universe I'd be accommodated. I love spontaneous trips with no reservations or expectations. It's how Shady and I danced through Costa Rica for three weeks when we first met. Months later, after moving in together, her Toyota was rear-ended and our lives and expectations were crushed between another car and a bus. I went from pushing the limits to pushing her wheelchair as she slowly, but never fully, recovered.

Despite the struggle that ensued, feeling so deeply in love made me believe that anything was possible and contributed to my courage to change the way I practiced and lived. Through the frosted windowpane, I'm transfixed on the falling snow, remembering that feeling in my heart of being more receptive, as if connected to something greater.

I close my eyes and I'm back to that sunset in Shady's arms in Costa Rica. The gentle Pacific waves swirls around us. There we lay, half in the soft sand and half in the crystal waters, cast in the reflecting moonlight as Venus magically appears between two dark birds while a hint of orange still lingers from the setting sun. The next day we lay in a hot river flowing out of the edge of a volcano. I lean over and kiss her. Our bodies entwine like the roots of the rainforest and the warm water rushing over us washes away any doubts.

A quarter of a century later as I write this I can still feel that moment in my body. Seeing through the eyes of love, or connecting with your heart, is like walking into another dimension. Life changes, we forget to slow down and marvel at this creation and each other, but an open heart, mixed with nature's magic, is unforgettable.

When we slow down and take time to reflect and still the mind, we can make our life one of infinite possibilities. Releasing judgment, expectations, and our "plans," we find a place all our own that has great power. This is all very new to me. By the firelight I read an old edition of Whitman's *Leaves of Grass*. "As I Ponder'd in Silence," he writes, celebrating his connection with everyone, "I am large, I contain multitudes." I too want to feel powerful within myself, *and* connected. Odd how this feeling of connection with everything comes when I am alone and away from everything familiar.

Closing the book, I bundle up and move out into the snowfall walking toward the edge of canyon in darkness. The incredible canyon hole, like a great abyss, reflects its majestic splendor, and it feels as if it lies within me. I move closer to the edge until my toes are dangling off. The wind cuts against my face and snow swirls all around me. I stand at the edge of the world, disguised no longer and stripped naked by the moment. And it's glorious.

▾ ▾ ▾

The morning feels like a new dawn on many levels. At sunrise I descend along a snowy trail that reflects only my boot prints commingled with bunny paws. Suddenly I notice the sunshine sparkling along the path like diamonds, while newly risen rays of light create a shimmering cascade of brilliance along the rocks and sloping canyon. The jewel-clad surroundings had been there my entire hike, but when my mind was filled with chatter and thinking about my life, I failed to see my true surroundings. As I look around me it's as if I am Dorothy in *The Wizard of Oz*, first opening her door to the wonderment and colors of Oz. The future seems brighter, like the diamond snowfall along the path. We rarely take the time to appreciate what we have right before us.

No one is poor, o Bhika
All have got rubies in their bundle
But how to open the knot, they do not know
And thus, remain paupers.[1]

These saints also say that the first step to God-realization is self-realization. I take a stick and write in the snow: I AM HERE.

▾ ▾ ▾

---

1. Cited in Julian Johnson, *The Path of the Masters: The Science of Surat Sahbd Yoga* (Punjab: India: RSSB, 1997).

CHAPTER 10

Reawakening

Last night, as I was sleeping
I dreamt—marvelous error—
that I had a beehive
here inside my heart.
And the golden bees were making white combs
and sweet honey
from my old failures.
–Antonio Machado

Joyous singing and shouts drifted through the high grassy veldt and up the hillside outside the village of Cofimvaba. The round walls of the huts dot the South African landscape, reminding me of the hogans and the vistas above the pueblos near my home in New Mexico. Villagers mingled with admirals and freedom fighters-turned-parliamentarians renewed old friendships as a choir swayed with the hypnotic songs of freedom. We were here to celebrate life. Chris Hani would have loved this day.

Haywood Burns

Cape Town, South Africa—April 1996
Two years had passed since receiving my dose of infectious energy from the historic 1994 South Africa elections and I'm back to drink at the well. But I wasn't ready for a dose of "the bitter with the sweet." Days after arriving for a gathering of international human rights lawyers, several friends of mine, true freedom fighters who had all touched my life at home and in South Africa, died in an auto crash outside Cape Town.

Lost were Shanara Gilbert, a quiet law professor, scholar, and activist from Philadelphia, who always had a smile for me; and South Africa's Felicia Roberts, a recent returning exile, who ran the electoral office in Bop. Felicia's courage, grace, and fortitude in fighting for a free and fair election, and her return to help rebuild her nation, had been an inspiration. That afternoon we'd eaten together, discovering great pleasure in the fact that we were both vegetarians.

The third victim was Haywood Burns, my friend and a mentor, a living example of walking this earth with a powerful and open heart. Haywood always had a kind word to say and wisdom to humbly share with me, whether on a stroll through the Pecos Wilderness, from the outfield in a softball game, or after dancing with a band of ragtag National Lawyers Guild diehards into the wee hours of the morning.

Simply waiting for things to get better was unacceptable to Haywood—the consummate active witness. "In the end, time will not make a difference," he'd say. "It is action in time that will." When invited, Haywood would travel anywhere to speak and said, in describing his path, "Nothing was going to stop me from resisting what I saw as wrong." Haywood often quoted with wry approval Anatole France's dictum that the "law, in its majestic equality, forbids the rich as well as the poor to sleep under bridges, to beg in the streets, and to steal bread." His sense of humor, poignant analysis, and commitment to social justice was such a breath of fresh air in the stogy practice of law.

When conflicts arose I watched Haywood, who had worked with the Rev. Dr. Martin Luther King, Jr., become the consummate peacemaker, seeking to build understanding and practice tolerance. He told me, "Listen. Learn to listen well and doors open." Haywood radiated an infectious and contagious joy for life. Yet he could be a courageous warrior representing the black radical Angela Davis against charges of kidnapping, and murder, speaking in opposition to Supreme Court nominees before the Senate Judiciary Committee, and seeking justice for inmates from the Attica prison riot.

Haywood taught me to take the less-travelled path and to go where you can make a difference. At the end of his first year of law school in 1964, Haywood had been hired for a summer job in the Civil Rights Division of the Justice Department. Meanwhile, voting rights workers were flooding into Mississippi for "Mississippi Summer," registering rural blacks to vote, many for the first time, in the face of the poll tax and other exclusionary practices. When the Department of Justice refused to send him to Mississippi, Haywood quit and went down to join the civil rights activists and to teach.

His haunting prophetic words to us at the International Association of Democratic Lawyers (IADL) general plenary on the day before his death are etched in my memory. Standing tall from his seat he smiled and spoke of his marvel at his experiences "watching people coming across the hills and the ages, dragging canes and Ivy poles and walking on crutches to vote" for the first time; at having Mandela visit and speak to us that very morning; at seeing freedom fighters— formerly "worldwide usual suspects"—now occupying the halls of parliament where dreaded apartheid once ruled. As if feeling complete he paused, smiled again, and said, "I could die now I think. But in the meanwhile, let me ask a question." It would be his last.

The night before a group of us from the States gathered at Dullah Omar's home for a small birthday celebration. Dullah, the Minister of Justice who had been Winnie Mandela's lawyer and a defender of labor unions and the banned ANC, was a friend from my earlier days of working on the ANC's proposed constitution. He liked to say he'd been living "in exile" during apartheid, as he was denied a passport. Dullah survived government hit squads' attempts on his life, including one where they tried to swap his heart pills with poison. Yet, he had become the man who helped draft and promote the Truth and Reconciliation Act through Parliament and was largely responsible for the upcoming hearings.

I loved Dullah's warm heart and commitment to justice. He always graciously gave of his time, even flying to Miami at my request to participate in a workshop I was organizing on the Truth Commission. I'd given him the name Reverend Omar, as a hotel employee heard him referred to as a "minister" and was, with all sincerity, calling him the "Reverend fellow in room 608." As a devoted member of the South African Communist party and a Muslim, it was quite ironic. We laughed hard and it became a standing joke between us.

It was Adjoa Aiyertero's fiftieth birthday. Haywood spoke lovingly, telling how much he deeply appreciated her. Adjoa, the Executive Director of the US National Conference of Black Lawyers (NCBL), an organization that Haywood cofounded, interrupted him to simply say to him, "No, Haywood. It's all of us that appreciate you." What an opportunity to put in words something we all felt so deeply and have it said to a friend just before his untimely death.

The phone rang at two in the morning with the painful news. A young South African friend had been driving the three to dinner. Remarking that the driver reminded him of his son, one of his five children, Haywood began to speak of his family when, suddenly, their automobile was broadsided by a speeding truck. Shanara and Felicia were killed instantly. The driver walked away. Haywood died that night at the hospital—fifty-five years young.

Dazed, I move through the hotel corridor to join my other friends from the States in Lennox's room. Lennox and Haywood had been like brothers. Entering the room, I was taken aback by Lennox, always a pillar of strength and coolness, seated on the bed, stunned and redeyed from weeping. Haywood had died in his arms at the hospital. We all held each other and took turns letting our grief flood over us. I found myself once again looking for answers from a senseless situation and questioning a God who takes away those who lived with such love and compassion.

The days following his death felt numb—like a bad dream I couldn't shake. On the tarmac at the Cape Town airport, six of us help deliver Haywood's body onto the plane home to America, sobbing as we sing a departing song and remove the new South Africa flag that draped his coffin. I could not grasp that within a moment Haywood, so full of life and love, was gone. Images of him and his wife, Jennifer, rolling over in laughter in each other's arms, comes to mind, and my thoughts go to Shady and my boys as I realize that any breath could be our last. Suddenly the thousands of miles between us seem larger.

We sent Haywood's body to America, but his powerful presence lingered and we were determined to take steps to commemorate our friends through a celebration of life. Haywood loved a good party. Within a day we organized a grand memorial service with a South African choir and words of support and love from many South African freedom fighters, now judges and ministers in the new government. Sadly, they were highly experienced in burying loved ones. As I enter the hall a soft voice is singing, "Lets' bring heaven down here. I don't want to wait for the angels."

Kadar Asmal approaches the podium: "We share in this tragedy as they shared in our enduring tragedy that unfolded over so many years." He praises each of them for "walking the extra mile." Looking skyward, the Minister of Water and Resources, who lived in exile in Ireland for twenty-seven years, lamented that these three were "tragically plucked from our midst. The good die young." he said. "The good and the beautiful die young." Then, summoning each by name he said "*Hamba kahle*," a Xhosa farewell greeting: "Go well. Good journey. Goodbye."

Justice Albie Sachs, seemingly stunned at the loss of his friend Haywood, who had supported him years before as a "lonely exile treading the earth looking for support and understanding," praises Haywood as that rare American who truly understood the international perspective. The usually animated Sachs is melancholy and his voice takes us to an earlier time long before he donned the robes of a South African Constitutional Court Justice. He described his visits with Haywood in New York:

> I was introduced not simply to the ideas of constitutionalism and human rights but the lived experience of American people who themselves were fighting for their human rights on their own soil in their own context. So the bridge was not simply an intellectual bridge between what we were trying to overcome—apartheid in this country—and what American lawyers felt as part of international universal ideas, it was a human heart-to-heart . . . a kind of bridge.

I knew what he was saying, as that bridge, that heart-to-heart, is beginning to steer my life and explains what had taken me to Africa.

Sachs remarks that in a fragmented and atomistic society, "Haywood somehow managed to pick up the warmest, the best, the most generous, the most insightful qualities of all the different communities and sectors and through him I was able to be in touch with a kind of United America that I found hardly anywhere else." It reminded me that the world so rarely gets a glimpse at the caring and compassionate heart of America.

Then, chiding himself for a touch of "South African arrogance," Sachs concludes with something I knew would be lighting up Haywood's face, saying that "Haywood could have been a wonderful member of our movement, because he had that openness, that generosity, that breadth, that didn't make him tame, didn't make him weak, didn't make him non-combative, but somehow made him a little bit ahead and always capable of bringing people together—a great unifier." Tears rolled down my cheeks and all I could think of was home.

But it was when Dullah took the stage that our common humanity became ever so clear. "Friends, ladies and gentlemen, and comrades. We consider ourselves very rational human beings, but are often seen as people without feelings, concerned only with the world and changing the world. And sometimes we are afraid to cry."

As if having shed many a tear for fallen friends he said, "I was pleased to see Lennox cry. I am sorry to say that but it symbolizes that we are human beings with feelings."

Wiping away a tear, he, too, describes one night in Haywood's New York City apartment where they discussed the meaning of being a revolutionary. "We concluded together, that a revolutionary, though so often demonized, was simply one who believes in the transformation of the world, committed to the transformation of the world. A kind of transformation that seeks to ensure that the human condition is altered so we create a world that is fit for human beings to live in." He describes how Haywood, Shanara, and Felicia fit that mode:

> . . . teaching us that lesson, of internationalism, universalism, recognition of a common humanity, that we are all brothers and sisters in one world. That we need to care for one another, there must be compassion, sharing, that human beings are not fated or destined to make war with each other, to kill each other.

But he, like other South Africans, had learned long ago that "The struggle for freedom never proceeds along a straight line. There is no linear development to freedom."

It was Justice Sach's expression of our common dream that touched the deepest: "We are all part of a great continuum called 'human solidarity' that can transcend national boundaries—a worldwide movement aimed to alter the human condition and make the world a beautiful place. Our greatest tribute to them is to see that the world never forgets . . . to dedicate ourselves to the same objective." They would want us, Sachs continued, "to commit ourselves to do things in our own lives, wherever we are, in big ways and little ways but knowing that there are people who are also doing those very little things that together will create a mighty ocean and that ocean will water the world and make it a better place to live in. Long live Haywood, Shanara, and Felicia."

The applause was so thunderous that it carried all the way to heaven.

The Roar of Awakening

In the days ahead, Dullah could still sense the weight we were carrying. He called and invited me to the celebration in Cofimvaba. "Eric, you must come," he said. "It will help with the healing." He was right. I needed something to shake off the pain. What better elixir than being with Nelson Mandela in a tent filled with historic freedom fighters who had become the healing balm for a nation torn asunder by apartheid. With the auto crash fresh in our minds we nervously drove all night along darkened two-lane highways without center lines to reach the Transkei by early morning, cringing as each oncoming headlight served up a stark reminder of our loss.

Cofimvaba, Transkei, South Africa—April 1996

For decades, Chris Hani's mother would rise early each morning to walk several miles from their Cofimvaba home to fill a large jug of water from the river, place it on her head, and return home. Hani had dreamed that one day this village of his birth would have running water and its people would rise from poverty. Holding tightly to his dream, he had withstood imprisonment, torture, and attempted assassinations to lead UmKhonto weSwizwe, the military wing of the banned African National Congress. Chris was known for his warmth, laughter, and his love of children, Shakespeare, and the classics. But most of all he was known for his fierce thirst for freedom.

For over thirty years Hani struggled to free all South Africans from oppression. One year before the historic election of Nelson Mandela, he told the future president that he had now "become a combatant for peace." Then, as he left his home one sunny morning, an assassin's bullet took away his life. It never, however, destroyed his dream. I remembered how, just days before, a Cuban lawyer reminded us that Jose Marti said that "Death isn't really death, if we have done life's work well."

Chris Hani was beloved by millions and would have likely been in line to succeed Mandela as President of South Africa. Now, three years to the day since his murder, President Mandela was arriving to Cofimvaba, where many of Hani's relatives and boyhood friends still lived, to honor his slain comrade. Mandela had spoken to our group just the week before with the sobering reminder that rights and freedoms are "illusory, unless you change the everyday living standards for the people." On this cloudy windswept day we were celebrating the power of real change, the inherent link between us and the womb, the "origin of all things," said organizer and new cabinet minister Kader Asmal, "a memorial of flowing and living water to salute Chris Hani."

I was beginning to understand how my sadness was something shared with those around the world who have lost heroes and friends, but that one's work, one's active witnessing to the needs of the world around them, can make them live forever in our memories and inspiration. Kadar continues: "A fitting remembrance for one who left us early. We are remembering you here where you threw your first stone, remembering you here in living water. It will be his moment. He shall live forever. Here to celebrate Chris Hani in water." But as always the micro reflects the macro, as Kadar builds to a crescendo reminding us that a greater purpose exists beyond the life of one man: "This is not just a tribute to a great man, but an example of what is happening in our country. The second wave of South Africa. A water revolution is about to break over our land. The invisible people of South Africa have become visible." Little did I know that this Cofimvaba water tap would extend so deeply into my cloistered heart and make visible the hope that can seem elusive when life reminds us not to nail ourselves to the seat.

Just then yelps, clapping, and stomping shake the hillside. The breeze makes the fields of grassy veldt dance as President Mandela emerges from a helicopter. Shouts of "Madiba" filled the air as he enters the large blue and white tent. The crowd sways like ripples in the sea, and I suddenly feel how everyone, including myself, is connected to each other and to the land. These people have suffered so much, yet they still laugh, sing, and share deep joy. How is it possible? In the village of Cofimvaba, something was reawakening deep inside me.

Some have said that the civilized twentieth century began with Nelson Mandela's release from prison in 1990. Emerging from his decades of isolation on Robben Island, he ascended to the presidency, determined to make all his countrymen free by encouraging them to recognize their fundamental human connection. "The chains of any one of my people were the chains on all of them," he said. Mandela knew that the separation between them would only perpetuate suffering for everyone. With his release from prison, South Africa began its collective metamorphosis.

Mandela had a knack for making everyone around him begin to believe in our common humanity, whether a township dweller or a white rugby player. "The oppressor must be liberated just as surely as the oppressed," he said. "A man who takes away another man's freedom is a prisoner of hatred . . . the oppressed and oppressor alike are robbed of their humanity." I had studied Gandhi and knew by heart Martin Luther King's words, "All life is interrelated. We are all caught in an inescapable network of mutuality, tied into a single garment of destiny. Whatever affects one directly, affects all indirectly." But it was on this hillside that I began to *experience* what this meant on a heart level.

Mandela's golden silken shirt shines like precious metal and his smile is just as radiant. He's home, back in the Transkei, in a hillside village like those he'd run through as a boy. He was with his people, who had shared the triumphs and tragedies of his life for so long. Madiba speaks for some time in Xhosa. The several hundred villagers listen intently, holding onto each word. The teachings of the Hindu Lord of Good Fortune Ganesh tell us that it is "only in the presence of the tribe can we be healed." I watch Mandela look into their eyes and touch every heart, including mine. Though I could not understand Madiba's words, the feeling shakes me profoundly. As he smiles, it's as if he's been speaking to me.

The shock and trauma of Haywood's death and the last few days dissolve and I no longer feel alone. Here on the Transkei hilltop I feel bound together with the villagers and Mandela in the web of life—in the continuum of King's "moral arc of the universe that bends toward justice." I sense the hearts around me beating in unison like the Native American festival drums I would hear late at night coming from Jemez Pueblo in New Mexico. Effervescent smiles become contagious, and I begin to understand how deeply we all yearn to connect. For so many of us, our isolated lives have imprisoned us as we desperately seek our freedom. Haywood became free not through death, but through the active way he bore witness to life and refused to accept our inhumanity toward others. As Albie described him days earlier, "It had a lot to do with his ideas but even more to do with his person. He lived it, he felt it inside his soul; he was a free liberated citizen of the United States of America."

After Mandela unveils the memorial to Chris Hani, a deep feeling of gratitude and connection with the love of the people around me wells up inside. I feel a strong urge to thank him for more things than I can name. The crowd surges forward and I work my way in. Determined to reach out, I extend my hand across the crowd. Mandela is still some ten feet away, but suddenly his eyes meet mine and he smiles. As if sensing my need to connect, his hand reaches out and our fingers clasp above the sea of joyful people. With my eyes held in that warm and gentle gaze, the sound of the crowd seems to fade away. I'm speechless and can only mouth the words, "Thank you." Then our hands separate. But the feeling remains, just as I imagine the grass remembers the breeze after it has passed.

On that cloud-covered and windswept day on the hillside outside Cofimvaba, I feel renewed as a proud and smiling Nelson Mandela reaches down and turns on the new freshwater tap. As the water emerges, the silence suddenly gives way to shouts and dancing. It seems like anything is possible. A true roar of awakening.

Heinrich Zimmer tells a story about a baby tiger in the opening of his book *The Philosophy of India*. The baby tiger grows up with a herd of goats. In the process he forgets about his tiger nature and adopts the ways of the goats. Later, he is helped to reconnect to his tiger nature and at that point he roars with awakening. The "roar of awakening" is the discovery that we are more than we think we are. It's awakening from a dream and finding we are in a completely different reality.

I left Cofimvaba to attend the first hearings of the Truth and Reconciliation Commission in the Eastern Cape and for life-changing meetings with Archbishop Tutu. It seems hope is contagious. My reality has shifted. I'm leaving the herd to find my true self and my life will never be the same. We can tap into our hearts and reshape our world. After all, water now flows in Chris Hani's village.

▾ ▾ ▾

CHAPTER 11

Desperately Seeking Justice

Then you will know the truth, and the truth will set you free.
–John 8:32

Johannesburg, South Africa—April 1997

"Leave your bags in the car," the fruit stand vendor cautions us as we exit our van. She has gentle eyes and appears concerned. We've arrived to buy fresh vegetables in the downtown Johannesburg market district. I feel conflicted. What if, when we're out of sight, someone breaks into the van and steals everything? Could it be a setup? In retrospect it proved a friendly warning, but having heard about crime in South Africa it just wasn't clear who to trust.

If I'd been thinking, we would not have been in this neighborhood. Judy Scully, a law professor and co-chair of our newly minted International Truth and Reconciliations Commission (TRC) monitoring project, and two law students, have arrived to be international observers with our project. They opt to put their bags and fanny packs securely under their coats. But unbeknownst to us we're being watched.

As we circle the block, small clusters of South Africans huddle close to the flames that leap from fifty-five gallon drums. I notice the bundles of bedrolls and items of the homeless stored atop bus stop stalls. Many shops are closed but there are hundreds of people in the streets. It stands in sharp contrast to the country lodge our hosts have secured as our base during the TRC hearings next week in small towns outside Johannesburg. We buy some items in a small shop and I'm ready to return to the lodge and cook up an unforgettable veggie feast. As we make our last turn back to the car I'm thinking of exotic spices and a Cape Pinot when I hear a scream: "Put me down, you fucker."

Turning back I see Amy, one of the law students, has been hoisted onto the shoulders of a young man and is being carried back down the sidewalk. Suddenly knives flash around us, bodies are leaping out from all directions, and as if in slow motion we are in struggle to save ourselves and our belongings. I run over and grab Amy's leg, shouting for him to put her down and pulling her back off her assailant's shoulders. They had already, with the precision of a sushi chef, reached under her coat and snipped the straps of her bag.

I turn back and see Rachel hit the ground and I hear a young boy, no more than fourteen, pulling on Rachel's passport and money belt. I grab hold of her leg and pull in one direction and a surreal tug-of-war ensues. He seems quite nervous and wants the bag more than to hurt us. We could have been stabbed or killed easily in the attack. "Just give me the bag," he shouts at us as the strap finally snaps and he and the other assailants run off. I perform a token run after them (what was I thinking?), mostly to try and muster support of others in the street to stop them. No one comes to our aid.

We huddle there together. Judy had been lifted off the ground and held around her neck, but the straps of her bag were pulling against her windpipe and she had been gasping for air. We pick up our torn bags of groceries and move swiftly toward the van. "Sir," I hear a woman say. Turning, I see a short elderly woman with soft eyes and a sad look of embarrassment. "Your tea," she says, having salvaged my box of Rooibos tea that I had just bought in the market and had dropped during the attack. I take the tea but am too stunned to speak. She nods as if she had seen it all before and wants no part of the teenage hoodlums haunting her neighborhood. A simple act of kindness in a sea of violence and indifference, but it brought me out of the shock.

Some lost cash, a few passports, and cut clothes, but we're all in one piece—though within we feel sliced and diced. Our host from the National Association of Democratic Lawyers (NADEL) is outraged and angered when he hears about the attack. He feels responsible. When he hears where we were he says, "Downtown? By the Holiday Inn? My God, *I* don't even go there!"

He implores us "Please. Please, no more excursions without telling us. You are our guests here and we want you to be safe. People are desperate. We have a long way to go to peace."

He mumbles something in Xhosa under his breath. I'm not sure if it's about us crazy Americans or the youthful attackers. It's my third trip to monitor the TRC in the past year and it strikes me as ironic that we've come to be observers of truth and reconciliation and become ourselves victims of the violent pain that still haunts South Africa.

Where's the Justice?

When I first arrived to chair the International Monitoring Project of the Truth and Reconciliation Commission (TRC), I was greeted by an op-ed piece in the Cape Times that read in part, "This is as explosive an issue in South Africa as the Nuremberg trials were in post Nazi-German." But unlike the post-WWII trials and prosecutions, South Africa chose another route. Chaired by Archbishop Desmond Tutu, its mandate was to assist in "healing the trauma of a nation" and to come to terms with its past. After the new post-apartheid government was sworn in it passed the "Promotion of National Unity and Reconciliation Act" calling for a search for truth that "can create the moral climate in which reconciliation and peace will flourish" and "prevent the shameful past from happening again." If South Africa was to survive and thrive it could not melt into a battle between racial and cultural groups, but had to find a more unified path. But at what price?

It was not a universal desire to accord a heartfelt forgiveness to the perpetrators of gross human rights violations that drove the TRC, but a political compromise to avert a bloodbath. After the provisional Constitution called for an election, the security police balked, saying they were promised a general amnesty by then-President DeKlerk and without it they were not going to preserve the peace during the election. Why usher in a new government that would mean their own imprisonment? Thus one of the greatest models in creative and human-based conflict resolution arose from a nation held hostage. Our gifts sometimes come in strange packages.

Amnesty had to be addressed, but how to meet these needs and still secure a sense of justice was a challenge. A general amnesty, as if the past never happened, results in a blanket amnesia that does little to help get at the truth. The ANC was not willing to forgive and forget. Therefore, they negotiated a new form of "individualized amnesty" from civil and criminal prosecution, even for murder or torture, but it required the perpetrators to file their own petitions for amnesty and reveal everything they had done, sometimes in a public hearing.

An amnesty court was set up to review the applications and make two determinations: 1) whether the actions carried out to meet a political objective, and 2) whether they in some way proportional to that objective. Sadistic killings for personal gain did not warrant amnesty. Those acting to defend the regime or fighting for an ideology or a free South Africa could be absolved of all liability. Suddenly, the two sides found a commonality of pain arising from their sad history, as there were applicants from both the ANC and the government security forces.

By requiring full disclosure, the victims would not be ignored and the blanket of denial covering much of the white community could be lifted. Justice was restorative, aimed at restoring dignity and, as Dullah told me, "We had no choice. The alternative was a continuing cycle of pain. To reconcile we had to come to terms with the past on a morally accepted basis." It was, he said, "part of an attempt to assist the healing process for a nation." I had my doubts but was primed to see if this strategy could truly heal such a fractured society.

I could not shake the feeling that when amnesty is granted someone should be held accountable or take responsibility for their actions. My lawyer brain was whispering "Someone should pay." Besides, international law requires each nation to prosecute gross violations of human rights, so isn't a process of amnesty for heinous crimes an affront to international norms of justice? Yet many behind the TRC had been victims themselves, so clearly they had the moral authority to stake new ground.

Constitutional Court Justice Albie Sachs lost his right arm to a car bomb set by the South Africa Defense Forces in retaliation for his anti-apartheid activities. He told me: "What's my arm worth? There's no price on things like that, and to me it would be very demeaning to try and put a monetary price on what is really kind of a part rooted in the liberation struggle. What people want is some sort of acknowledgement."

My friend Dullah, himself having experienced attempted assassinations and imprisonments, was instrumental in the statute's drafting and implementation. He told me "I don't distinguish between wounds, many people are in need of healing, and we need to heal our country if we are to build a nation that will guarantee peace and stability." The goal, he'd say, "is building up a human rights culture in our land. While there is a commitment to break from the past, we must forgive, but not forget and build a future based on respect for human rights."

Mandela, himself a lawyer, reminded us at a gathering in Cape Town that money alone never provides full healing. He said, "We do know that reparation cannot make full amends: there can be no correlation between the pain and frustration of victims and their families and any remedial measures." From years of litigation I also knew this to be true. Something more was needed. A new higher ground. Thus the grand theatre and healing exercise began.

Higher Ground

Truth commissions were nothing new, with recent examples from Chile, Haiti, and Uganda, but this one was the most powerful to date. Besides its unique requirement for individual amnesty, South Africa empowered its commission with subpoena power to compel witnesses to appear and documents to be produced, a simple requirement if the truth is to be revealed. It included open hearings, and, in a tip toward transparency, published names of both victims and perpetrators. Victims would be allowed to testify in their language of choice, especially important in a nation with nearly a dozen official tongues, and those attending would get headsets and simultaneous translation. No easy task in churches and community centers where most hearings would take place.

Archbishop Tutu sensed my uneasiness—I was a lawyer used to seeking justice and punishment, He explained that South Africa had been so divided and traumatized that the usual justice of retribution or vengeance would have been "justice with ashes." Like King and Gandhi's power behind acts of passive resistance, there was a palpable power within the TRC model that was shaping up to go beyond the usual measure. I'd felt such admiration and respect for peaceful demonstrators who rejected violence, vengeance, and battle, and challenged our government with their bodies and hearts. I've litigated or resolved hundreds of conflicts and seen how they come in all shapes and sizes, so it made sense that solutions needn't come from the same box. Why couldn't a nation choose peace and nation-building over traditional justice?

Over the years I'd seen the importance of speaking one's truth to power. Contrary to popular perceptions about plaintiffs in litigation, most clients who arrived on my doorstep were not after tons of money. They arrived wounded, and I could see the pain beneath the anger. They wanted acknowledgment, their dignity restored, and the truth to be known. It has taught me that there is something innately human, almost spiritual, about seeking and exposing the truth.

Justice Albie Sachs said the work of the TRC was "putting a higher premium on truth than prosecution. Encouraging the rascals and the villains, whichever side they might have been on, to acknowledge what they did is more important than sending X or Y to jail." But it remains an experiment in truth, as he often added. "Whether it's right or not, it's really one of those cases where history will tell." We were all wondering as the hearings began.

Coming Clean

When standing next to his TRC co-chair, the much shorter Archbishop Desmond Tutu, Alex Boraine looks like a giant. As a white South African he symbolizes the unity and inclusiveness that Mandela and the new government seeks to reflect in the new "rainbow nation." A retired minister, he has studied truth commissions and travelled the world to discover their strengths and pitfalls. In the TRC Cape Town offices a few days before the first hearings, the affable Boraine reminds me that "we can respond ruthlessly, but with truth as our weapon." The goal, he says, "is to "restore the moral order," and gazing out the window as if lost in time he frames the nobleness of this grand experiment in nation healing: "Can we help them rediscover their human and social dignity?" Glancing back, he catches my eyes and as if knowing we all have something to hide, says, "It's a catharsis when people come clean, don't you think?"

The TRC pamphlets and posters proclaim "The Truth Hurts, But Silence Kills." I thought of my own country and in the article I wrote that night for the *Albuquerque Tribune* I reflected back to my countrymen across the sea:

> Sadly in the United States we have never had a similar truth and reconciliation process—documenting and actually listening, as a nation, to the pain of the victims of repression. Whether it was the McCarthy period of the 1950s, the victims and descendants of slavery, racial terror, Vietnam, or the policy

of genocide waged against Native Americans, little has been done to heal our own wounds.

Homegrown oppression has too often been swept under the rug. Our children are rarely taught about it, and victims have been ostracized and left to scream in silence. Those of us who tell a different tale have been labeled traitors, un-American, or even communists.

In America we must begin talking to each other and actually listen to the pain of what it feels like to be poor, hungry, or homeless. We need to hear from our youth about their frustration, boredom, and despair with their schools, community, and their future. If we can put a face on the pain and break our apathy and denial, perhaps we won't turn our backs and live with such problems. I asked a young South African woman from a local township who was heading to hear the testimony how she felt about the TRC. Her response was wise: "There is no alternative if we are to be one nation." What I was learning from these brave and courageous people was reframing my approach to activism and making me come to grips with our social truths.

The hearings begin this week and the world is watching. Months before, Boraine wrote to me to express gratitude for our efforts to organize international observers for the TRC hearings. He said, "We value international solidarity." But it feels like I should be thanking him. When we reach across cultures, continents, and hearts, it's a two-way street. All are enriched by the recognition of that connection. But it's also said that "the truth hurts." Boraine's comment to me about "coming clean" haunts me. Is it because, as scientists say, the observer is never separate from the act observed? What did I need to reconcile or forgive?

I feel my foundation shifting. Archbishop Tutu once described to me the historic change South Africa was undergoing as being transformed from "a repulsive caterpillar to a gorgeous butterfly." It has been metamorphic but also contagious, for like the caterpillar, transformation begins only when we digest our self, letting go of our prior form. It's never easy, as the struggle of breaking free from the chrysalis we've built around us is a necessary step in order to fly. As we gathered in the Eastern Cape for the opening hearings it felt like heading into the fire. My own experiment with truth was about to shake my core and transform me as a lawyer and as a human being.

▾ ▾ ▾

CHAPTER 12
Opening to Truth

We want to disarm human hearts and human beings,
one by one, country by country.
–Mairead Corrigan

Mdantsane Township, Eastern Cape, South Africa—April—1996
The crowd is electric. Decked out in white, Archbishop Tutu leads the celebration under the glare of television lights. It was the day before the gavel came down on the first hearing and I'm in a church service in the nearby township of Mdantsane. Everyone rises, hands raised and swaying back and forth as Tutu shouts repeatedly, "We are all free! Black and white." He pronounces blessings for the victims and perpetrators and for the TRC, telling stories of Christ and the Devil, but always returning to themes of freedom and justice. The packed house sings songs of peace as the service is beamed live over the South African Broadcast Corporation. Praying aloud in English, Xhosa, Sotho, and even Afrikaans, Tutu uses every opportunity to convey that the Truth and Reconciliation Commission is a process for all. While lighting a fire for the TRC, he's also cleansing the soul of a nation.

Many eyes fall on the widow of activist Matthew Goniwe, seated just a few rows in front of me. She had been married to of one of the Craddock Four activists who disappeared in 1985 after a note from the State Security Council called to have them "removed from society." After being tortured by the police they were killed and their car and bodies burnt beyond recognition. Nayameka Goniwe, known by her friends as Nyami, had publicly said that she was uncertain about supporting the TRC and testifying, as she had been disappointed by "inconclusive" State inquests over the years and still held out for justice.

Even on the eve of the opening session, no one knows how many people will come forward to support the hearings. Statements and applications for amnesty and reparations are still arriving and there is an air of caution. These first hearings are meant to instill confidence in the public and prod others to come forward and share their truth.

A New Dawn

East London, South Africa—April 15, 1996
The sun rose like any other day, but it was a day unlike any other. I'm in the town of East London, a small South African coastal city on the Indian Ocean. They consciously chose this region to launch the hearings as it was the birthplace of both the black resistance movement and the first black educational institutions of higher education. The government fought brutally against resistance in the area making it known that whoever destroyed the Eastern Cape will rule the country.. Nearby villages birthed leaders like the Mandelas, Steve Biko, and Goven and Thabo Mbeki.

Biko's story had been memorialized in the film *Cry Freedom*, which spread outrage against apartheid around the world. Many knew the story: Biko's call for black consciousness, Biko's arrest and beatings and the fateful drive hundreds of miles to Pretoria while bleeding to death chained in the back of a police vehicle. His family had gone to court to challenge the TRC as unconstitutional, describing the TRC as a "vehicle for . . . political expediency" that "robbed" them of their right to justice. Several high-profile activist families had joined the challenge and sought to stop the TRC and its amnesty provisions. Not everyone was in the mood for reconciliation.

On the eve of the hearing the Constitutional Court ruled against stopping the TRC hearings, but the Biko family would have nothing to do with the TRC. Healing such divides would be a challenge and reminds me of how controversial the TRC process is even to those who suffered. I thought of Tutu swaying the night before in the church and speaking of togetherness, but I'm feeling that his words are aimed at the heavenly heart more than the reality on the ground. Despite calls for unity it still feels like a deeply divided nation, and we are about to open old wounds.

Entering the century-old East London city hall auditorium, I feel the excitement and tension. Stained glass windows of green and purple cast a natural and magical glow along the wood beams that line the walls. Two South Africa flags extend out from the balcony encircling the words "Healing Our Past." We are invited back to the tea room where witnesses mingle with commissioners and the TRC staff. The Archbishop is scurrying about greeting people and seeing to last-minute details. His expression changes rapidly from a broad smile to a pensive brow. He and Dr. Boraine take their seats in the hall as people are still filtering in. All the TRC, including the seventeen commissioners, are seated in front of the stage, but there are no grand entrances or legal formalities.

We've been given the "Day Programme." It lists the names of the witnesses, the facilitator of the questions and the support Briefer assigned to each witness. It reads like a surreal horror script as it describes the "Nature of the Violation": "Injured in Bomb attack, Death in Detention"; " Torture"; "Shooting, Torture Beating"; and on and on. It's clear we're heading into the storm.

We're given seats up front as honored international guests. There are seven of us. Five lawyers and a law student from the US, of diverse races and ages, and another law student, from Belgium. We exchange smiles down the row as the buzz is running right through us. None of us would ever forget these four days.

The witnesses file into the hall and everyone stands as they enter. Archbishop Tutu approaches them at their seats. He's shaking hands with each and every witness and their relatives, often lingering, holding their hands in his and welcoming them. I can hear him saying "thank you," and it's clear he means it deeply. The TV cameras follow him, sending a message across the nation and around the world that these "victims" are valued. I can see from their nods and smiles that this gracious moment is also going straight into their hearts.

You can hear a pin drop as the Archbishop lights a candle in memory of all who have died as a result of the conflict in the past, while a "roll of honor" of those who had fallen is read. The whole hall breaks out in song. *Lizalis' idinga lakho* (Let your will be done). The Archbishop bows his head: "O' God of justice, mercy, and peace. We long to put behind us all the pain and division of apartheid together with all the violence which ravaged our communities in its name. We ask you to bless this Truth and Reconciliation Commission." I'd not expected such a formal show of religion at a government event, but I closed my eyes closed and clung to every word. While Tutu's references to forgiveness for those who "repent and confess their guilt to almighty God" and his ending with "Jesus Christ our Savior, Amen," would usually have made me uncomfortable, I could feel that this gathering had both a practical application and an inexplicable spiritual dimension.

In his opening remarks the Archbishop thanks those in South Africa and "around the world" who have prayed and are praying for the commission and its work. "We are charged to unearth the truth about our dark past; to lay the ghosts of the past so that they will not return to haunt us." Looking into the camera and into the hearts of the nation he says, "We will thereby contribute to the healing of a traumatized and wounded people—for all of us in South Africa are wounded people—and in this manner promote national unity and reconciliation." As Michael Ingaltieff of the *New Yorker* later wrote, "Every South African citizen was contaminated by that degradation, that deadness, that offense against the spirit." But would these hearings help cleanse the spirit of all South Africans, or would they reignite the outrage?

Nohle Mohapi, Steven Biko's secretary, opened the hearings and described how her husband Mapetla, a member of the Black Consciousness Movement, was killed in police custody and the authorities covered it up as a suicide. His crime was he worked with the elderly and the youth teaching them that the country "belonged to all of us, black and white." The police tortured him on several occasions and wanted him to admit to being a terrorist. "They were subjecting him to electrical shock treatments," she said "and cigarette burns on his feet. They would place sacks over his head nearly suffocating him into confessing."

I was quickly growing numb. My heart ran for cover, and we were on just the first victim. Nohle then described her own detainment. For six months she was "thrown in solitary confinements with ants, lice, and no washing water." Her words hushed the room into silence and I could feel the solitude, the fear, the damp walls. "I was fastened to a grill, beaten and choked. They wanted me to confess. They kept repeating over and over 'Do you want the same thing to you as happened to your husband?'" They wanted her to admit that Steve Biko was a terrorist.

The Commissioner asks what she wants and she replies that she "wants her children to know what happened and that their father didn't kill himself." Then she pauses and admits that she carries "hate and the heavy load in the heart. Even if you don't forget he is dead, the children will never wake him." She asks nothing for herself. Across the hall we feel her wounds still running deep, the loss of a father to her children and a part of their mother still so raw.

A Bomb in the Building

As Nohle is recounting the horrors of her detention the Archbishop is handed a note. He then says: "Ladies and Gentlemen. We have received information of a threat that requires that we search the building. It does indicate the kind of things we have to deal with in South Africa. It makes all of us aware that there are some people that will stop at nothing to try and prevent this commission from carrying on its work."

Reconciliation had begun with a bomb threat. You could see both anger and concern on Tutu's face. Soldiers enter with bomb-sniffing dogs as we move slowly without panic toward the exits and mingle outside on the sidewalk. The look on most faces is serious, as many had too often seen bombs tear apart their dreams. Yet few say they are surprised, nor do they seem shaken by it. The mere threat of violence pales in comparison to the story we're hearing.

When we return to the hall the Archbishop, clearly bothered by the interruption, announces it as a hoax, but then tells the world that "if there are any more bomb threats we will not respond to them." The hearings must go on. Such courage, I thought, but also wondering how safe we'll be in the days ahead. Lynne, a lawyer from Seattle, looks over at me with large eyes, as if saying, "OK. Here we go." But to Tutu there is so much riding on this process and they have to demonstrate that they will not be intimidated. Sitting in the hall, the possibility of an attack never fully escapes my mind.

Three women then testify how their husbands, who were active in the Port Elizabeth Black Civic Organization (PEBCO), all disappeared on the same night in 1985. Several witnesses had last seen them in police custody. It has since been revealed that they were killed by the military's infamous special unit hit squad. One widow described how her house was firebombed as a police van sped away. "Did you report it to the police?" she's asked. "How could we report the police to the police?" she replies. The audience laughs nervously and I see many nods around me.

"What are you seeking from the Commission," she's asked.

"We want them to confess and tell us why they murdered, to say who were the murderers, to reconcile so we can wash our hands," the widow tells us. There is something powerful and innately human about bringing light to the unknown. She continues, "We can never have them back, but don't want them to remain disappeared."

Next to testify is a white man with one arm—a victim of a spray of bullets at the High Gate Hotel that killed his friends and maimed him for life. He has seemed to be in his own world, and out of place in the mostly black audience. Yet he describes the shooting in detail and admits he wants justice. He seems less drawn to forgiveness than the other witnesses but says that if amnesty were granted to the perpetrators he would accept it.

On some levels he represents the attitude of many whites in South Africa who are being forced to accept the reality of the "new dispensation." Still, perhaps after hearing some of the other witnesses and sharing their pain, he says he truly "wants to hear their side of the story and try to learn the motive for such brutality." His description of years relearning how to dress, shave, and bathe reveals a consequence of violence that he revisits each day. I think of the countless victims of US bombings over the past year in Bosnia and Herzegovina and how silent we have all been on the human consequences of our choice to use violence. Learning about the impact of an attack on the life of a victim may stop someone in the future from pulling the trigger. I was getting an early lesson in the power of truth-telling, and how so little is simply black and white, good and evil. It may have been the church service and all the praying, but what kept going through my head was John 8:32: "Then you will know the truth, and the truth will set you free."

Ubuntu

The Interim Constitution and the statute that formed the Truth and Reconciliation Commission says "there is a need for understanding, but not for vengeance, a need for reparation, but not for retaliation, a need for ubuntu, but not for victimization." Days before, I'd read in the *Cape Times* Tutu's remark, "We are ready to forgive and build a new kind of country. This was only made possible by God's special gift to South Africa, the gift of ubuntu." I had never heard the term "ubuntu" until preparing for the hearings and was curious about a term characterized as God's gift and included in their progressive constitution. I needed to learn more.

I'd scheduled a meeting with the Archbishop after breakfast in East London in order to record a greeting to lawyers and law students who wished to join our project as international monitors. We meet in the back of the hotel restaurant with the crowd of diners buzzing in the background. His large gold cross clangs against the edge of the table. I'm nervous. Here is a man at the center of attention of the TRC and the world week taking time for me in his crowded schedule during this historic. When we sit down I fire up the recorder and get down to business.

"Archbishop, thanks for meeting with me. I wanted to record a greeting to monitors who may be thinking of coming to South Africa to observe this process—"

At that point he interrupts me by reaching across the table and placing his hand over mine.

"Yes of course," he says, smiling with his playful grin. "But first . . . Let's say hi."

I'm blown back. In the haste to get him on to his busy day I'd not taken the time to connect, to meet as humans, or to even say hello properly. I was all business. What a gift he's sharing in that simple moment, demonstrating that a genuine connection in any encounter, be it business or pleasure, is more rich when we take the time to honor and acknowledge each other: The power of saying "I see you" is immeasurable.

I blush and say, "Hi," and look deep into his eyes. He smiles and suddenly we're just two grinning humans meeting on more equal ground.

He records a beautiful comment for us to use in our outreach that spoke of the process and international solidarity: "It's important to have people like yourselves, lawyers, students, and other people with appropriate skills and expertise to come and monitor so that they can attest to the fact that so far as humanly possible, this very difficult process is being undertaken with integrity."

He then invites everyone to "Come be part of this exhilarating experience. Watch as this repulsive caterpillar becomes a gorgeous butterfly."

I could not have asked for more. But I have another question.

"I have read the statute that says 'there will be ubuntu rather than victimization.' I don't know that term ubuntu. Can you tell me what it means?"

The smile returns. "There is no direct translation in Western terms. Ubuntu means I am human through my relations with others. You are a person through other persons. It speaks of social or communal harmony as a human person is seen as corporate. The solitary individual person is in our understanding a contradiction in terms. Ubuntu says I am human only because you are human. If I undermine your humanity, I dehumanize myself. Ubuntu speaks of warmth, compassion, generosity, hospitality, seeking to embrace others. You must do what you can to maintain this great harmony, which is perpetually being undermined by resentment, anger, or a desire for vengeance."

Then relating it to the hearings: "That's why you have these extraordinary expressions here of people saying 'I just want to know who I should forgive.' And its people who have undergone quite horrendous things. You wonder how they have the capacity to laugh and be human. That is ubuntu."

Having listened to the victims I understood what he meant. It's more of a feeling and understanding than a easily definable word. Ubuntu is part of the African worldview of our nature, arising out of the Nguni group of languages. In Sotho languages in Africa it is called *botho*. In fact it exists in many nondominant cultures around the world. I would learn that the Navajos have a similar term, *Ke*, and Buddhists, aboriginals in Australia, the ancient Hawaiians, and the Mardu of New Zealand all have similar philosophies that view us as interconnected in a web of life. In the Brazilian rainforest the term *Tzai* (pronounced "chi") means "half of what's in you is also in me, and half of what's in me is also in you." They say "we are all branches of the same tree." I recall from my Grand Canyon escape Walt Whitman's "Song of Myself": "I celebrate myself, and what I assume you shall assume. For every atom belonging to me as good belongs to you." Ubuntu was anything but new. We had simply buried this innate wisdom along the march to conquer and control.

But I would discover that ubuntu is far from simply a philosophy. It's a way of life. Tutu modeled it in his respect toward everyone in the hearings and for me in that simple greeting when we connected in the cafe, giving me a deeper experience of its application. It's what he says "comes from knowing that he or she belongs in a greater whole, and is diminished when others are humiliated or diminished."

It explains why my self-assurance and hope feels as if it's growing, even while my heart is breaking from the graphic truths laid out for all to see.

▼ ▼ ▼

CHAPTER 13

Courage Under Fire

Each day we should practice a small act of courage so that when the big things arise it's just a matter of habit to be courageous.
–Congressman Dennis Kucinich

The stories from the TRC hearings are a mix of shock and inspiration. The descriptions of torture, burning people alive, and a system focused on fostering separation tear at the heart. It was a calculated campaign by the apartheid government, dubbed the "war on terror," to justify torture and extreme measures against the "enemy." Sadly reflecting back on it today it sounds all too familiar. Guantanamo on steroids—the closest to "evil" I've ever encountered. But the stories of forgiveness, deep listening, compassion, and blurring the lines of who is the enemy taught me much about the world of conflict in which I danced back home.

As the witnesses testify, I see many people in the audience, eyes closed, faces in their hands, listening to every word. Men wipe away tears and groups of people huddle together, as if for warmth, while the victims recount the deep pain from the threats, intimidation, and assaults. Perpetrators testify in hard cold tones about using generators to send electrical shocks through the body or beatings with iron pipes, as the victims describe through tears the rapes, torture, and dismemberments. What emerged was that no political party had a monopoly on pain. Human suffering was human suffering whether it came from a grenade tossed by a Zulu or PAC fighter or an iron pipe from the police. Both left orphans and nightmares in their wake.

I connect to these stories by deeply listening and bearing witness. The testimony takes on such vivid colors and images as people recount the deaths in great detail. The time of day, what someone was wearing, the memory of a last touch. "I threw myself over him. I can feel the wetness of his blood—I felt his last breath leave him," one mother told the TRC as she lost her only child to police bullets. One victim described how she had not gone back to the room in which she was tortured "to fetch her soul," and that she believes it's still sitting in the corner where she had left it—where she had been curled up after the violent attacks. As an observer it feels as if my heart has doubled in size, but with a noticeable hole.

The description of torture by the widows of the four Craddock activists plunges through the hearts in the hall. The entire audience cries out at the description of acid being thrown on their faces and their being fingers cut off. A widow left with fatherless children but no grave, no place to lay flowers, pleads to the Commission, tears streaming, to "get his remains, even if burnt to death, even one bone to his body, because no person can disappear without a trace."

At the end of the second day of the hearings Tutu thanks those who so courageously came forward and "opened their heart and soul to all of these people and to the world." I head back to the hotel thinking of how we are going through something profound. Despite the graphic nature of the incidents there is a sense of hope that emerges when voice is given to the unspeakable. I type out my story for the Tribune alone that night in the hotel room. It is late when I get to sleep . . . hoping I won't dream.

The next morning a tall, blond Afrikaner woman approaches the witness table and takes the oath. I'd noticed her blond hair and quiet presence as she waited that morning for the hearing to begin. I'd been speaking to her casually at the break in the tea room. Her name is Beth Savage. Like my own mother, she'd been a librarian, and said she was nervous but looking forward to telling her story.

It was November 1992 and she was part of a Christmas wine-tasting party at the King Williams Town Golf Club when someone tossed a grenade into the club. The attack was part of the intensification of the struggle of the armed wing of the Pan Africanist Congress (PAC). As one other victim of the attack noted, blacks and whites "were on both sides of a boiling point." Four people were killed in the attack and Beth was badly wounded, requiring open-heart surgery and removal of half her intestine. She describes how she had to learn to walk again, had to be bathed and fed by her children, and was in intensive care for months. Even within the ICU she began to have nightmares of the face of her attacker appearing at the window.

Beth testified that the attack had been even more upsetting because she was raised in a family that opposed apartheid and she had been taught to respect all races. Her father went into a great depression after the bombing. "It broke his heart," she said, wiping away a tear. She still had shrapnel lodged in her body. But it was what it embedded in her heart that was so miraculous. She testified that "through the trauma of it all, I honestly feel richer . . . a growing curve. I think it's given me the ability to relate to other people who may be going through trauma." She admits she does not know how she would have reacted "if I had been in their situation."

Asked about her feelings if the perpetrators were given amnesty, she said, "What I'd really like is to meet the man who threw the grenade in an attitude of forgiveness and hope that he could forgive me too for whatever reason." Her genuine tone and eyes showed she was not just parroting this idea, but that it was something she truly wanted to do. Months later I'd learned that after she eventually met Xundu, the perpetrator who applied for amnesty and who was now a major in the South African Defense Forces, she no longer had nightmares about the incident. Something was released on a deeper level.

The willingness to forgive in these moments was unparalleled in human history. One husband and father, Sicelo Mhlauli, was stabbed multiple times by police, who also poured acid on his face. Police chopped off his hand and preserved it in a jar of alcohol, which they later used to intimidate detainees. They called it "the baboon's hand." Mhlauli's nineteen-year-old daughter was courageous as she testified about being eight-years-old and seeing the police came to her house joking about her father's death, knocking around the house and shouting at her mother "like talking to a dog." She recounted how proud she was when her mother responded, not with anger, but by saying, "I am a human being, so are you, so you don't need to speak the way you do." Ironically, the officer said, "The truth will come out someday." Despite learning of this degrading torture and death, she said, "We do want to forgive, but we don't know whom to forgive."

Stories of peace and our common humanity are sprinkled throughout the countless tales of horror. One mother whose son was killed by the police summed it up this way: "We do not want to see people suffer in the same way that we did suffer. We would like to see peace in this country . . . We do not want to return the evil that perpetrators committed to the nation. We want to demonstrate humaneness towards them, so that they in turn may restore their own humanity."

Such testimony moved Nyami, the widow of Matthew Goniwe, and she decided to actively get involved with the TRC. As she testified toward the end of the East London hearings I watched the country hang on every word. She described their loss and heartache at Matthew's murder. Why had she come forward? It was, she said, the experience of sitting through the first days of the hearing and "feeling so humbled by the experiences of others."

It affirmed for me that when people choose to be active witnesses and tell their stories or engage in the process of change, it moves others to do the same. It awakens the active witness to give back to their community. Years later, Nyami was elected the first female mayor of the Inxuba Yethemba Municipality, the town made famous by the Craddock Four. Her inauguration was marked as a historical event for the Eastern Cape.

The Arch

Much of the tone and success of the TRC is attributable to its chair Archbishop Desmond Tutu. He understands that laughter and tears are both part of being human. During the first day of hearings one witness, Nomonde Clata, a widow of one of the murdered Craddock Four activists, reaches a painful point in her testimony and lets loose a wail that breaks the silence in the hall—a proxy cry for all of us. The Archbishop adjourns the hearing so she can compose herself and when he returns, rather than just diving into the graphic story, he leads the hall in a singing of Senzenina. I later learned from people around me it translates as "What have we Done?"

Tutu has shown himself again and again to be the consummate peacemaker. His compassion helps drive the commission and maintain its healing focus. His empathy with witnesses is moving. He tells the widows of the Craddock Four: "We are proud to have people like you and your husbands and the reason we won the struggle is not because we had guns, but because of people like you. People with incredible strength. And this country is fortunate to have people like you. This is one example why we are going to make it." He tells the daughter of a murdered activist, "Your father is looking down and is so proud of you." He then says something to the widows that could be sincerely comprehended only in the context of these unprecedented hearings: "Thank you for your contribution to our struggle, and thank you, even though it was certainly reluctantly, thank you for sacrificing your husbands. Thank you."

But even one as strong as Tutu has his breaking point. On the third day of testimony we're listening to a heart wrenching story from wheelchair-bound Singqokwana Malgas. We all feel worn thin from the days of painful stories. Malgas was hard to understand, as his speech was slurred by a stroke. He had been an ANC member, was incarcerated on Robben Island, and been tortured many times. He describes the "helicopter method": police would handcuff the prisoner's hands behind his back, manacle his ankles, suspend him upside down and spin him around. Malgas has difficulty telling his story, and he suddenly puts his hand over his face and breaks into tears.

This wounded soul puts Tutu over the edge and the Archbishop suddenly shakes and begins sobbing. All eyes move to him and the cameras broadcast his pain to the nation. He's bent over the table with his face in his hands and weeping. I heard he said later that he felt as chairman it was not appropriate for him to collapse in tears, but I have never been so moved and proud at such a public honest response of the heart. Leadership is not always about strength, but must come from being authentic and human. Tutu has taught me that on so many levels. It is safe to be vulnerable and show your humanity. Even the sweet way he would say before the hearings that he had "butterflies" in his "tummy" brought a smile to me, even while he waded knee-deep in the horror.

People across South Africa were awakening as a result of this process in creative and heartfelt ways and Tutu always looked for ways to demonstrate that the nation was moving toward healing. During the next set of hearings in Cape Town the Archbishop shared a poem written by a member of the public about the hearings the week before in East London. I watched the faces in the hall as the audience listened with attentiveness and appreciation. As Tutu read, people nodded and the room seemed transfixed on something greater:

The world is wept.
Blood and pain seep into our listening; into our wounded souls.
The sound of your sobbing is my own weeping;
Your wet handkerchief my pillow for a past so exhausted it
    cannot rest—not yet.
Speak, weep, look, listen for us all.
Oh people of the silent hidden past,
let your stories scatter seeds into our lonely frightened winds.
Sow more, until the stillness of this land can soften;
    can dare to hope and smile and sing;
Until the ghosts can dance unshackled, until our lives can
    know your sorrows
And be healed.

He then summed up something very powerful for me that helped carry me through this often gruesome and painful process. He acknowledged the "depths to which we are able to sink in our inhumanity to one another," even the "sadistic enjoyment of the suffering." But he reminded us that with ubuntu there is "another side, a more noble and inspiring one." Leaning into the microphone he tells the hall and the nation:

> We have been moved to tears. We have laughed. We have been silent and we have stared the beast of our dark past in the eye. We have survived the ordeal and we are realizing that we can indeed transcend the conflicts of the past, we can hold hands as we realize our common humanity. . . .

When I returned to South Africa months later, a piece of America's "dark past" emerged front and center: the hearings revealed the US government's hand in apartheid, presenting me with my own need to forgive, leaving a crack in the wall of separation between us and them as some of the "unshackled ghosts" of my own government's history made its way into this story, and "their sobbing" truly became "my own weeping."

▾ ▾ ▾

CHAPTER 14

Knowing Who to Forgive

The problem in defense is how far you can go without destroying
from within what you are trying to defend from without.
–Dwight D Eisenhower

My last trip to Cape Town felt like coming home. I'm staying with my friend Johnny DeLange, his wife, and their three cats who take to any open space in my bed. Johnny, a long time ANC activist lawyer, is now a Member of Parliament and chair of the Justice Committee. It's remarkable that he has not changed in the past two years since his elevation to the halls of Parliament—though he seems to have a nicer suit. We stay up late drinking and exploring the tales of our two countries, at times not so different, both facing the challenges of division, automation, and globalization. The talk turns to the TRC.

"The hegemony of the police has been broken and many have come forward," Johnny says. "However, the armed forces, particularly those who were or are at the top refuse to take any responsibility and remain for the most part silent." Those who carried out the orders are beginning to feel angry toward those who gave the orders and who "duck and cover," ready to let others take the fall. The hope, Johnny says, is that this split creates a whirlwind of truth to tear down some more barriers. We both agree that this genie cannot go back in the bottle, or, in an expression fitting of the DeLange household, the cat is out of the bag. Johnny smiles: "There's no turning back."

As formal observers of the TRC we're only scratching the surface. When I recently began to question whether our presence is making a difference, I received a note from Archbishop Tutu that lifted my spirits: "The interest and support of the Monitoring Project has been an encouragement to us at the TRC." Perhaps the fact that we care, that we are bearing witness to their effort at healing, and that we might in any small way "encourage" them is itself a marvelous victory. We are modeling ubuntu by giving of ourselves to others and not pretending that what happened in Africa was separate from us across the ocean.

I suspect that somewhere in our collective consciousness we also carry the pain. It is exciting to facilitate dozens of lawyers and law students to come to South Africa to experience firsthand this attempt at healing conflict and, we hope, to have them return home with a recharged "essence of being human." For lawyers it opens them to new possibilities in looking at conflict resolution and defuses some of their us versus them training. In the end, the experience is recharging my ubuntu—my sense of being linked with the rest of the world. Once you experience the sharing of tragic circumstances through personal story you are bound together forever in the healing process.

I'm moved by the humanity behind the powerful stories, but during the second year of TRC hearings I became furious, not at the perpetrators but at my own country. For what stood out in the Crossroads KTC hearings was not merely the barbaric acts, but the revelation of the role the US military played in fueling the violent and torturous strategy of the Apartheid regime.

Africans around me in the hall seemed unfazed by the revelations. Much of the world that has over the years borne the brunt of our massive export of weapons, coups, and bombs are rarely surprised by discovering the US fingers in another nation's oppressive pie, but I felt like fleeing the hall or shouting, "Not in my name."

The Red Sea

In June 1986, more than sixty thousand people lost goods through arson and had their homes burnt down. Dozens were killed. One group of older men chased people they suspected were ANC supporters from their homes and violently hacked them to death. Called *witdoeke*, loosely translated as "the Fathers," they were encouraged by the police, who even opened fire for them to clear the way, and who ended up supporting the slaughter of hundreds at KTC in Crossroads. These are the stories that haunt the nation.

I listened intensely as a twenty-two-year-old woman finds her sister's body and with the mix of pain and poetry I've experienced so often here, describes her pain to the nation saying: "It was as if the sun had set during the day." Or the father in search of his son stepping over bloody and burnt bodies in the mortuary and in the last room finding him laying in the corner on the floor. He breaks down weeping, "On my chest I'm black and blue." The funeral was sprayed with gunfire and tear gas and people dropped the coffin in the street and ran to safety.

"We were pulled from the car and beaten, kicked, grabbed and poked with axes," the beautiful young woman tells us in a soft wounded voice. "We were taken around Crossroads. We saw bodies floating in the water and could see human hands and headless bodies floating." She calls it "the red sea in Crossroads." They had tried to hang her three times from a tree but she did not die. What they did to her after made her wish she had. Sometimes it's as if I've awoken in a horror show. It's when you realize that the stories are real that your heart feels kicked in as well.

Some brave white South Africans stood up to the onslaught, but most simply ignored it or disbelieved the events as they unfolded. Reverend Fitch, a white minister, is called to the stand. It's clear that those who were witnesses to the violence were still in need of great healing. The police blocked people from fleeing, he says. "They were laying barbed wire to keep people fleeing from returning to their homes. I heard the cries coming from the shacks, babies in the burning shacks, but no one could reach them." He weeps, recounting with frustration his helplessness to save them. "It has come back to me in a dream the past few days as I begin to remember. I still hear those cries."

"I remember the warm blood on my hands," he says, holding them out before us. "I held a man in my arms with a deep slash in his neck. A Casspir (an armored police vehicle) came within a few meters and I waved to get their attention and even made eye contact with the driver. He drove on and the man died in my arms." The police then returned to arrest him, but he protested strongly, "These hands have held a dying man today, I've prayed for people, and witnessed these events." He shouts at them demanding, "What am I being arrested for? What am I being arrested for?" He was making such a ruckus that they released him.

As if representing the guilt of the silent who turned a blind eye and passively accepted what was going on, he says, "If whites had the humility, honesty, courage, and insight to see through it we would not have allowed it to be so totally manipulated and to become blind agents of oppression." The Commissioner asks him what factors contributed to the manipulation of the whites. "Fear. Because they were denying reality. And this denial, the ostrich mentality, leaves your rump exposed." I understood, longing for our world to pull its head from the sand.

The McCuen Strategy

The police have been subpoenaed to appear and I watch them standing clustered in the corner. They're laughing. This morning I feel more angry than forgiving after the graphic Crossroads testimony. How can I put myself in the shoes of those who perpetrated such heinous crimes? They should be in jail, not in uniforms and suits. Yet, looking closer, the faces of evil appear more human and sad than I'd expected.

A mid-level warrant officer takes the stand. He is clearly nervous. He swallows a lot and I watch his leg tapping below the table as he describes their infamous Joint Security Management Plan and the "Clean up Operation" they were running in Crossroads to break the support of the ANC and "to create a happy and contented community." I can't tell if they are simply lying racists, paternalistic men living in a fantasy world, or simply delusional. I'm not wearing my most empathetic hat this morning.

Mr. Schelhase, the Chief Superintendent of Housing and part of the Provisional administration set up to "take care of" the Crossroads situation is called to the stand and is sworn in to tell the whole truth. He describes with a cold display of indifference how it was "in the interest of the Development Board that an attack take place. . . .isolate the comrades and get rid of them." He confirmed that the State Security Council, led by the State President, was kept abreast of their actions. But then he brought it home for me in a way that made my blood boil.

"Why did you not do anything about it?"

"I admit I didn't go to too much trouble to try and prevent it. We were following the McCuen strategy," he said.

"And what is that?"

"It was the work of US Marine Lt. Col. John J. McCuen and he has made a study of revolutions and counter-revolutions all over the world, and set up theoretical guidelines for a State or a government to handle revolutionary situations." My ears perk up.

"We were taking the older 'fathers' and molding them within the McCuen strategy." I picture the red sea and the murder spree that had just been presented and wonder how this could be a sanctioned practice by a US military strategist. He tells us "all our operations in terms of management, administration etc, had to be molded within the McCuen strategy. It was a direction. It was a model in which we had to operate." It included eliminating the terrorists if necessary. He then leans in and coldly says the Fathers "wanted 'law and order'." The room buzzes as people see through the absurdity of the claim and have painful memories of the axe wielding group attacking people throughout the area. The Apartheid regime adopts the age-old fatalistic policy that somehow violence can lead to peace.

Lt. Col. John J. McCuen had written the book *The Art of Counter-Revolutionary War* while serving on the US Army General Staff in the 1960s and it was for years on the US Department of the Army's "required reading" list. He argues that the only way to win is by establishing groups of indigenous "counter-insurgent insurgents" who fight "fire with fire by . . . annihilating or expelling the enemy."

It turns out McCuen's book became the bible for the South African counterinsurgency campaign in their brutal occupation of Southwest Africa's Namibia. The McCuen strategy then became the apartheid government's scheme to fight what it dubbed the "Total Onslaught" back home in South Africa. Keep the survivors more worried about their own security and survival so that they have little focus to carry out the organization's revolutionary program, he writes. Col. McCuen's strategy became the justification for the apartheid regime to keep dividing and destroying its own people.

Despite the fact that such policies failed miserably in Vietnam and Central America this divide-and-conquer strategy drove the apartheid machine, became the template for spreading black on black violence, and served as the blueprint for forced relocations and murder. Torture becomes a means for, as McCuen writes, "destroying every individual who is captured, as well as his or her sense of solidarity with an organization or a community." I felt sickened.

As the testimony about KTC and the McCuen strategy wound down I notice that my hand is shroud in yellow light from the church's stained glass panels. My skin seems soft and vulnerable and the moment seems oddly filled with light and hope. But just for a moment. If I open my heart I can't shake the images of the hands and heads floating in the "red sea" at Crossroads. A butchery so devoid of humanity. A graphic example of unleashing counter-terrorists to do your bidding. A nation awash in the battle between us and them—to keep their separate world intact and not have to open their eyes, homes, or pocketbooks to those in need or those they perceive as different.

CIA documents, such as a 1985 Report on South Africa, describe the road needed to limit the power of the protesters. It states, "government divide and rule tactics will remain potent factors limiting the ability of these groups to challenge the government." In the final report of the TRC the Commission make note of this special relationship between the apartheid regime and the CIA. "US influence was evident in the co-operation between the security forces and the Central Intelligence Agency, which considered South Africa a local ally against the Soviet Union." It notes that the head of intelligence and founder of the Bureau of State Security General van den Bergh was trained by the CIA.

Oddly, Col. McCuen died recently just a few miles from where I grew up outside Detroit. But his push to violently torture and murder the revolutionary "enemy" lives on. His *Art of Counter-Revolutionary War* was republished in 2005 to be applied to Afghanistan. American national and military strategies stressed the need to enable our allies to counter Al-Qaeda and its ilk and deny them sanctuary by creating an environment inhospitable to them. One can only think of Abu Ghraib, torture, and targeted assassinations to know his approach is alive and well.

McCuen's obituary reflected his take-the-battle-to-the-enemy attitude: "Jack was a fully loaded cannon in every way regardless of mission or assignment and would always achieve victory as all warriors do! . . . A fine soldier—one who could always take one more step and fire one more round." But I'm drawn to the last line, which reads, "survived by his pet dogs Tanker, Tillie and Ruby."

I know the lesson for me is to learn to forgive McCuen and US policy makers, lest I be dragged into that vortex of hate and anger. It's never so simple. As Aleksandr Solzhenitsyn said, there is no purely good or evil, as it "runs through the heart of everyone and who is willing to destroy a piece of their own heart." Yet in the days of drone attacks, targeted assassinations, and the endless war on terror it remains an increasingly formidable task. Are we getting ahead by fighting "fire with fire"? Why are we still immersed in us versus them thinking— the west versus the rest? Sadly, McCuen's ghost is still advancing forward, "firing one more round."

▾ ▾ ▾

CHAPTER 15

Making Flowers Grow

Forgive, forgive, and then forgive some more.
–A Course in Miracles

South African TRC Hearings—1998

The Chief was attacked with stones and had his body burned by vigilantes. I leaned forward to hear his soft-spoken son testify in Leandra. A commissioner asked, "Do you know who was leading the group that attacked your father?" A buzz filled the hall and I leaned over to ask an elderly woman what people were saying. "They were reacting," she said, "because the killer is outside the Commission hall right now . . . in full police uniform." The relationships within communities remain complicated.

Healing cannot be evaluated in a cold, quantitative winner/loser manner in a process whose objective is reconciliation and peace. One of the most transformative moments our monitors observed took place in Richards Bay in Kwa-Zulu Natal, where black-on-black violence between the ANC and the Zulus had been intense. A black man in a grey suit, strikingly tall and good looking, takes the stand and describes his role in a hit squad by the local police force. He has applied for amnesty for his involvement in over seventy violent attacks on people in the community. Recruited at age eighteen, he quickly rose in status and rank. He calmly described his work targeting ANC members. It took three days for him to recount everything, at which time he said, "I know that I never can return to my community, so life will have little meaning for me."

He then turned to a woman seated in the front row, now in a wheelchair, whose legs were lost in a grenade attack he'd orchestrated at a bus stop. He says he'd known her his whole life and did not know she would be there. "I can't take away your pain or the suffering you will endure for the rest of your life but I can take responsibility for it. I can say I am truly and deeply sorry that I did this to you and to the many others in the community."

Tears began to fall down the applicant's face and the woman in the wheelchair leaned over to bury her head in the chest of the woman seated next to her. The hall was silent, then a deep mourning cry erupted from the nearly five hundred people in the audience. The applicant was handcuffed and led away by security to be returned for the night to prison. No one in the room moved but everyone cried openly, including our four white monitors attending.

The next day as his testimony concluded, the community members returned and an older woman dressed in bright African colors and beautiful beads rose and asked to address the commission. She talked about the evils of the past and the sadness in their hearts. She said the community had discussed the brother's application and said that if he is granted amnesty they would forgive him and he could come home. The man burst into tears.

Such powerful human stories change the lives of the individual, community, and often everyone within earshot. When acting from a point of compassion it can change the trajectory of one's own life. The TRC was like the boy walking a beach after a storm who sees thousands of starfish washed onto the shore. He can't possible save or heal all of them, but he begins to meticulously throw them back to sea one by one. As the story goes, an older gentlemen passerby scoffs at the boy, "There are so many of them. You are just one person. How do you ever expect to make a difference?" The boy smiles, picks up another starfish and tosses it into the sea "It makes a difference to that one."

Forgiveness

I first met Linda and Peter Biehl in New Mexico, a place they called home before their daughter Amy, a Fulbright Scholar attending the University of the Western Cape, was giving some student friends a ride home when she was pulled from her car and stabbed to death by an angry mob in the township in Gugulethu. My son Sasha went to a new charter high school in Albuquerque named for Amy Biehl. I was speaking on my South Africa experiences at the school, and Linda and Peter came to hear me speak and to share part of their story. We bonded instantly and Shady and I joined them for lunch.

Over green chili enchiladas they told me how they had attended the amnesty hearings for those who had killed Amy and had spoken in support of their applications. They actually had taken the time to meet the families of the murderers. "It's strange how things turn out," Peter said, his eyes still bearing a sadness that only a parent who has lost a child could understand. But he'd light up when he talked about what they did to reconcile with the perpetrators. "It's what Amy would have wanted. It's what she lived for."

Linda and Peter could have been passive victims, but instead they chose to be active witnesses. They created the Amy Biehl Foundation, which educates in forgiveness and supports projects in the very township where Amy was killed. They started several businesses there for troubled youth, and even employ two of the killers of their child. They had learned about ubuntu, though they were living it by example before they knew the term, and we talked about how it had changed our view of the world.

The Biehls commitment has been a reminder to me, an anchor when feeling angry or hopeless. Though they lost a daughter, they have saved hundreds of young people from criminal violence and the dead ends of township life. Courage to move forward breeds more courage. I left lunch feeling perhaps humanity has a chance. The TRC had provided a forum that gave the Biehls and hundreds like them a unique opportunity to forgive and heal.

I'd grown up believing that forgiveness was weak; that it was more important that one pay for the crime. But the hearings demonstrate that forgiveness is actually a necessary step in releasing anger. It is powerful medicine. It does not mean condoning wrongdoing, but it gives the perpetrator a chance for a new beginning. It's the closest thing to magic I'd encountered to date.

It is said the heart is a muscle that needs flexing to feel. In the years I'd cloistered it away, shielding it from disappointment or pain, it grew weak and detached. A closed heart embraces fear, rejects love, and isolates us from our ubuntu essence. The TRC hearings were filled with great pain, but simply sitting and listening empathetically to the stories, I could feel my heart opening.

Being here is like samurai training for lawyers. I'm beginning to understand that those who come to me in trauma or after great loss can be helped to choose a new path, release judgment, and even overcome the erroneous perception that someone or some circumstance has broken their heart. The TRC witnesses demonstrate that one's heart could be left battered or in need, but their resilience after great tragedy and stress shows that a heart does not break. Nor should our faith in our power to make a difference.

The TRC allowed me to remember our common humanity and that there is great power in caring about the plight of others—even if separated by thousands of miles. It's as Atticus Finch said in *To Kill a Mockingbird*, "To understand someone you have to climb down into his skin and crawl around in it for a while." This is empathy, something scientists are discovering is a human trait for which we are softwired. The TRC witnesses showed me the power of forgiveness and of being able to tell one's story. As one young man, who had been blinded when a policeman shot him in the face, told the TRC, "It feels like I have got my sight back by coming here and telling you the story."

I was witnessing the powerful choice South Africa was modeling for the world: the refusal to be consumed by resentment and hate, but to embrace a different path. Much of this ability to forgive was intrinsically wrapped up in accepting the notion of ubuntu, that we are interconnected. President Mandela used to say that "the chains of the oppressed wrapped equally around the oppressor as well." The TRC was not going to create a society that embraced and sang Kumbaya around a campfire. But the process itself had a redemptive power essential for giving the nation any chance of creating an atmosphere conducive for peace, right relationship, and what they called a "human rights culture."

Planting the Bomb

It was 1988 and Albie Sachs was an ANC activist in exile teaching law in Mozambique when he left to his car to head home. As he opened the door someone called out his name and he turned away for a moment. That moment saved his life as the car bomb planted by the South African Defense Force operatives exploded, taking some of his hearing and eyesight and severing his right arm.

Albie, now sitting on the South African Constitutional Court, could have been bitter, angry, and vengeful. But he, too, chose a different path. Over the years I'd seen him at clubs or parties dancing with great passion and joy. His thirst for life and freedom clearly motivated him, but there was something deeper. He once told me and some colleagues about a unique moment for him in the TRC process.

One day in his chambers in South Africa, Justice Sachs had a visitor named Henry.

"Can I help you?" Albie asks, looking up from his desk.

Henry glances down and seems quite nervous.

"I wanted to tell you that I'm the one who planted the bomb in your car."

Albie was stunned. He had helped create the laws around the Truth Commission, but this hit such a personal core. Here was the man who had disfigured him. He was left without words—an unusual experience for the loquacious Sachs.

Henry said he was applying for amnesty for the crime and that he was sorry for what he had done and he hoped that Albie would support his amnesty petition and forgive him. Sachs gathered his composure and told Henry to go and tell all that he had done to the Commission and they would see.

Some months later Henry ran into Albie and he told Sachs that he had gone to the Commission and had told them everything. Henry made reference to others he had tried to kill abroad, using their first names, almost as if they'd become friends. What a strange twist in the tale. Albie reached with his left arm and shook Henry's hand, forgiving him.

Later he sought to discover what had happened to Henry. Someone who had known him told Albie that after he had spoken with Albie, Henry went home and literally wept for days.

Albie told us, you can't take back what happened, you can't replace the arm. "But you can make flowers grow from it."

Albie's story and the entire TRC process convinced me that we can choose to be victims of the illusions of us versus them, red and blue states, and the politics of fear, or we can take control of our lives and practices, refusing to accept hate, anger, and vengeance. A tug-of-war requires two sides willing to pull. When we drop the rope the war ends.

But to cause systemic change more lawyers have to look in the mirror and ask the tough questions. During a speech on the TRC to the

Albuquerque Bar Association luncheon, I challenged hundreds of my colleagues to go a little deeper: "Do our attitudes of vengeance, bitterness, and hostile combative litigation build us up as a culture or tear us down? Does the process add to social harmony or divide us further?" Few lawyers take the time to consider such matters, but I became determined to reframe the way we resolved conflict and opening up the possibility of making flowers grow even from a field of ashes.

▾ ▾ ▾

CHAPTER 16

Falling Down as Heroes

*The world is moved along, not only by the mighty shoves of its heroes,
but also by the aggregate of tiny pushes of each honest worker.*
–Helen Keller

Robben Island, South Africa—May 1998
I'm following the path taken by Mandela, Mbeki, and Sisulu toward the prison on Robben Island. Hundreds of ANC activists were wrapped in chains, isolated, and removed from society to this secluded and infamous prison. Now reopened as a political tour site, it remains mostly unchanged from the time it housed Mandela, though the controversial proposal for a gift shop has stirred the pot.

With Table Mountain in the distance, I traverse the same waters families were allowed to cross once or twice a year to visit their loved ones whose only crime was their thirst for freedom. Our guide, who himself had been a Robben Island political prisoner, says it's the same boat that was used to bring him to the island ten years earlier. Who could have imagined such a transformation and role reversal?

Passing through the gates into the main prison we visit the room where interrogations and torture took place. The descriptions from the weeks before come alive within this space so imprinted with pain. My guide pauses, and the crackle in his voice as he describes the room's history shows that certain memories do not fade or totally heal with time. I think of my first trip six years earlier, when prisoners were still slowly being released, and seeing the joy on their faces as they fell into the receiving arms of their families and comrades.

The eight of us on this tour speak very little, as if in church, introspective and respectful. I didn't known what to expect. "Did you ever hear the voices of children?" asks one visitor. The guide lights up, "Oh yes. Sometimes you would hear in the distance the children of the warders playing and it would be so wonderful . . . like a breath of fresh air." He recalled when someone visiting would bring in a baby and how they would just want to "hold that baby just to feel close to the living."

We board a small bus for a drive around the island, passing herds of leaping springboks and a flock of nearly a thousand penguins. Seeing penguins in Africa has always been a mind twist, having been raised on images of Africa being tropical jungle and desert. We enter the lime quarry and I'm met by the powerful reflection of the same sun that damaged prisoner Mandela's eyes. I can almost hear the digging and feel the anguish of so many souls. It would be like my visit later that year to Hiroshima, where the ancient souls still seem to be crying.

The most moving moment was standing at the cell of prisoner #46664—Nelson Mandela's tiny home for over seventeen years. It houses a cot, which fills most of the space, but for eleven years he slept on a straw mat on the ground. As the group moved on I lingered at the cell door. The bars were cold and I remembered reaching out to Mandela the year before in Cofimvaba and how his finger tips were so cold. I could sense the thousands of times he must have leaned against these doors, hands wrapped around those bars, dreaming of a new South Africa.

This dream has been so contagious. A few days before this visit, the *Cape Times* ran a photo of Mandela visiting a children's center in the township of Gugaletu. Four children are wrapped around his waist in the tightest, most loving embrace imaginable, as if they were clinging to hope for the future itself. As I move past his cell, his broad smile in response to the children's embrace lingers as I imagine him also listening to the children playing and laughing in the distance . . . dancing off the heart of the one who was waiting, waiting to be free.

Social Truth

Over two years I made several visits to South Africa and read testimony from dozens of other hearings. I felt connected to the stories, but also through the wounds in my ubuntu-connected heart. How does one forget the soldiers who burned the body of their victim in a barbecue pit for several hours while they drank and talked beside it? Or the government's Chemical and Biological Warfare program of forced sterilizations, poison whiskey, and the fascist experimentation to find bacteria that would only target blacks. A doctor was even attacked with underwear infected by the government with poison in retaliation for his anti-apartheid leanings. Information came to light of the release of botulism, cholera, and the production of other chemical drugs into local communities. One cannot listen to such things and not be shaken to the core.

At the end of a long day of painful stories, Archbishop Tutu told us that it is "a catharsis not just for the witnesses, but for all of us up here." But at times it also felt like more trauma or a re-injury of things that perhaps should be forgotten. That is the delicate balance with truth. There is an African proverb that says, "Truth is good; but not all truth is good to say."

On my last day of hearings, I climb into the hills bordering Table Mountain, which rings Cape Town. It's one of the most beautiful settings in the world. After listening to days of testimony of man's inhumanity to man, the fresh air seems so enlivening. Here there is no black and white, no victims and perpetrators, just an interspecies dance of the divine. From the top of the hill I can see Robben Island on that windswept piece of land that heads toward Antarctica. I stand and stare for some time, thinking of Mandela's cell but also his words: "Freedom is indivisible—the chains on any one of my people were the chains on all of them; the chains on all of my people were the chains on me."

It's what motivates me as an active witness, as I have always felt a kinship and responsibility to people around the world struggling for justice. But Mandela also warns us that "to be free is not merely to cast off one's chains but to live in a way that respects and enhances the freedom of others." I want to integrate such an intention into my life and my work as a lawyer. To date something has been missing.

Mandela was the ultimate *active witness*—he knew our task is not merely to watch the world spin by, but to live in a manner that enhances the world. Even the theme of the recently enacted United Nation's *Mandela's International Day* "is to inspire individuals to take action to help change the world for the better, and in doing so build a global movement for good. Ultimately it seeks to empower communities everywhere."

Watching the boats round the Cape, I know it's time to reflect upon this ubuntu journey. My notions of conflict, justice, and healing have been turned on their heads. Was there justice in this unique transition to freedom? Some killers walked free, while others, most notably the Chris Hani and Steve Biko perpetrators, were denied amnesty and went to prison. President DeKlerk and others came before the TRC, feigned ignorance, and went away scott-free. The architects of apartheid, a crime against humanity, still sit by their pools and embrace their loved ones. The contrasts between rich and poor and black and white remain stark.

But we forget that there is a type of *social truth* that relates to a person's experiences more than the forensic manner in which we prove criminal cases or seek justice. In a nation of denial and silence this truth-telling has great value. This was the truth the TRC pursued. It helped rewrite the history of a nation—and along the way it opened the heart of a lawyer from Albuquerque to new possibilities.

Tomorrow

Unlike my experiences in US courts, the Commission was highly witness-friendly, expressly guided by the principle that "victims shall be treated with compassion and respect for their dignity." Having "briefers," individuals trained in psychology or social work assigned to each witness and sitting next to them as they testified, sometimes stroking their backs or holding them if they broke down, changed the tenor of the proceeding. This dose of humanity was mocked by the media or opponents who dubbed it the "Kleenex Commission," but after hearing their stories, who could deny their tears?

Freedom is often about more than merely rights. The country as a whole was craving to move forward, to simply live in peace. Victims often said that by testifying and learning of the fate of their loved ones there was a "heavy load removed from our shoulders." What price can be put on such a release? On my last night in Cape Town I run into Albie Sachs at a jazz club. Speaking of young people, he says, "Someday our children will look back and wonder what all the fuss was about. They will lead boring normal lives. This is what we have fought for . . . their chance to have life this way."

One aspect of the TRC was to have reparations, most often in the form of monuments built to the victims of apartheid, to help ensure that what happened will never be repeated. But how many times will these stories have to be written until it never happens again anywhere? *Nunca Mas*, Never Again, was the cry of the Commission on the Disappearances of Persons released to the Argentine Government in 1984. As truth unfolded in Argentina the Total Onslaught Policy was shifting into high gear in South Africa, and so much horror followed. Between April and June 1994, around the time Nelson Mandela was sworn in as president of South Africa, an estimated 800,000 Rwandans were killed in the space of one hundred days. We must keep telling these stories so they help weave a new moral fabric, and as the world grows more connected through telecommunication, Facebook, and other social media outlets, I am cautiously hopeful that we will reawaken to our common humanity.

The goal was not to *achieve* reconciliation but to *promote* it—and for anyone connected with this historic transformation it was clear that South Africa experienced a metamorphosis. Albie Sachs told us one evening about his swearing-in ceremony as a Constitutional Court Justice. Mandela, the newly elected President of the Republic, told him that the "last time I was in court was to hear whether or not I was going to be hanged." The new heads of the armed forces and the Minister of Defense are all former leaders of the military wing of the ANC, and are now being saluted by the very soldiers who for years had sought to capture them and kill them. Such shifts give us all hope for new possibilities.

South Africa, however, is not a magical utopian and peaceful place. The apartheid era legitimized violence, and it's a legacy that is hard to shake. But learning how the government manipulated and fueled the violence puts some perspective on its root causes. On a personal level, it placed our attack by the gang of young men in Johannesburg in a larger context and helped replace the feelings of fear with a droplet of peace. As individuals we can change more quickly than institutions or nations because our perspectives and attitudes are fully within our control. I was living what the constitution proclaimed: there shall be ubuntu rather than victimization.

Yet there are, as Mandela says, "many more hills to climb" and he warned us: "Unless there is real change in the circumstances in which ordinary people live, then that freedom will remain a promise and many of the rights proclaimed in the constitution will remain formalities."

Walking home through the sunny skies of a warm Cape Town winter day toward the end of my last visit to Africa, with the majestic Table Mountain aglow at dusk, a child approaches and asks for food or money. "How old are you?" I ask. He answers, "Fourteen." It shakes me. I think of my son Khlari, who will be fourteen next week. This boy's soft vacant eyes remind me of the millions of children around the world who are forced to live in such conditions. "Where do you live?" I ask. His stare is the answer. It seems that home is not a word he knows. He must live where he can. What will *truth* mean for these children? The commission, in its final report and recommendations to the president, cautioned that "unless there is real material transformation in the lives of those who have been apartheid's victims, we might just as well kiss reconciliation goodbye." The universal truth remains: We cannot eat or drink from the well of truth and survive without more.

Each part of our world must confront its truth, its history, and its pain in order to heal. We need to listen to each other and become active citizens of the world, witnessing with our heads and hearts and our actions a new and more peaceful ubuntu-based world. South Africa has a way to go to find its internal peace, but we can take the experience of the TRC and the forgiveness it brought into our lives and create our own *experiment with truth*. This is what I was to carry home.

Just as feeling love and opening my heart made death and violence all the more poignant, these stories and my experiences in South Africa have convinced me that in the end it makes loving all the more essential. Tutu was fond of saying that he came away with an "exhilarating realization" that although there is much evil, human beings nonetheless "have a wonderful capacity for good." Deep in the legal system it is easy to forget this truth.

My most profound moments came not from meeting Mandela, Archbishop Tutu, and other heroes of the transformation, but from the testimony of the brave men and women before the TRC who opened their hearts and soul to their country and the world. The TRC, despite its goal that there shall be "ubuntu rather than victimization," still divided people into victims and perpetrators. But the word "victim" was a misnomer. What I witnessed was a string of powerful heroes and heroines, like Nonceba Zokwe, whose son was killed by the police in 1988. She was now a grandmother, having raised thirteen children, and she spoke so powerfully.

The commissioner is moved by her courage and willingness to forgive. He asks, "Mama. You give us power, and I want to ask you where did you get this strength, so that other people would know in times of trouble that they have to be strong?"

She describes growing up with relatives who would "share with anyone who came by because there are no strangers in this house of ours." She was given strength by the "examples of the brave people, the heroes," the people who died for freedom and "fell down as heroes."

"If these people could survive the struggle, then I also could survive." In the end she added: "My womanhood gives me strength." The listeners hang on every word, many of us wiping away tears, as she sums up the crossroad of my journey to date with, "I think tomorrow you will have to decide for yourself who you are and what you will be tomorrow."

▾ ▾ ▾

PART III

The Spirit in the Dark

. . . and in her starry shade
Of dim and solitary loveliness,
I learn'd the language of another world.
–Lord Byron

CHAPTER 17
Listening to Mother

*Deep Ecology is rooted in a perception of reality that goes beyond
the scientific framework to an intuitive awareness of the oneness
of all life . . . ecological awareness is truly spiritual.*
–Fritjof Capra from *The Turning Point*

*Success requires more comprehensive ways of perceiving,
understanding, and appreciating the relationship between
people and nature. . . . that we not simply change the land,
but that we change ourselves.*
–Aldo Leopold

The poet Wallace Stevens used to say that "truth depends on a walk
around the lake." I've tasted this truism as a child running full-throttle
down the Sleepy Bear sand dunes toward Lake Michigan, when staring into the embers of a burning campfire or catching a glimpse of the
setting sun over the western lava beds from the foothills surrounding
Albuquerque. But surrendering to the beauty, wisdom, and mystery
of the creation, without trying to figure it all out, is something easier
said than done for such a left-brained lawyer, even one experiencing slight spiritual rumblings. What allowed people in South Africa
to forgive and still hold onto love and hope despite such tragedies?
Was there truly a space between the notes—Rumi's field "outside the
realm of right or wrong"—that we each could touch?

As a young boy, my father would read to me the story of Ferdinand
the Bull, who was more content lounging in the field and staring at
daisies rather than bullfighting. It taught me to love nature and modeled a different way of being, but years later, as a new lawyer, and even

today with climate change threatening the planet, I'm left wondering where the peaceful bull fits when the daisies are dying.

The Rhythm of Life

Tikal, Guatemala—December 1990
Not having formulated a spiritual life, I'd always a sense of transcendence in nature, and of course sex. After my wife Demetra and I ended our experiment in marriage, I dated like it had just come back in style, thirsty for the connection I'd been missing. Adventure came with Susan, a twenty-six-year-old, tall, bright Missourian, raised in an eclectic home akin to Isabelle Allende's *The House of the Spirits.* She and I rendezvoused at the airport in Mexico City and headed to the Caribbean and south to Guatemala. I'd been so busy in trials that I needed to change my energy and just play.

Passing through Belize City on the bus we spent hours downtown clinging to our backpacks in a city reeking from open sewers and desperation. Not quite the respite I had been seeking. The next day we snag a minibus to escape the city and head to neighboring Guatemala, but our van slowly fills with carbon monoxide from a missing tailpipe. The beer and tequila from the night before only magnify the message and my discomfort. But as we exit at our destination—the ancient Mayan ruins in Tikal in northern Guatemala—my lungs explode with a dizzying fresh shot of rainforest oxygen.

The trees appear to extend above to heaven, like the majestic California Redwoods or even the dome of the Mexico City cathedral. Here the sky is clear blue, yet the sound of raindrops fall from the canopy, dancing on the ground creating a crystal shimmer against the eye through refracted rays of sunlight. Despite the lack of topsoil, roots cling to rocks, trees, and even flowers that lie in their path. Such passionate and sexy growth takes place with life and birthing going on everywhere.

Venturing deeper into the jungle, the moist smells and sounds take my breath away. The courtrooms, the battles and what *they* are doing to *us* melts away. We move down the trail listening to a cacophony of insects. Sweet Honey in the Rock's whispering song came to mind, "Won't you listen, listen, listen, listen, listen to the rhythm."

Listening is our greatest human attribute and plays a key role in being an effective lawyer, partner, or parent. Nature reminds me that it's more than merely hearing something. Listening is rich and abundant, coming from all our senses and experiences, including symbols, memories, even our dreams. Here, so far from my comfort zone and feeling like a guest in a larger story, the jungle provides me the chance to practice this expanded form of awareness.

Like many around me I'd been self-absorbed in my patterns and footprints, glued to what we're told is "all the news fit to print," accepting that winning against the powers-that-be was the path to social justice and living a full life. I'd not listened deeply or even been aware there were messages around me.

After two days in the jungle I drift asleep in the hammock. An earthquake shakes me, but rather than hide, I choose to ride it out in a doorway of an old house. As I embrace the experience rather than fear it, the earth continues to shake, but I notice it now has a reggae beat. My world had been turned upside down with my divorce and so many courtroom battles, but as the earth shakes I feel a sense of peace by accepting what the earth brings my way, instead of fighting it.

But then it grew darker. My young son Sasha was choking. I'd put him down hard on his back and when I lifted him up his eyes were rolling back and he was stiffening. I reached for his tongue, but it didn't appear stuck. He was drifting away. I awoke in a sweat. It was a dream, but nothing is more frustrating for a parent than being unable to save your child from harm's way.

I suddenly felt the thousands of miles between us. Was he in trouble? Not wanting to wake Susan, I quietly slip outside into the moonlight and head to the pay phone outside a small tienda in the village. My fingers are shaking as I dial the number. My ex-wife answers and at my insistence she goes in to check on him. He's sleeping fine. I slide over to the star-drenched beach and soft surf and ask myself, "What did it all mean?"

As the ocean sweeps across my toes I remember that dreams, like all storytelling, have a broader message, an internal *I Ching* with endless pages and symbols. Learning to listen to these soft reminders is the key. It's the awakened hard ones that can hurt a lot more. Clearly Sasha needed me to be more involved in his life, to listen more to his struggles, and to be there for him. I live such a bifurcated life, one week a dad and the next a globetrotting bachelor. It was clearly time to get home.

But if we're all connected, then our dreams may also be signposts for more global messages. In the countryside I've seen so many young children awash in poverty despite all the food programs that say there is enough to feed the planet. Perhaps my inability to stop Sasha from choking was symbolic of the frustration we all feel when we choose to open our eyes and hearts and acknowledge that each minute across the planet dozens of children are choking, struggling for their last breath, as they die of hunger.

Today, living from ubuntu, I understand that these children are my children, and I have the choice to either become paralyzed in pain and hopelessness or use this awareness to inspire me to be an *active* rather than *passive* witness to their plight.

A Labyrinth of Red

Jemez Springs—New Mexico, 1999
Some flee the city to forget, but I come to the canyons of Jemez to remember. Outside the sky is deep turquoise, like an O'Keeffe painting, white billowed clouds shaped like the Sphinx float above the canyon wall casting shadows on the dancing pinions. It's spring, and the nimbus giants rise up, stretching out their buckets of rain to once again tease our desert thirst. My urban mind can race so quickly that I fail to notice the moment—the robins dancing on the frozen pond or even my own heart beating, simply and without rhyme or reason. I'm discovering that if we stop to listen consistently with the beat of the planet something about life becomes clearer.

My yearning to daily integrate at home the awareness I'd found in nature led to my using a recent settlement to buy land in the red rock canyons of the Jemez mountains, within earshot of the Pueblo drumming. It became my escape, a place to breathe anew. After a day of helping clients traverse their workplace struggles, or pushing against a wall of resistance in mediation, I'd find my respite building a home of straw bale and radiant mud floors, with majestic views up the pinion-dotted valley.

At night the stars are so thick it feels like the cosmos is dripping directly into my veins. During the day the wildflowers, shrouded in red clay, dance in the wind. As the sunlight illuminates a billion tiny pebbles and crystals within the sandstone, I'm reminded of the richness of this world. It's this depth of observation and awareness I want to carry into my daily life, pulling back the curtains and revealing the gemstones that are always present. As the twentieth century is winding down, it's with this reverence for each boulder as unique that I spread the red rocks into place until the circle is complete.

A labyrinth takes us off our linear path. From ancient European cathedrals to the spirals of the petroglyphs, they have been used for contemplation. But the pattern I've chosen for my Jemez hilltop, based on the Chartres Cathedral in France, takes me in one direction, then suddenly another, passing where I'd been, close to the center then far away, until suddenly it leads to the core—the center of life revealed. Like life it is a meandering but purposeful path, always guaranteeing you'll end up home.

I once walked a different type of path, where Gandhi's footprints are cast in stone. The New Delhi home had been converted into a museum of the great mahatma of India. Haunting black and white photos from his days as a young lawyer in South Africa to his great march to the sea lined the walls. In the garden I slowly put one foot in front of the other along the path from the sitting room to the spot where his assassin was waiting.

Pausing as I approached the last footprint, I found myself frozen in time as tears filled my eyes and a great loss lingered. But on this path I knew what I must do. I stepped past the place he fell and kept walking forward, knowing it's the step we all must take: be the change we want to see.

The labyrinth takes this reflection deeper as the circle is a universal symbol for unity. Weeks later, after laying the last stone, I walk the finished path feeling my soul hungering for some connection to my intuitive nature, to the myths of our times, something outside the body. As friends visit and walk with me in silence I'm reminded how thirsty we all are for more tools of transformation, more ways to find peace and reflection.

Passing friends along the paths, we smile and bend just slightly and glide past each other, continuing on as we do in life. Patience is my lesson of the month, as I know I will get there if I just keep my eyes on the prize. I hold my friend Viviette's baby as she walks the path we would decades later revisit, not knowing that I would someday explore with her the famous labyrinth of Chartes Cathedral, reach the center together and have her step into my heart so deeply. For now it's the words of the old lama who walked from Tibet over the rugged Himalayas to India that fits perfectly with my labyrinth experience and my life to date. When asked how he was able to make such a difficult and treacherous journey he said, "I put one foot in front of the other . . . one step at a time."

Rising up to Paradise

Kealakekua—Hawaii, 2000

> *Rising up to paradise, I think I'm gonna shine.*
> –John Perry Barlow (The Grateful Dead)

Swimming without thought of the wild sea around us, we reach the dolphins. My wife and I'd escaped the crazy testosterone-charged household with our boys and headed to the Hawaiian waters. Shady, who at times has trouble walking, swam the mile out to sea without kicking, likely channeling her childhood swim-team prowess. We gave no thoughts to sharks or what we might encounter along the way. The line between reckless and spontaneous is often quite thin. In the bay, halfway to the Captain Cook monument in Kealakekua, I felt like singing as we arrived at a huge pod of dolphins traveling as a family, little ones in tow.

Shady, a natural healer and teacher, started chanting harmonic overtones and I joined in. The dolphins responded and circled back, suddenly taking on their dreamtime state where one side of the brain goes to sleep as they continue to swim while still holding some awareness with the other half—totally reframing for me the power behind a "half-brained" idea. Rhythmically rising up in groups in a circle around us, fins flashed the surface and gently rolled back down. Through our masks beneath the water the ocean too became dreamlike as they rolled and dove down, flapping to propel themselves forward in unison, sunlight cutting down in shafts of light.

We are in many ways like the pod of dolphins, a family of man, swimming in dreamtime in the bay. As mammals we share similar traits such as patterns in behavior, large brains, and complex cognition. But they actually use a larger percentage of their brains than humans, and I witness something we've lost along the way. A sense of group harmony, a feeling of belonging, or a knowledge that everything I need is already within me when I swim with others.

Tropical paradises reflect for me a deep acceptance of all living things in the air and an inspirational slower pace. In Costa Rica, Shady and I laid on the jungle floor watching sloths move through the treetops of the rainforest's canopy. We smiled at the slow simplicity of the moment and how, despite the ruckus of us tourists below, they stayed above it all and rushed for no one. They had their own pace and rhythm, and their deep focus with each step made the name "sloth" a misnomer.

In Mexico I'd marveled at the wings of the stingrays that swam beside us stroking the water like a symphony conductor leading the orchestra through a stanza played in adagio. Before leaving Hawaii we swam with sea turtles, whose grace, like wings of the ray, stroked with a powerful rhythm and brought my mind into focus. Like my higher or true self, they surface occasionally to take a breath, blow some bubbles, and then descend to actively explore life below.

Exploring new ways of practicing law and defusing the notion of the adversarial process, has set me apart as a lone wolf, making the sea turtle the perfect legal totem, as they too feel caught between two worlds. They draw their breath of life from above, but they refuse to leave the simplicity and beauty of the sea. It's as if they've seen something terrible and chosen not to step out. They send a message through their silence, that the world we've created is missing something ... is not safe.

All my nature experiences have provided me great lessons for both my legal practice and all my relationships, but the sea turtle's messages run deepest:

- Choose my environment or cases, rather than having them forced on me
- Love each breath as I feel blessed to continue to swim with the beauty of life
- Swim effortlessly, despite carrying a heavy (case) load
- Appreciate the uniqueness of everything and every client I meet, for no two shells are the same
- Take care of myself as I know that I too carry my home on my back, for the body is my temple that journeys with me and houses my connection to a greater universal energy (though it still remains an enigma to me)
- Act boldly, choosing beauty over conformity

Mixing with the mystery and beauty of nature, far from the court-room and chaos, is where I feel the most relaxed, connected and willing to embrace the unknown.

Fairy Dust

Osaka, Japan—May 1998

From the majestic ancient palace in Osaka, we walk out into the Ume orchard where the ancient plum trees are in full bloom. I'm in Japan to present workshops with local lawyers on Human Dignity in the Workplace, when a few of us escape to tour the castle. Petals softly fall over us like snow, and glancing over at two lawyers from my delegation, I'd swear they'd been hit with fairy dust.

Ted, a large New Yorker steeped in the concrete forest of city life, is literally frozen in his path with an amazing grin, as if he's been joyfully sprayed with Love Potion No. 9. He's caught in the aromatic conversation between two deep red blooming Ume trees. Petals cover his shoulders and his head as the dance of the pollen, the flower essence of life, takes us out of our bodies. Ted later tells me that it was like everything stopped and nothing else in his life mattered.

We all should experience these moments, what I'm now seeing as regular CHE courses: Continuing Human Education. These moments of aromatic delight and visual splendor are images to keep close to the heart, like the feeling of young love, or a first kiss; always there to bring a smile and remember how we are not separate from a greater story. The world needs to slow more often while we honor its beauty, the intimacy of our surroundings, if only to remember. For the flowers come but once a year and for a short time.

This can be done anywhere at any time. When I breathe nature in deeply and remember the connection, this crazy world of us versus them and the forces of hate lose their power and significance. I feel more alive, and such moments convince me I'm part of the dance. It's how we choose to be in the world around each of us that makes the difference.

As my friends stroll out of the Ume garden, I move into a grassy meadow behind the castle. I've been taking Tai Chi for many months, but am just beginning to understand it on a deeper level. No one is around and the stillness invites me to practice. As my hands start to push I feel something through my legs, ringing my torso, a realization that we humans have forgotten how to walk on the earth. I shift effortlessly all weight from one side of my body to another, and as my surroundings slip away it is as if two mountains are moving, but with a connection miles below the surface. Turning, with hands floating, I feel as if I'm moving with the grace of the deer in the forest, or the giraffes as they floated next to my car in Africa.

Something as simple as how we walk can determine our perspective and attitude about life and the world around us. Each step not only counts, but is sacred and reflects the power of being grounded in the moment. It's all connected. As my hands come to rest at my side I see an old Japanese man standing across the lawn watching me. His wrinkled coat and lean frame have known both sorrow and joy. He stares at me, smiles, gives a short bow, turns, and shuffles into the Ume orchard. I bow back and when I look up he's gone.

When life seems anything but gentle or fluid these experiences in nature provide me an anchor to the new story, or in reality a very ancient one; for when I close my eyes, my dream state can take me below the surface to float up and back in perfect harmony. Remembering the crystal snowflakes of the Grand Canyon or the red rock canyons in Jemez, my troubles lose their significance and I feel a part of something greater.

Fritjof Capra, in the *Tao of Physics*, said, "because of the interconnection of all things with one another . . . the universe has to be grasped dynamically, as it moves, vibrates and dances."[1] Ubuntu says we as humans are all connected, but ecological thinking, the core of today's sustainability movement, expands this relationship to everything around us: humans, animals, plants, and the earth. What we have done to the planet we have intrinsically done to ourselves, and it is up to us to cultivate and practice an awareness of being intimately connected with all of the natural processes around us. My dance with nature confirms that to make any sense of this crazy world, we too must tap into the vibration of nature. The rhythm of life is a powerful beat.

▾ ▾ ▾

1. Fritjof Capra, *The Tao of Physics: An Exploration of the Parallels Between Modern Physics* Shambala (Boston 1975) p. 195.

CHAPTER 18
Going Deeper

Man continues to wander in the dense forest of his intellect.
–Philosophy of the Masters

Beas, Punjab India—1992

It is an eight-hour train ride from Delhi to the village where my wife's guru resides. She has been on this path for over thirty years and after her recent car accident she needs help to get to India. Staring out the faded windows I'm numbed by the sights of people living along the tracks, tarps over their families, more outstretched hands, eyes lost in time and to the world. What type of God allows the people to suffer in such conditions? Why aren't we all outraged? Perhaps we all collectively run from problems rather than face them, not understanding why or what we could do to make a difference, dropping a coin into a beggar's cup, not to change the trajectory of his life, but so he'll quickly be out of sight. . . out of mind.

Religion is an art form in India. Everywhere you look are temples or street rituals, flowers or wandering sacred cows. It's where Muslims and Hindus have clashed so violently, and where Gandhi had opened up paths of ubuntu against great odds. Yet, religion remains a mystery and an enigma to me. As long as I can remember I've been religious-phobic. In New Mexico Catholicism is practically a state religion. Our county was forced, kicking and screaming, to remove the crosses from its emblem in the 1990s. The Ten Commandments remain cast in marble at the entrance to District Court. "Thou shall not covet your neighbor's wife . . . nor his ox, nor his donkey" for that matter, lest you end up confronting a jealous God, or I imagine at least an irate husband. Over the years I've found myself lost in religion's swirl of contradictions and faith in the absurd.

I'd lost two workers in my office to AIDS. Walter and Dan. It's hard to accept a compassionate God when watching friends slip away so young. Walter's parents never accepted he was gay or admitted he had AIDS. In those days he would not have gotten a Catholic funeral because he was such a sinner. So Walter's "sin" was kept hushed, replaced with a wink and a prayer. The service talked more about Jesus than Walter, a religious show that felt like pure hypocrisy.

Still, I was beginning to take spirituality out for a spin. Here in the Punjab I watch volunteers feed three meals a day to nearly a million people who attend *satsang* to hear the discourses and be in the guru's presence. All are welcome, people of any religion or none. They are quick to point out that it's not a religion. "Our religion here is love," one speaker says. I feel like I'm on another planet.

I am resisting the idea of a teacher. One evening Babaji, as my wife's teacher is called, is discussing the notion of a guru. It seems unique that he never uses that term for himself, nor asks for money. He doesn't even make any claim to being spiritual. "When I meet someone who gives me peace of mind, gives me happiness, he is my teacher," he says. I realize I have learned from people who over the years who have left me feeling more connected to my own heart, like the comrades in South Africa, or courageous sanctuary workers I defended for sheltering refugees from the wars in Central America.

Perhaps it's not about one teacher but about learning from the world around us and from the experiences that give us that peace of mind. Each encounter gives us a chance to grow, to smile, and to share love. Looking into the mirror I understand it has much more to do with my receptivity than a dearth of teachers. The lessons abound, and entraining with a teacher must not be about surrendering yourself to him or her, but about building a relationship that can be a great template of love to reflect out into all our relations in the world.

I find his Babaji's freeing. All too often I have tried to place a label on something that was happening to me, but in hindsight I would miss out on what is actually happening while trying to figure it out. He smiles, "Don't get caught in a web of words. It's about experience. True faith comes only from experience." Or maybe from a good laugh.

Holy Laughter

After weeks of discourses and lessons in love, we're on our way to Sa-mode Palace in Rajasthan. My head is spinning with tales of camels, temples, and tigers, a true storybook journey. The plane from Del-hi to Jaipur was bare bones; all one class, few amenities. Just before take-off a group of six Tibetan Buddhists clad in their deep burgundy robes board the plane, filling the first two rows. As one turns sideways I see his familiar glasses and know it's the Dalai Lama.

"Of course," I thought. "He lives in India. How cool is this?"

"Please fasten your seatbelt," the stewardess instructs me. Little did I know that I was in for a ride.

It had been only three years since the Dalai Lama was awarded the Nobel Peace Prize. His acceptance speech in Oslo brought the world closer and was filled with ubuntu:

> Because we all share this small planet earth, we have to learn to live in harmony and peace with each other and with nature. That is not just a dream, but a necessity. We are dependent on each other in so many ways, that we can no longer live in isolated communities and ignore what is happening outside those communities, and we must share the good fortune that we enjoy. . . .we are all basically the same human beings, who seek happiness and try to avoid suffering . . . For if we each selfishly pursue only what we believe to be in our own interest, without caring about the needs of others, we not only may end up harming others but also ourselves. . . .As interdependents, therefore, we have no other choice than to develop what I call a sense of universal responsibility.

Here is one of my heroes in the flesh. Carpe diem. I've got to seize the day and meet him. After we're airborne, I catch glimpses of him through the seats. What was he doing? Was he meditating? I won-der what he's reading? Questions abound. Can I go over to say some-thing? What would I say? Stop staring, Eric! Looking around, I appear to be the only person noticing our special guest.

As the seatbelt sign fades so does my apprehension. I'm deter-mined to say something, if possible. If he's in deep contemplation, I'll steal a rock-star glimpse and head into the bathroom. I move toward the front of the cabin and turn the corner within a couple feet of his seat. His body methodically moved from left to right, his eyes were fixated as if in a trance, his glasses filed with an odd green iridescent glow, and his fingers, which had spun so many beads, supported his thumbs as they pressed first left than right.

"Holy shit," I say almost out loud, my mouth nearly dropping to the earth below. I could not believe my eyes. I'm in the presence of one of the greatest most renowned spiritual leaders of the twentieth century and what is he doing? Was it a secret Tibetan ritual? No. His Holiness the Dalai Lama, the Nobel Peace laureate and exiled leader of the Tibetan people, was zealously playing a handheld video game!

Suddenly he either sensed my presence, or heard my gasp of surprise, and he looked up from the screen. His infectious and joyful smile spread across his face in a moment of pure joy and excitement as if to shout, "Isn't this fun?!" And he resumed playing. I stumbled into the restroom.

An uncontrolled laughter burst from my lips. What was I expecting? But what a smile. We hadn't exchanged a word, but I felt as if I had shared an intimate moment wherein a genuine, honest connection of the heart said far more than any words. They say that one look from a saint can change your life. But it's not what we take from a glance, it's what he gives. I had been given a plateful. As I exited the restroom he put the game into his robe and stared ahead. I need not say a word.

Upon returning to my seat I feel speechless. All I tell Shady is: "He was playing a video game!" and something about that smile. We land, and I watch out the window as he leaves the plane to a limo waiting on the tarmac. What a gift! We carry so many judgments. If we're caught enjoying something childish, something out of character, we feel embarrassed . . . almost ashamed. But here was someone who was doing something that brought him pleasure without reservation, nor fear of public perceptions. When he saw I was looking at him, he didn't stop playing, didn't clear his throat and turn serious. He shared a smile of pure joy and returned to play. Being yourself—being true to your feelings—is more powerful than maintaining our image. It was a holy moment. I could feel him radiating happiness and contentment in that moment our eyes met. It remains a constant reminder to me when I get too serious or fall into any sense of self-importance or am quick to judge another.

I also understood the lesson I'd been given in letting go of expectations. Life is never quite what we expect. It's far from linear and we cannot draw conclusions about what enlightenment looks like, what politicians should act like, or even what awaits us around the corner. I had an idea of what a spiritual leader would be doing with his spare time and at 30,000 feet, my expectations were eclipsed with a smile.

▾ ▾ ▾

CHAPTER 19
Moving From Darkness to Light

Come to the Edge they said.
No I'm too scared.
Come to the edge.
No I'll fall.
Come to the edge, and I did
and they pushed
and I flew.
–Guillaume Apollinaire (1880-1918)

The Dalai Lama video game encounter served to propel me further out of the lawyering box. After depositions in litigation against Honeywell in Minneapolis, my client and I ended a day of intense questioning not by drowning in liquor, though it came to mind, but by renting roller-blades and cruising on the bike trail around one of the majestic city lakes. As my long coat and tie trailed behind me in the wind, I thought of that lesson in fun and joy on the Jaipur plane and could tell from the smile on my client's face that we had already won by not letting them pull us down into the muck of litigation. A year later she received a half-million-dollar verdict and I received a most unusual bonus.

Albuquerque, New Mexico—1993
It started innocently on a cold blistery December night. I'm poring through files when the phone rings. It's Shirley, who'd skated with me around the lakes.

"Remember that man I told you about, from Brazil? You know, the one with the light," she excitedly told me. "Well he's back and I got you and me in to see him."

The guy with the light, I thought. Now which one was he? Oh yeah, the one who emits light from his body. Not your usual client phone call.

"When is it?" I ask, still half lost in the mound of papers for the morning.

"Tonight," she says "and I know you are meant to be there."

"Tonight?" I laugh. "Sorry, Shirley, but I've got so much on my plate right now. I wish it was another time."

She would not be dissuaded. "Eric, you cannot miss this. He's the guy who went on TV in a G-String to prove the light actually came from him," she replies with great seriousness. "It could give you some needed energy. Maybe it will help you with your work."

"Help me," I thought. Lord knows I could use it. I'm spending these days with a hostile Federal judge who thinks discrimination only re-lates to good taste or refinement. The other day the judge told my client to "shut up," a sign that he was not impressed with our case. Maybe I could use some light or at least a shift of my energy out of this surreal lion's den.

"Alright, I'll go," I said. My head, like a pesky inner critic, kept say-ing, "Are you crazy?"

We meet that evening at a large adobe house in the tree-lined Ridgecrest section of town. Shirley meets me at the door and we join twenty or so other adults of all ages. There is a buzz of excitement in the air. A woman emerges from the kitchen and begins to speak. She is Mauricio's wife, Kimberly, and she tells us that when he was nine years old—Mauricio was now near seventy—a mysterious blue light followed him home and he could not escape from it. The lights did no harm and waited for him each day. Mauricio would resist it and run, but each day it returned. Eventually Mauricio learned to let go of his fear and trust in something greater and the light would appear at different times and a voice would tell him he should help others.

"This is not about healing," she says. "It is just something he shares with you for you to take from it whatever you are needing." By this time it feel like I need to get back to planet earth. It's a bit Twilight Zone for my spirituality tastes. Mauricio's young wife describes that we will go in two-by-two and then we can quietly come out and lay in the other room to realign.

I watch the first couple go in and close the door. Shortly after the door closes, beams of bright light suddenly shoot from under the door. A few minutes later the first pair stumbles out and are led to another room to lie down. "Oh boy," I whisper to myself, "What have I gotten myself into?"

When it's our turn Shirley and I enter the room. Mauricio greets Shirley with an embrace like an old friend. He's a short, stocky man, looking more shopkeeper than mystic. I notice his rounded fingers and his gentle smile. He speaks only Portuguese, so there was little talk. We lay on the two massage tables. Suddenly he begins at my feet and works specific points up to my forehead. As he touches my body a remarkable bright light beams out from his hands. Although cautioned to keep my eyes closed, I can't keep from peeking, like taking glimpses at a full eclipse. The electrical charges pulsate through my body. His sleeves are rolled up and his hands empty, yet brimming with light.

When he finishes sharing this energy with us, he stumbles silently back to the corner chair, breathing hard, his face still, as if drained of life force. As we stagger out, I glance back at him sitting motionless—his soft, placid gaze fixed on the ceiling. We lay down for some time in the next room in a sea of pillows. There's heat coming from the "third eye" in my forehead. I quietly slip out and head for my car. My body tingles and I feel slightly dazed, but I'm being pulled back to ply my trade. As I drive home, I wonder, "What will tomorrow bring?"

The next morning I leave for court feeling charged up, literally, and ready to go. All seems quite normal until late morning. I'm examining my client on the stand, below the giant bald eagle plaque and the judge's scowl, when the room starts to spin. Gripping the podium I'm amazed at the visuals. My client continues to talk, but I can barely hear him. What's happening to me? I wonder. Have I been electrocuted? I imagine asking the judge for a recess, saying, "Sorry your honor, but I saw this shaman last night and I'm currently hallucinating," but opted to hang on (literally still gripping podium) for the impending recess. Grace intervenes as the judge declares an early lunch break. As I sway back to my chair the room appears to return to normal, but I feel like I'd kissed a Duracell.

The afternoon was uneventful, as if I'd simply been given a reminder about the power of the unknown and the path before me. Mauricio's graphic demonstration of Qi—our energy or life force—charged up my body, but the experience opened me to look at the world through limitless eyes. Einstein spoke of this place: "Out yonder there is a huge world, which exists independent of us as human beings, and which stands before us like a great, eternal riddle." Sometimes, especially for us over-rational lawyers, it takes something completely out of the box to let go and trust in the infinite. On that fateful evening, I laid the groundwork for moving beyond the intellectual understanding of ubuntu to having faith in my connection to everything.

I didn't suddenly become a totally new person working with a deep heart connection in my work and life. I'm not sure it works that way. Too often we want overnight change and in our disappointment at not moving mountains we miss the messages. Like his wife had said, I should take what I needed from the experience and Mauricio's light rekindled the lessons I'd taken from India and my other spiritual dabblings to date:

> *Faith:* Follow your instinct, even if it cuts against the grain.
> *Surrender:* Don't pretend that we really understand what's going on.
> *Let go:* The boldness of letting go of the parameters of our beliefs is dynamic.
> *Listen:* Listen from within and without, for a sound, for a moment, or the light that will set our deepest self into motion.
> *Keep Growing:* Turn the legal system on its head.

I had gradually come to see that there is a whole other realm of existence and relationship that we've barely touched or begun to understand. While building a career and "fighting" for social justice, a huge part of me was abandoned like a forgotten bride at the altar. I was being drawn to a new way of practicing law that would reframe conflict and seize the opportunity to heal—a synthesis of my legal work with my spiritual exploration and ubuntu.

The evening with Mauricio was like rediscovering the spirit in the dark, while, like the dolphins' dreamtime, trying to keep a part of my brain in a state of awareness. It's stretching my emerging sense of spirit, but as Rilke put it so succinctly, "In order to have creative experiences" we have to "live from a deep place." It was no surprise that the courtroom turned upside down, for this confirmed my choice to re-pattern my legal practice and my view of the law.

But the past still clung to my bones. Could I, while working within the adversarial legal system, let go of expectations and blame and rise above the muck? I would need a whole new set of tools to be the peacemaker, to place compassion and love on the mantel with winning for the client. Months before his assassination, John F. Kennedy reflected on our commonality with the Soviets: "For in the final analysis, our most basic common link is that we all inhabit this small planet. We all breathe the same air. We all cherish our children's future."

I felt excitement at the prospect of applying my lessons in human dignity, spirituality, and ubuntu into my work. We are more alike than we know. Time to feel reborn and serene, to smile like my grandson Lucean, who runs about naked pushing the giant wheelbarrow, filled with joy in every breath.

▾ ▾ ▾

CHAPTER 20

The Past Will Set You Free

I was thrown out of college for cheating on the metaphysics exam;
I looked into the soul of the boy next to me.
–Woody Allen

Santa Fe, New Mexico—August 25, 1998

Dark and foreboding, the vacant eyes behind the wooden masks follow me as I pass through the Santa Fe Plaza. It's Spanish Market and the downtown streets are full of craft vendors, mammoth crosses, and food booths. The art is heavy, almost contorted, with an odd mix of inquisitional themes and angels. Christ is everywhere, hanging from crosses or etched in coffee mugs.

A cluster of Native Americans are stretched out along the ground under the Palace of the Governor's portal in the same place they've been relegated to for centuries. Since briefly ruling the roost after the Pueblo Revolt of 1684, they have seen themselves squeezed into smaller and smaller spaces. Here, beneath the shadow of J Crew and the Gap, they sell jewelry, pottery, and blankets to the thousands of tourists passing by each day. Historical appearances keep them stooped over on blankets strewn across the ground rather than tables, but at least it is prime retail space. Santa Fe, once a quiet artist colony with a unique cross-cultural mix, has morphed into rows of upscale restaurants and art galleries, metaphysical products, designer clothing, and Häagen Dazs franchises.

I'm surrounded by craft booths and savoring chili-laced grilled corn while Spanish mariachi music drifts from the plaza. Despite the commercialization, there are few cities in America that look and feel like Santa Fe. My relationship with Shady has hit a roadblock and my once certain future seems to be slipping away. Perhaps I have spent too much time trying to understand my connection with the world and neglected the woman right before me. A part of me hopes I'll discover some inner guidance on this trip north. But I realize something or someone is calling me.

I stumble upon the recently opened Georgia O'Keeffe museum tucked down a tiny side street. Entering, I am struck by the colors and how nature spoke to her so deeply. O'Keeffe taught us that beauty lies in our angle of vision, right before our eyes in a flower or in a cloud across a near perfect sky. A quote on the wall from the free-spirited artist who adopted northern New Mexico as her home reads: "Nobody sees a flower really; it is so small. We haven't time, and to see takes time—like to have a friend takes time." Breathing deeply, I know it to be true. I need to take the time to see the world around me, to feel my connection to it and to others. But something is haunting me and keeping me back. O'Keeffe's painting of the sky through a hip bone reminds me that there is a passageway within that I must discover.

Choosing to Fight

Leaving Spanish Market, I'm heading into the nearby Pecos mountains to camp for the night. A sign on an old wooden porch stoop off Cerrillos Road catches my eye: "Psychic Healings." Maybe it is time for me to go, as Babaji said, "a little deeper." Entering I'm greeted by a short, roundish man whose receding hairline and dress placed him more in an accounting office than a psychic parlor.

"I saw your sign on psychic healings?" I tell him, the words rolling off my tongue as if I was merely responding to a Help Wanted sign.

"Oh, I'm sorry," he says, "The psychic is booked until 7:00, but I do past-life regressions if you're interested."

Ah, Santa Fe—no wonder they call it *The City Different*. Now we're talking.

The past life guy's name is Charles and he explains, "I will talk you into a pre-hypnotic state and ask some questions, but the prior experiences come from you. I think you'll find it interesting."

What a leap of faith for me. Perhaps I was beginning to believe in past lives, having heard about them from the guru, the Dalai Lama, and in books by Santa Fe's famous resident New Age queen,

Shirley MacLaine, but I had not known anyone who really had been "regressed." I wondered to myself, "Could I go back in time?"

Why not? You can't ask for a sign and then "wilt upon its stage" when it shows up. Fate had brought me to his doorstep and there must be a reason the psychic was booked. I paid upfront and said to Charles, "Let's regress."

I stretch out in his client chair, a cross between a La-Z-Boy recliner and a dentist's chair. Do they have catalogs or stores for past-life regression furniture? I never figured myself as a candidate for hypnosis as my monkey mind rarely quieted, and "letting go" has not been my forte. But Charles's soft voice put me at ease and soon he asked what I was seeing. What a ride! Over the next two hours I floated in my mother's womb 150 years ago, died twice, was at my daughter's birth in 1895, felt the blood of war on my hands, lost a wife and daughter, and saw points in time where I had cloistered my feelings and made choices that still haunt me today. Where were these stories coming from?

"Look down," he says. "What do you see?"

"Boots. Old boots." I can literally see the mud on them.

"Who are you?" I hear Charles ask.

"My name is Martol. I live with my wife Pitanya near the Baltic Sea."

"And how are things?"

"Amazing. We are so happy. I love her so much." Part of me is saying, *What? Where is that coming from?* But a part of me feels so at home, so familiar.

"And what is happening?"

"It's a room, women are around. Its our daughter Titania being born." I feel a tear rolling down my cheek. I am flushed with joy. A proud moment in time. My sweet Titania. *Wait, who?*

"What happens next," Charles asks, as if he knows something is brewing.

"She's three. Playing in our yard. I see a group of three soldiers on horseback approaching. They say I need to go to war, the nation is calling. I'm torn. I don't know what to do. I know what happens if you refuse military service and don't want to go to prison, or worse."

"What do you see now?"

"Pitanya and I are fighting. She says we should all just leave and run away. She says I owe it to my family not to go. My instinct is telling me to flee with my family, my joy intact, but I don't have the courage to say no." I feel a lump in my chest like being hit by a brick.

"What do you do?"

"The next morning before sunrise I kiss my sleeping daughter, who's lying next to our bed, and leave to war without a word to anyone." A part of me is seeing that along the way I also closed the door on my heart and feelings in order to cope with the pain of leaving. "And then the horrors."

"What do you see?"

"I'm curled up in a ditch or perhaps a foxhole. Bodies all around. There's blood puddling at my feet." Why didn't I follow my heart?

"Do you go back home?"

My mind floods with a series of sped-up images until I see I am there.

"Yes. A few years later I return to my house but it is empty. I wanted them to forgive me. I needed to see my daughter's smile. They're gone. I'm grieving so much and frantically looking everywhere for them." It's much like my seeking joy in my life today. Here I was more than a century ago feeling disempowered and a failure as a parent from leaving my family.

I hear a voice, "Where are you next?"

"A cold room. It feels like my deathbed. My insides feel rotted out, from drink and pain. There are stiff white sheets over me and the smell . . . chlorophyll." I can actually smell it.

"Must be a hospital. I've been here for some time. I'm cursing God. How could he let this happen?"

The hostility toward anything God-related would follow me into this life. Perhaps such things explain why I was born into a house of atheists.

I gasp and Charles simply says "What?"

"Two angels are here and I'm being swept into a room."

"What does it feel like?" his voice coming closer.

"Calm, non-judgmental . . . pure love." I'm forgiving myself for leaving, checking out, shutting down, and for lacking courage.

This frantic search for my wife and the joy of the years we did share together feel quite real, as if the feelings were still a part of me.

Charles asks, "Is she is here in New Mexico?" Wow, that's something I didn't expect. And from somewhere I hear myself say "No."

But she is somewhere. Does that mean she is worth finding, a soul mate from another life, an unfinished love? Or is it just that the loving inside me is unfinished and truncated and it's time to open my heart?

I open my eyes and the session is finished. I see Charles sitting against the wall smiling. "You really got it," he said.

I could barely speak. I never expected to regress into anything. I muster simply a quiet "Thank you" and stumble into the twilight with the late summer August thunder rumbling in the distance.

"What the fuck was that?" I said aloud to myself. How did that story come from my lips? I think of my relationship with Shady and whether there is someone else I am suppose to find or be with, a soul mate. Is it all true or just signposts for my current life? Alexander's line that "Those who don't know history are apt to repeat it" comes to mind, but I didn't know it meant *my* ancient history. Did this explain my antiwar work for decades and how I resonated so deeply with pacifism and conscientious objectors?

In the end I've decided it's simply about love and choosing to reflect it in our daily lives. I so deeply yearn to share its magnificence —not squander the opportunity. Clearly the stories help explain some of my current feelings of disempowerment as a parent and spouse.

The saints say we are given a chance to be together with people in this life to work through past karma. Now is the opportunity to be together in love, regardless of the past. I am beginning to understand that our spirit is composed of beings of light and love. We wear these body suits in our different roles over time—and "overtime." How the world could benefit from a true spiritual awakening that views everyone as souls traveling through time. Race, sex, height, color, culture are all simply coverings the soul is wearing—You are not your clothes!

Yet I'm resisting simply folding the past into the present. The guru always said to not spend much time dwelling on such matters as they are a distraction and beyond much of our understanding. What rings clearer to me is the simple and profound teaching of Richard Alpert, known as Ram Dass, in the title of his guidebook for living: *Be Here Now*. I don't want to chase after the past but long to be deeply here in the present, to embrace the unknown before me with gusto. Howard Zinn described this well: "The future is an infinite succession of presents, and to live now as we think human beings should live, in defiance of all that is bad around us, is itself a marvelous victory."

A friend once described my past-life scenario as similar to the story in Dr. Zhivago, but I'd never read Boris Pasternak's book or seen the film. But I was not surprised, for my reflection depicted the universal human quest to reunite with our beloved, to search for truth, connection, and love, in the face of painful separation. Too many die separate and alone, never coming to know their true ubuntu selves.

Pecos Mountains, New Mexico

I settled that evening into a meadow full of yellow dandelions, Queen Anne's Lace, and daisies deep in the Pecos Mountains. The forest is teeming with life, a connected celebration of creation. The trees feed the nation of insects and birds and the flowers intoxicate the butterflies, which I watch on the edge of the water as they spread their crimson wings, embossed with a circle, a constant reminder of nature's grand symphony. A still, reflective pond mirrors my state of mind.

My dreams that night affirm my choice to move forward. I'm afloat at sea. Two bobbing floaters are thrown into the sea to test for pollution. Suddenly the boat starts moving away and the test containers are being left behind. I step to the edge of the boat, realizing I have a choice. I can dive in and attempt to retrieve them, but I risk getting left behind by the boat. At that moment the message came: "Let go of the past. You don't need them. Don't chase after things left behind." In other words, "Don't let yesterday use up too much of today." I need not leap overboard to swim after the past. It's old news. Measuring the pollution of our prior struggles ties us to the past, while acceptance brings peace. Awakened, I light a candle and see Shady's eyes reflected in their radiance as they brightly illuminate the tent, warming my heart, and I'm grateful for it without lamenting the past or speculating about the future.

"The best thing about the future," Abe Lincoln said, "is that it only comes one day at a time." I'm taking to my spiritual seeking with that in mind, trying to accept that I cannot predict what lies ahead or what it means for my world and my legal practice. Yet, my dabbling in the spirit in the dark proves that lessons can arrive in strange packages.

Knocking from the Inside Out

Tokyo, Japan—1998
I tried Buddhist meditation classes, but the optional rituals of bowing and prostrating seem forced and out of place. I remember the guru's lessons that spirituality is not about ritual, but inner experience, and I feel a spiritual connection echoing inside me, Yet around the world, religions have built temples of brick and mortar and sometimes engage in the oddest rituals, like when I ventured into the "Money Washing Temple" after hiking up the hillside of Kamakutra in Japan.

The scene was surreal. Hundreds of people were placing money in reed baskets at the edge of a pond. They were not peaceful, they scurried around with a frenetic energy. I take a bamboo-handled cup and pour water over my thousand-yen note. After washing it an elderly Japanese woman with a toothless smile shows me how to shake it out over a burning pile of incense. People are leaving eggs as offerings, banging a gong attached to a rope, clapping—with both hands (Zen joke)—and clasping their hands in prayer. All around me fortunes and hopes in the form of yen bills are tied to the trees like ribbons, as offerings for prosperity. I wonder who is watching me as I post my note and close my eyes, but all I see is an old guy on a cloud with a long beard shaking his head in amazement—thanking us for the cash.

At times such rituals feel more like folly faith, but then I give up trying to understand and ask myself, Who am I to say what works? The Buddhist notions that we are all united, that nothing has an essence of its own, and that people cannot be segregated by race, sex, or religion, is providing a bridge between my politics and my emerging sense of spirituality.

Perhaps my political work has been more spiritual than I imagined. The link between the three universals—interdependence, responsibility, and compassion—is the root of progressive politics. Religion is perverted when it is used to justify state violence or the abandonment of someone who is gay. John Lennon famously made the point some years before: "people got hooked on the teacher and missed the message." I'm much more drawn to the message of saints who play video games, or laugh.

Indianapolis, Indiana—1999

After a long day of work a flyer catches my eye: "His Holiness, the XIV Dalai Lama, will perform the Kalachakra for World Peace, a traditional Buddhist ceremony, in Bloomington, Indiana. This 10-day event is a profound ceremony that unites people from around the world in a peaceful spiritual activity so as to affect people and the environment in a significant manner." World peace, that radiant smile, and a chance to take my young sons and expose them to something different and constructive. I knew I had to be in Indiana. I clear my appointments and book our tickets.

I've always wanted my sons to think out of the box, explore the world from a different angle. The Kalichakra was a step beyond our reading at bedtime the wise and insightful *Tao of Pooh*. At the ripe age of eleven, Sasha has taken to occasional meditation and, unbeknownst to me, had been dropping into a Buddhist center in Albuquerque with his friend Willie. They would do chants and sit. One afternoon he tells me he has committed to the path of the Bodhisattva and that he had wanted to be a Buddhist since second grade but had thought they couldn't have sex. He was relieved to learn otherwise. My heart is doing somersaults. For the next several months we dive deep into our *Free Tibet* phase with Sasha even starting to learn Tibetan. What draws a child to such things? Talk about past lives and sanskaras.

Khlari's sense of spirit, on the other hand, remains elusive. But he has an ability to focus and break through the bullshit, which will serve him in the years ahead, even against great struggles. When he could barely speak he stood between his mom and me near our kneecaps when we were bickering over something stupid and simply said, "No more games." It stunned us into looking at our insensitivity and meaningless banter. As a young teenager one night he takes me out in the moonlight to see the iridescence of a large spider web. Sharing this wonderment with my son is love incarnate; there is no greater moment than right here right now. I'd been so consumed with work that I'd been like the person Rainer Maria Rilke describes, imagining a man looking out his window at summer's end, "having been busy with everything except the one harvest that mattered." Finding the work/life balance is essential element to staying connected to our humanity.

The boys and I travel to Indiana. They get to see the Dalai Lama, but we were all quite restless with the whole ceremony/ritual scene. The endless chanting, bells, and prostrations did not help my restless mind, though we all love hanging out in the market sideshow of incenses, scarves, and Tibetan crafts. The trip proved to be much more about holding a space with my children than diving deep into peace and spirituality. Or maybe—*that* is peace and spirituality?

▾ ▾ ▾

PART IV

Reframing Conflict

To win 100 victories in 100 battles is not the acme of skill.
To subdue the enemy without fighting is the acme of skill.
–Sun-Tzu, *The Art of War*

CHAPTER 21
Non-Violent Advocacy

*My joy was boundless. I had learned to find out the
better side of human nature and to enter man's hearts . . .
to unite parties driven asunder.*
–Mahatma Gandhi

Throwing papers across the table at my client, the opposing counsel
from the Washington, DC firm uses the deposition to make snide and
angry remarks about our allegations of defense contractor fraud. The
goal is to shame, blame, and intimidate my client and to pull me into
a fight. Instead of engaging him in battle I choose to use the power of
compassion to diffuse the situation. I say, "It appears that Mr. Holmes
is tired, so we're going to take a break." He goes ballistic.

"I'm not tired. Your client is the problem. I'm not tired. There is no
need to break," he shouts.

Softly but firmly, and looking at the dazed court reporter tran-
scribing every word, I repeat, "No, he appears tired and we're going on
break." While exiting I can still hear him repeating like a schoolyard
bully, justifying his behavior, "For the record it's Mr. Sirotkin's break,
not mine. I'm not tired. I'm not tired."

As the dust settles we return and Holmes is remarkably subdued.
We finish the deposition and he returns to Washington and passes
the case to the much more affable local counsel. I never hear from
him again professionally, and the case settles, but for several years he
sends me a Christmas card.

I could have chosen to engage him in his tirade or make threats
about how he was treating my client. As a lawyer it's easy to just say,
"Fuck them," and be sucked into the blame game and battle. Instead

I went with a nonconfrontational method that included concern for him. He was ready for the fight, but my peaceful approach was more powerful. Years of courtroom drama taught me that responding with anger or a counterattack creates more damage to the parties and to that part of my heart that remembers we are all interconnected—the plexus where we dance with the divine. What good is one's religion or spirituality if it's not reflected in our work, relationships, and daily life? This is starting to be fun.

Through my explorations of peacemaking, interconnectedness, and spirituality I was beginning to feel that I, like the lotus flower, could live above the muck. It's akin to the verbally abusive man coming to see the Buddha and hurling insults at him while the Buddha just sits there calmly. Finally, the man asks the Buddha why he does not respond to the insults and abuse. The Buddha replies, "If someone offers you a gift, and you decline to accept it, to whom does the gift belong?" If someone is irrational, abusive, and combative, you can mentally decline to accept "the gift." Let that person keep their anger and insanity, and don't let it affect you. I sent Mr. Holmes home with his gift and I pondered whether "lawyer burnout" could be a response to years of accepting unwanted "gifts."

What Brings You Joy?

The healing messages I'm witnessing and experiencing around the world are becoming the *evidence* I need to muster the courage to become what I'm calling a "nonviolent advocate." It's as if a huge hole in my heart was filling by stepping out of the battle and the legal boxes and reconnecting to what it means to be human. Successful lawyering, like anything else, often comes down to our attitudes. A few easy lessons in nonviolent advocacy made all the difference.

First, I changed my attitude toward conflict, integrating into my consultations with clients the old Chinese notion wherein they use the same symbol for "conflict" as "opportunity." It was no longer about what I could do *for* them, but an exploration *with* them of where we could go with the hand they'd been dealt so they could heal, learn from experience, and move forward.

Second, I needed to deepen my understanding of the client's hopes, dreams, and most precious needs. This not only gave each appointment new life but included inquiries beyond "the facts" that met the client in a very human place. If we treat our client as our equal, a peer and partner, instead of as a client, a file, a case, a plaintiff, a defendant, or a headache, we become what Deepak Chopra calls "two people seeing the spirit in each other." This is a higher way to be in any relationship.

In my initial consultations I began asking, "What brings you joy?" A simple but powerful question that established a human basis for our relationship. Without such information how could I know what their needs and desires were? When things got stressful in the case I could draw upon this knowledge to ask them to get out for that walk in the woods, or go horseback riding. Their reconnection to things that had meaning for them helped them heal and made them stronger witnesses in their cases.

Third, in order to find peace for my client I had to model the role as peacemaker. Arlo Guthrie in *Alice's Restaurant* feigns being crazy in an effort to get out of going to Vietnam. He goes for his draft board psychological exam and starts jumping up and down shouting "Kill, Kill." Soon he looks over the table and the psychologist is also jumping up and down and they're both yelling "Kill, Kill" and the therapist pins a medal on him saying, "You're our boy."

Lawyers and their clients often fuel the fire in similar ways. The client comes in and says, "I want to *get* so and so," and the lawyer nods and says, "We'll get him, no problem."

"I want them to pay," the client says.

"We'll make them suffer and pay," the lawyer retorts, until they both are essentially jumping up and down together shouting "kill, kill," and the client stops, shakes the lawyer's hand and says, "You're hired!"

The lawyer has played into the client's neurosis and anger, rather than serving as a healing force and modeling a different way to look at the conflict.

Fourth, I learned active listening. At Shady's suggestion, I finally read *Parent Effectiveness Training* (P.E.T.) and came to appreciate the power of active listening. I recommend this book for law students to learn how to achieve authentic contact with others. Gail, a forty-something secretary came to see me and as I listened I'd reflect back what she was saying. She told me, "I can't believe I'm sharing this with you. I have never shared it with anyone." I watched her lighten throughout the session, as if a great burden was lifting, and I hadn't even filed any suits or started the case for her.

Fifth, I remember the goal is to heal the conflict, not win the war. After twenty years of practicing law, Gandhi wrote, "My joy was boundless. I had learned to find out the better side of human nature and to enter man's hearts . . . to unite parties driven asunder." His efforts to bring about "private compromises of hundreds of cases" did little to diminish him, but instead he says, "I lost nothing thereby— not even money, certainly not my soul."

Sixth, I reframed my language to find common ground. People respond better to win/win language, dialogue, and understanding, rather than to blaming and finger-pointing. Both sides have their truths. I changed my approach from threats to expressing an aspiration for a win/win resolution, my goal being to get my foot into the door and work then on a more human level. Trained in mediation, I learned to reframe the dispute in order to move the parties to common ground. A chart I incorporated into my earlier book, *Labor and Employment Law*, laid out the magic that applies to any of our conflicts or efforts at reparation wherein we move:

FROM Emphasizing the Past	TO Looking at the Future
FROM Personal Attacks and Threats	TO Attacks on the Problem
FROM Saying It's the Other's Problem	TO Defining It as a Shared Problem
FROM Inflexible Demands	TO Aspiration

I changed my initial contact letter with the employer pointing out that "we" have a problem, that I wanted to find a way for both sides to move to the future, and that my client aspires to move ahead with his life and career successfully. Little to argue, there and I found that more employers would respond with curiosity and a desire to avoid costly litigation. In the past I'd tell them, *You* fired them because of their sex and *you* are in violation of the law, causing them to circle the wagons and puts up defenses rather than listen, let alone have a discussion or seek a peaceful resolution.

At the beginning of my campaign to change the adversarial process, I felt like a lone wolf, or more accurately a lone sheep among wolves. Yet everywhere I went lawyers were craving for a new way of relating to each other and the law itself. Dissatisfaction surveys were at an all-time high. I was not only re-patterning how I practiced but I felt stronger, more connected to my clients, and more present.

A Spiritual Journey

Nonviolent Advocacy (NVA) has become more than a practice. It's a spiritual journey. When you take your heart and soul into your work, everything changes. Matthew Fox wrote:

> Spirit means life, and both life and livelihood are about living in depth, living with meaning, purpose, joy and a sense of contributing to the greater community. A spirituality of work is about bringing life and livelihood back together again. . . . We can be in our professions without being of them, that is, without selling our souls to them. (*The Reinvention of Work*)

In the law profession it breaks down the notion of us versus them simply by seeing yourself and the other side as great souls. By changing your angle of vision to one reflective of your spiritual ubuntu nature it leads you to act with what my friend Gary Zukav calls "authentic power" and act and say what your soul wants, rather following your drive to win at any cost. Picking up *Philosophy of the Masters*, I opened to a random page and there it was: "Man continues to wander in the dense forest of his intellect." I was beginning to see the clearing ahead.

▾ ▾ ▾

It's no surprise that, after dabbling in spirituality, and my encounter with ubuntu in South Africa, I would turn to holism. Being holistic embodies this understanding of the interconnectedness of all things, while keeping in view our individuality and uniqueness. I discovered the International Alliance of Holistic Lawyers (IAHL) and together we explored having our work take us deeper into ourselves, forcing us to deal with the events that brought both the lawyer, opposing counsel, and the client to the dispute, and examining its impact on our life and the inner conflicts that must be resolved in the process. Interacting with holistic-minded lawyers from around the world confirmed for me the power of moving beyond win/lose and looking at the fairness of the situation for all concerned.

But what does a law practice, let alone the world, look like if you take the us versus them out of the equation? I began picturing the robes of the lawyer changing from the business suit to the outfit of the Aikido master, who repels an attack, not by violence, but by using the perpetrator's own force to guide them aside and out of harms way. I laugh, thinking about bowing to the witness before slowly but compassionately pinning him to the ground.

The term "holistic law," while accurately describing the approach, was a difficult term for me to openly share. It reminded me of the comic strip I'd seen of a man in a white shirt and tie asking a client, "So, Ms. Smith, why did you choose a homeopathic lawyer?" Of course we were not diluting the law with tiny pills,, but many people thought the idea of holistic lawyers was strange. I admired my friend Bill van Zyverden's shingle that read "Holistic Justice Center." Bill, the founder of the IAHL, got teased for practicing "wimpy law," but he would simply smile and say, "No, I'm just practicing law from my heart." But his office was in Vermont, far from my less tofu-oriented streets in Albuquerque. I was still in the closet.

Whether we call it holistic, ubuntu, peacemaking, therapeutic jurisprudence, collaborative law, or nonviolent advocacy is not important. The goal is to practice in a way that connects both the practitioner and the client on a deeper level. By recognizing that every person I met, be it the judge, client, witness, or opposing party, held something for me or gave me the opportunity to show compassion and feel my own humanity, how could I not but stay enlivened and excited about my work? It becomes a pathway for my creativity, ingenuity, and growth.

Too often we wait for the system to change, rather than "be the change we want to see." Van Zyverden laid down the challenge to not settle for less. We have to "see beyond the walls" of the legal system, he says, and "begin to live our lives in accordance with the greater laws of life." Trust in the power of the heart. "If we do so the current system will expand to accommodate our growth, our caring and compassion." But little did I think that I'd get a reminder about compassion and holism from the devil himself.

A Little Beachfront

Havana, Cuba—April 2000
Fidel stood tall in his green fatigues before me in the great conference hall. The crowd from around the world cheered wildly as he was introduced, as if the tall bearded lawyer turned revolutionary needed an introduction. Here I was, many years after my first visit to Cuba, sitting twenty feet from the man most Miami Cubans refer to as the devil incarnate. Stepping to the microphone, he softly thanks us and apologizes that he has not brought a speech. Then, in Fidel fashion, he speaks for three-and-a-half hours. It was the most mesmerizing and informative talk about the state of the world I'd ever heard.

Detailed statistics on the cost of military hardware in America, the number of cars per person in the US, Europe, and Japan as compared to Latin America, or how twelve million people in the world die each year from preventable disease, roll off Castro's tongue as he speaks without a note. Growing more animated and bouncing up and down with excitement, he challenges us to redefine freedom: "Is it freedom to decide what soft drink to drink, the latest toothpaste or bathroom deodorant to use?" No wonder we have an embargo. Corporate America did not want this guy on a cross-country campus speaking tour.

"We are not perfect," he admits with a degree of reflection that you can readily see in his eyes, as if he carries a load of both triumphs and regrets. He says that as human beings we have the ability to choose a meaningful path, reminding us that "the capacity of a human being when it gets enthusiastic due to certain values is incredible." Then, gazing out across the room he leans forward and I can feel myself leaning in to meet him as he says, "You can see it in the soul of a person."

I'm smiling from ear to ear. Holy Fuck. This is not what I'd expected.

"The world needs much more reflection. More common sense," he continues. "A terrible hatred is unleashed . . . but the goal is to find a little beachfront in the soul of someone with a little human capital and take action: Few imagine the power of ideas, the power of the truth, the thing to do is to convey it!"

All this talk of the soul and preaching on the power of being an active witness was like being in church. Castro even describes how years before, while visiting the United Nations, he spoke from the pulpit of a Harlem church, noting with a Cheshire-cat grin that "If I'd not been a guerrilla fighter perhaps I would have been a pastor." Just then a child starts crying in the back of the room and Fidel smiles softly and says, "We have to protect the children."

His words strike a chord in me that often asks, What world are we leaving our children? When will we begin to live and make decisions consistent with the Iroquois' vision that "In every deliberation, we must consider the impact on the seventh generation?" Do we creatively mold our institutions based on "common sense" that reflects our common humanity, or do we continue the practices of isolation and separation? Cuba-US relations, with our policy of isolation and embargo, clearly represents the waning days of the age of separation. But my journey toward ubuntu consciousness has taught me that if I as a lawyer can become part of a new, more powerful story—restoring the essence of being human to our relationships—anything is possible.

Castro touches on a holistic approach in describing Cuba's unique approach to medicine, telling us: "We teach doctors not just about bones and procedures. They need ethics and values and ability to assimilate what it is to be a woman and a man. What turns us into humans." It's no different for lawyers as most of us have only been "trained in the bones," leaving the health and well-being of both parties and society out of the equation. By isolating conflicts into simply x versus y we miss the opportunity to defuse the roots of the dispute and make the world a more peaceful and connected place.

"When you have solidarity, not selfishness," Fidel added, "no one knows what can happen." The ultimate solidarity with everyone is not political, but ubuntu.

▼ ▼ ▼

On my return from Cuba, I continue to bring the South African Truth and Reconciliation Commision and nonviolent advocacy lessons home to my local colleagues through articles, lectures, and modeling within my practice. Family Court Judge Anne Kass, having read my article "Lessons of South Africa," wrote me saying, "Eric, you must meet Robert Yazzie. Navajo Peacemaking is ubuntu."

▼ ▼ ▼

Smiles of Hope. Soweto, South Africa, 1991.

With Andimba Toivo ya Toivo at his home in Namibia for the First Anniversary of its independence from South Africa occupation in 1991. Ya Toivo is a Namibian anti-apartheid activist, politician, and political prisoner, co-founder of the South West African People's organization (SWAPO). He served sixteen years in Robben Island prison with Nelson Mandela and became a Member of Parliament and Cabinet Minister.

A group coming across the field in the Transkei to our gathering with President Mandela in honor of Chris Hani who was assassinated the year before the election. Cofimvaba, South Africa. 1996.

Seeking the future. Township kids. Soweto 1991.

President Mandela preparing to speak at Hani Memorial, with Cabinet Minister Kadar Asmar. Celebrating first water tap for residents.

Speaking at Dongguk University, Seoul, South Korea with families and victims of atrocities during the Korean War. 2010.

Telling the President of the People's Assembly DPRK, Kim Jong Nam, that there are millions of peace-loving Americans who seek to live in good relations with North Korea.

Speaking to a gathering of a thousand North Koreans at the Sinchon memorial in DPRK, site of war crimes. Putting a face of compassion and forgiveness on America.

First delegation of US lawyers to the DPRK at the DMZ, 2003.

At Hiroshima ringing the bell of peace and feeling the imprints of cries and whispers there. Japan, 1998.

Kids in the DPRK, 2005.

Being greeted at Pyongyang University, 2012.

US and Canadians meet DPRK lawyers, 2003.

Delegates from the National Campaign to End the Korean War on heading to Congress for lobbying for peace. Washington, DC, 2012.

I'm holding the banner on the right during protests for ending the Korean War with a peace treaty. Washington, DC, 2014.

Bringing Ubuntu to The Women's March of Washington, Albuquerque, New Mexico edition. January 21, 2017. Photo by Maria Wolf.

CHAPTER 22

Stargazing

*As a peacemaker the lawyer has a superior opportunity of
being a good man. There will still be business enough.*
–Abraham Lincoln

"The answers are all there," says Philmer Bluehouse, director of the
Navajo Nation's Peacemaker Court. "We have eyes but we can't see, we
have ears but can't hear. We have learned to be adversarial and we can
learn to be non-adversarial. It just needs to be rediscovered." While
I'd learned about ubuntu across the sea in South Africa, I hadn't realized the same rooted wisdom was present in my own backyard.

Driving for several hours to reach Window Rock, the capital of the
Navajo Nation and central office for the Navajo Peacemaker Courts, I
was ready to have my eyes opened even further.

In the past few months I'd befriended Jim Zion, the solicitor to
the Navajo Tribal Courts, and Navajo Supreme Court Chief Justice
Robert Yazzie. They agreed to help me train a group of employment
lawyers in the power of peacemaking. As I'd temporarily suspended my trial practice, instead only helping clients through dialogue,
mediation, and alternative dispute resolution processes, it seemed a
perfect fit to expand my creative tool kit.

Both Yazzie and Zion had been to South Africa and told me that
ubuntu was the same as the Navajo *K'e*, which has been translated as
love, respect, solidarity, and a wide range of emotions that prompt
closure when there is a dispute. Both terms, Zion says, "are elusive
but I sense that in both Zulu and Navajo they refer to a relationship
process." A crime, he says, is a glaring example that "there is something wrong with relationships." While truth may be important,
peacemaking must be more about reconciliation if we truly want to

heal the conflict and the ripples it sends out into the community. We share our experiences from South Africa and I nod as he describes that it taught him "that restorative justice-peacemaking is an urge in many cultures and that we are only beginning to tap its dynamics."

Yazzie, a stocky man with piercing eyes and a bellowing laugh, speaks about peacemaking as if it were gospel. "It is a process we call *nalyeeh*," he tells me. There is a need to "talk out the action" and the hurt it caused "so that something positive will come of it." His words are balm for my aching legal heart. It's this positivity that I'm seeking with my work. In Navajo peacemaking it's about "the effects of what happened" on the victims, relatives, and the community. Yazzie and I talk about the TRC in South Africa and he points out its similar "ceremonial practice of turning abstract monsters into something tangible and concrete before you, and then dealing with them."

Chief Justice Yazzie, or as his friends like to call him, CJ, rejects the "revolving door approach to wrongdoings where the accused falls back into the same conduct and those hurt by the crime are left out." The Navajo Peacemaker Court, which he helped resurrect in 1982, has demonstrated results, sporting only a 10-15 percent recidivism rate, compared to 65 percent in the adversarial process. Apparently people change on a deep level when you listen, deal with the roots of the problem, and use our innate connection to the community to help people understand and evolve. Yazzie tells me, "The most important piece of paper in peacemaking is the Kleenex tissue paper for drying tears." I remember how in South Africa the TRC was often derided in the media as the "Kleenex Commission," but feel how different it is when such tears are valued and embraced.

Everyone I meet from the Navajo Nation welcomes me with genuine warmth. The universality of the peacemaking process says much about our relationship with others, our ubuntu nature. Another Supreme Court Justice, Raymond Austin, says, "K'e encompasses extensive responsibilities to others and respect for them. The others include spouses, children, immediate blood relations, clan relations, Navajos in general, and people at large. Even Father Heaven and Mother Earth, and the plants and animals are included."

I remember the Oglala Sioux expression *Mitakwye Oyasin*—to all our relatives—and the Brazilian rainforest Kaxinawa and their word *Txai* (pronounced "chi"), meaning "half of what's in you is also in me, and half of what's in me is also in you." The Navajos, Austin says, recognize their connection and responsibility to others: "One should act towards others as if they were our relatives. It's about mutual dependence and cooperation." A wrongdoer is not punished but shamed with, "You act as if you had no relatives." As if you've lost your way—as have we all.

This understanding of our connection to the community is embodied in Navajo culture from an early age. Chief Justice Yazzie likes to describe K'e with a story. "When the baby first shows signs of awareness of his or her surroundings and laughs," he tells a group of lawyers I have brought together for a course called Law and Healing, "it is a joyful event." But it's more than a happy day, as "the person who first hears a baby's laugh must sponsor a gathering to celebrate." At the gathering all the baby's relatives attend, and "the baby's *awareness* opens to a world of relatives and relationships. That is where the baby first learns about k'e."

I imagine we all are babes seeking a world founded more on relationship and less on conflict. As I'd learned in Africa, it's not about changing as much as stripping back the layers to uncover our innate ubuntu nature. There we forgive, love, and find unparalleled strength. But could it be applied to more traditional courts and conflict resolution? This is what has brought me to the peacemaker courts.

The goal of their peacemaking process is to achieve *hozho*, which is loosely translated as "harmony." Wrongdoings and offenses happen when something is out of place. A proceeding whose focus is peacemaking is directed toward regaining and maintaining harmony. It is like our notion of "restorative justice," in which an offender incurs an obligation to restore the victim—and by extension the community—to the state of well-being that existed before the offense.

"What makes Navajo Peacemaking so successful?" I ask Justice Yazzie.

A smile comes to his face and the knowing runs deep. "Traditional Indian justice works because it is a community view of life, not an individual win/lose contest . . . Individuality is exercised in the context of the well-being of the group."

It seems so simple.

"It gives justice by offering healing," he adds.

As he says this my whole being responds, as it strikes a familiar chord. Something was whispering to me that this could be the bridge between my quest for healing and my legal practice.

The western court system is based on force, coercion, and control from the top down. Even the judge sits up on an elevated bench. But Navajo peacemaking is based on the equality of all participants. "The adversarial court systems promote greater adversarial relationships and disharmony," Yazzie says, "rather than true justice. The ultimate goal of the peacemaker process is to restore the minds, physical being, spirits, and emotional well-being of all people involved."

Imagine if all lawyers took that on as their objective. Is this why Lincoln said the nobleness of being a lawyer is peacemaking? While the US court system is unlikely to convert to a peacemaking model, with more than a million lawyers and fifteen to twenty million lawsuits filed each year, how we choose to function within that process could alter the experience and the results for everyone it touches. As Yazzi speaks, I'm feeling more hopeful about my profession.

Even if the parties came with the intent to fight it out in court they can still be ordered to appear at peacemaking and witnesses can be subpoenaed to attend. Covering both criminal and civil cases, including assaults, domestic violence, wrongful death, and property disputes, the session involves not only the person accused and the one who suffered, but, as Yazzie describes them, the "tag-alongs" of the crime, namely the relatives of both. He avoids the term "victim," as he finds it too constrictive. The TRC statute echoes in my mind: "Rather than victims and perpetrators there shall be ubuntu."

"Perhaps America will learn," Yazzie says, "that there are other ways to deal with crime." I have wondered for years why we can't apply our creativity, not to being better warriors, but to reframing the very system of justice itself. Professor Larry Little Bear of the Blood Nation in Alberta described it once with a bit of native tongue-in-cheek: "The law shamans of White People must be very wise, because they can find the truth based on the lies of lawyers."

"But you must meet Philmer," Yazzie says. Weeks pass before I get my chance.

My Dinner with Philmer

"The entire western justice system must be reexamined," Philmer Bluehouse tells me. We're sitting in the portable building that serves as the administrative office for the Peacemaker Court. Philmer was in law enforcement, conducting criminal investigations, for over seventeen years. He'd seen the worst monsters of our humanity as well as the realities and limitations of the system. "We need a serious look at how justice exists, how adversarial and divisive it becomes, as well as how class, the haves and have-nots, fare in such a system." He speaks of a cultural outlook akin to ubuntu: "To the Navajo we are made up of the same substance that you are made of equally. Therefore, I have relationship with you and you have relationship with me and that relationship is very important."

"How does it relate to peacemaking?" I ask.

"It's simple. It doesn't matter which culture you're from. The creator established both the positive and negative side of life. At some point in time we elected to use the negative side of life almost continuously. You go into a court of law and there's 'fighting words' and a mental battlefield. There is power being discussed, posturing, and eventually bloodletting in terms of words. No healing when you think about it."

"What I've experienced is that it's so strongly violent," I concur.

"Very strong." says Philmer. "That would be the negative side; that would be the adversarial arena. In other words, when you take that journey to heal in peacemaking you can confront the dark, negative lawyer side and understand it for what it is, understand anger. If we understand we were angered then we have more power, we have more knowledge, and if we have that knowledge we are able to become better. In Navajo thinking we dare confront the dark side, we dare to understand, to know it for what it is gives us power over it. It's a journey, I call it *re-creation*. We have that power to recreate and the power to be peaceful, the power to try new things. In other words, we are discoverers and we will bleed unwillingly sometimes, but we will finally understand why and be better off for it. We then finally seek wisdom."

"So is it," I ask, "about rediscovering our awareness?"

"That's exactly right. There are three functions. One is a psychological focus. The other one is the biological focus of being proper. But the other one is the sacred focus or where the spirit lives—we call it 'that which lives within.' We don't know what it is but we understand it to be there, it's our life spark which is sacred, that holy stuff that is there. So these three components, psychological, biological and spiritual have to work together in order for us to function."

"Some lawyers are so detached," I venture, "but it seems so contrary to our innate nature, that sense of ubuntu the South Africans speak about; having a connection to the entire human community."

"The whole notion of ubuntu you describe," Philmer responds, "is to us found in the Creator. The Creator could not exist alone so he created all these things to co-exist with. In Peacemaking we do look for the idealism and the calmness and the nurturing and caring for each other as opposed to always being individualistic and having to outdo each other."

"I think it sounds easier than it is to put into practice," I add having seen how the western litigation system seemed to thrive on extracting a pound of flesh.

But Philmer is undeterred. "Everyone has the power to come back to that natural balance. We have that capacity, we can relearn that journey inward and rediscover those things within. We all have that basic common thread, that basic common denominator."

"I'd love a new way to be with my clients. What's the goal of your office at the start of a case?" I ask.

"At intake here at the Peacemaker office, we are diagnosticians, but even more like the stargazers. It is the start of their healing process."

"Stargazers—a new way of lawyering," I say to myself, so ready for this role revision.

"We might suggest they go get some ritual objects, get certain people involved or make offerings. We help people take their responsibility back as part of a healing process. When you sit with that person you are beginning this process. When they leave here they have to feel that they have accomplished something."

"How is that different from the full Peacemaker Court session?"

"The ceremony of peacemaking is like setting the table with food. It's also about getting all the bad stuff put on the table. Hate, stereotyping etc., so we can discard it, join the humanity circle. Pick the good, get rid of the bad. It's a journey to look at the bad and good and look at the qualities of both and find the common denominator, level and rebuild from that place up, it allows you to discard and retain some qualities within yourself. Your health and psychological mentality rebuilding process all have to be part of peacemaking process. The whole idea is to allow that to occur or at least to start it to touch that common thread. Allow them to get to that level and understand each other."

"Archbishop Tutu, in describing ubuntu, once told me that 'the solitary individual is a contradiction in terms.' But when someone kills or hurts someone else, how do you reach them to help them remember they are not alone?"

"We all have those basic instincts," he tells me, laughing knowingly as if he had toiled with his own demons. "Aggressiveness. We can't ignore it but we have to go to that level and understand it. Why were we in such a miscommunication mess? What are the reasons? Their parents may have to talk about BIA government school experiences and having their mouths washed out with Lye soap for speaking their own language. That's the way we were brought up and we might then impose it on our children. It's about understanding."

Philmer pauses and looks inward. "We're all damaged goods," he adds. Looking up he smiles again "But we can take the barriers down and look at the raw picture and not make it a shaming or victimization process but a healing process. We must discover why you are so aggressive, why so angry?"

"What changes can we make as lawyers?"

"We can relearn how to use peace language. Respect one another. To learn to have good relationships with one another, is about moving beyond being *individualistic* to *group-istic*. We always talk about our differences but rarely about our common denominators."

"But what about justice?" an old part of me asks. "Martin Luther King, Jr. said 'positive peace means peace with justice.'"

"Yes but justice means balance, harmony, and peace. The adversarial process doesn't do it. There's more justice in a win/win situation and that balance of good psychology, biology, and sacredness."

"But without cross examinations and a strong advocate how do you get to the truth?"

"Truth is a very critical word in peacemaking. You come there with a half-truth you will not get peace. There are strategies to overcome it. A person in denial is confronted by others who know him best. The mother, or sister says 'You've been lying about your drinking problem. We are here to help you understand why you have it.' Peacemaking is about uncovering the mystery about why something occurs. For that knowledge is power. It's why the box of tissues is more important than legal documents, for you're dealing with emotions, revelations of real issues come out. To take those and recreate the future. That is the goal of peacemaking."

"What does one come out with from peacemaking so they can truly reach the healing point?"

"The first phase of starting the peace is so critical and it is where we seek wisdom. If we move in that fashion and are able to understand that common thread—that we are in fact tied to the same basic root, to some type of creator in a spiritual sense. Fire, Earth, Water, Air each has a contribution to the other. So a relationship, relatives, relation to one another, teaches us that we need to co-exist. When you come to acknowledge it with respect and responsibility it's a natural progression."

"So relationships need to model that connectedness?"

"Exactly. There is relationship in everything. We look to nature to discover this relationship. It's not all positive relations. Look at water with fire. Now I'm not saying *firewater*," he says, laughing again. "Water will quash fire, but enough fire will create the H_2O to separate and create more oxygen for our substance. All this connectedness."

"What challenges did you personally face in order to fully accept peacemaking?"

"The biggest impact in this peacemaking process for me was when I first came to this area. I had good knowledge in organizing and administration, putting together structure. It was helpful to me but for two whole months I went behind the window rock on a path and sat in nature observing the interaction. The ants with pebbles, seeing where water had settled or the pollen on top of the water engaged in a chemical process with one another, interacting with each other. And the blades of grass and how they were moving. The air I felt around me helped me focus. It's a peacemaking process that was actually here in nature, and it too was doing it without having to have written rules to abide by. In a natural state, doing it because of these relationships, cross-pollination all happening in time without no commandment by a physical convention, a supernatural event. My taking a serious look at that was the first picture of earth and mother. In this concept of peacemaking, when you recognize relationship there is a certain responsibility to it. In the non-traditional world too often our institutions fail to see the relationship and fail to take responsibility. Respect, responsibility, and relationship are all needed for K'e to function."

The sun is setting and an hour of his time has spilled into three. My cup and heart are full. Standing I shake Philmer Bluehouse's hand and we nod at each other. He appears to know why I came. Instead of driving off, I watch the sunset cast its magical glow over the red rock arches of Window Rock, and I know deeply that we all must become peacemakers. It's part of the journey toward becoming more human and to reconnect with the universal great family.

Becoming Gentle

The essence of thriving in the practice law is empowerment and healing, as you can never control the other party, the judge, or the jury, but you can create a healing space for clients and help them grow stronger. Peacemaking is closely aligned with the efforts at truth and reconciliation in South Africa, bringing out all aspects of the impact on the parties and the community at large, but not dwelling or getting stuck there. We've scarcely scratched the surface of our creativity in adjudicating conflicts. There is so much to learn from one another when we take the time to listen.

The goal of restorative justice programs is to restore to the individuals some sense of wholeness, rather than merely punishing the offender or declaring a winner and loser. But it's a small fraction of cases that utilize such an approach in our retributive criminal justice system. As an undergraduate student I interned at a county jail and saw the revolving door of justice firsthand as repeat offenders never met their victims and were often locked away for their third or fourth time. It felt like quicksand. Even most civil litigation increased bitterness more than understanding. Bluehouse's statement that to be successful, justice must have some healing, felt vital and hopeful.

My conversation with Bluehouse put me in touch with someone who understood the link between nature, humanity, peace, and our ubuntu essence . . . and still maintained a sense of humor. I'd known that peace was much more than the opposite of war, but viewing it as an act of nature, the essence of relationship, was something I didn't see coming. Shady's work with the Chinese five elements came to mind, and though I did not know it would soon become part of my practice I marveled at how many cultures, separated by oceans and mountains, have drawn the same lessons about relationship from the Creation.

As lawyers, if we choose the path of the peacemaker, we can help ferry the parties toward reconciliation, moving them from their head to their hearts. A Native American story tells of a great peacemaker who travels among the people untangling their old traumas—or as it's said, "combing their hair." It is not always easy. Most people are simply afraid, have grown accustomed to the entanglements, feel it will hurt, or they simply choose to remain caught in their stuff. But the peacemaker is determined to comb their hair straight.

When my three-year-old grandson, Lucean, sees the hairbrush, he runs, or asks me, "Ampa. Are you going to be gentle?" We often approach our old traumas with a similar degree of hesitation. But it's all in the approach we take. When Shady combs out Lucean's hair she takes her time, talks with him, and slowly releases the tangles until he takes off smiling, his smooth long blond hair freely blowing in the wind. I took my comb and headed out determined to serve and help untangle from the destructive combative patterns of the past, now realizing that as human beings we have no other choice.

▾ ▾ ▾

CHAPTER 23

Earth, Wind, and Lawyers

*Our task must be to free ourselves from our prison by
widening our circle of compassion to embrace all humanity
and the whole of nature in its beauty.*
–Albert Einstein

Albuquerque, New Mexico—1999

The South Africans and the Navajos taught me to think and trust outside the box. When it came to law and healing, I was rewriting the way my clients and I viewed conflict. The challenge would be how to put this into practice in the belly of the beast. I'd sworn off trial work and envisioned my future without courtrooms, angry opponents, or arrogant judges. Something had changed. Through my explorations of peacemaking, interconnectedness, and spirituality I now felt that I too, like the lotus flower, could live above the muck. Of course, it was then that the call came:

"Eric, it's Dan Cordova. I need your help."

Dan had come to me to analyze his case a couple of years earlier but felt he needed to go to court. I'd referred him to another lawyer in town for the litigation.

"My lawyer just took a job with the Albuquerque City Attorney's office and I have a trial coming up. I'm screwed. Can you help me?" he pleaded.

I agreed to meet with him and upon review saw that he still had a strong retaliation claim. The usual scenario. An excellent employee with stellar reviews suddenly takes a stance for fairness or equality at work and his "disloyalty" results bogus write-ups, isolation, and, in his case, placement into dangerous situations. It didn't hurt that his case was against my old nemesis Public Service Company of New Mexico (PNM), which had been my first jury trial, and which I'd beaten in several subsequent trials. A bright and mostly progressive judge, Susan Conway, was on the case, and the symbolism—a new beginning, returning to my first-trial "foes," but with a healthier attitude—was too much to resist.

I was viewing the conflict through a new lens, the case moved at a more natural pace, and I felt energized instead of drained. My client and I were in sync and the opposing counsel's attacks on him seemed empty and futile. He'd complained about discrimination and was then sent into unsafe jobs on gas wells that could have killed him. Despite such heavy issues, we both walked lightly and remarked at the end of each day how we felt stronger and on the right path. I laughed and kidded with opposing counsel and the judge was clear and respectful. Something had shifted for me.

When the jury went out, Dan turned to me, a renewed sense of pride and peace on his face, and said, "Thank you. Regardless of what happens I know we did our best and I am very happy." At that moment I knew why I'd come back. We both felt at peace. It's about how we live and work in our daily lives, not the results. Winning his case and being awarded six figures didn't hurt either.

▾ ▾ ▾

At the height of my warrior period, I'd moved in with Shady, who was on a path to be certified as a body-centered Hakomi psychotherapist and was completing her studies at the School of Natural Therapeutics. We were in love, but in many ways we've approached life from different ends of the spectrum. It would take many years of heartache, struggle and regretful compromise in an attempt to experience a true synthesis of our work, lives, and hearts. Time would not prove our friend.

Teaching the analytical lawyer to actively listen and not struggle to "fix" things took amazing perseverance. However, it was through Shady's living example and the courses she taught in Holographic Repatterning that I first learned about Chinese medicine and Wu-Shang—the Dance of the Five Elements.

Shady taught her students that you have to be in balance within yourself to "hold a healing space" for others. I was living proof of this maxim; it was not until I opened my heart, ears, and spirit, and we focused on healing our relationship at home, that I was open to receive the axiom that forms the basis my true work: *We lawyers are healers who practice bringing wholeness, harmony, and humanity to parts of ourselves and others that are out of balance with the relationships surrounding us.*

Conflict is a form of imbalance. The Chinese five elements of fire, earth, metal, water, and wood became a bridge between the spiritual and the practical, opening a door to an analytical model to use with trials and legal work wherein every mood, behavior, action, and relationship is understood on another level. It took me deeper into my awareness of the nature of the problem and provided a roadmap to easily shift it so that people became more open, honest, forthright, and forgiving.

It's nothing new for the law to address balance. The entire premise of justice is reflected in the scales of justice that weigh the two sides of a dispute. Our legal system and governmental institutions are based on a system of checks and balances

Traditionally we lawyers have been trained to use fire (being charismatic, lively, and expressive) but not earth (nurturing, accepting, balanced, and empathetic.) When a witness presents attributes of a water imbalance (lack of smoothness in life, stuck, frozen, fearful, anxious, powerless, or unable to let go), you cannot approach it from fire. We know what happens when we try to confront water with fire. But earth naturally controls water (think of it as containing streams), and the empathetic questioner reflecting these earth element qualities will yield better results than the fiery one.

As a warrior lawyer I'd find myself focusing on the part and missing the whole, on "rights" and missing the person, on "the case" and missing the conditions underlying it. As I approached cases with the wisdom of the elements and an open heart everything shifted, and in the years that followed the verdicts and resolutions grew beyond my dreams.

Into the Fire

Roswell, New Mexico—2002

Facing off against the City of Albuquerque for my African American client, I knew I had my hands full. Not only were we assigned one of the most conservative judges in the region, Tenth Circuit Judge Bobby

Baldock, but we were trying it in the southern New Mexico town Roswell—of UFO fame—with an all-white and Hispanic jury. Usually I would settle such cases to avoid the prejudice and unreasonable rulings I'd expect from such a scenario. Instead it became a test for my Five Elements lawyering.

As we prepared the case, Jeanette DeAnda, my paralegal extraordinaire, and I evaluated each witness, juror, and judge on charts of the elements. This mapping revealed the qualities we saw in each and the elements needed to control or feed them. A scared and disempowered coworker, for example, reflected a water imbalance and needed to be approached with earth element characteristics to feel "supported" and "accepted," and metal characteristics to feel she was being "valued."

The city manager held key testimony to implicate the mayor in retaliation, but his earth element was caught in being "secretive" and we needed to strengthen his water element, the quality of "courage." This approach needed more positive elements of the earth, such as making him feel "welcome" in court and "loyal" to a higher source such as the city as a whole or the taxpayers, rather than just the mayor.

The mayor was "angry," a wood imbalance," "walled off," "hypersensitive," and "suspicious"—all fire imbalances. The best way to make an impact with him as an adverse witness was not with more fire but by asking questions that drew on high levels of integrity—metal elements—and questioning him with calmness and clarity, which arise in water.

These approaches worked to strengthen not only our presentation, but also enriched us on a visceral level. Witnesses and opponents were not enemies to be conquered, but human beings with imbalances, like all of us, that needed to be exposed and realigned before the jury of their peers. Our personal anger or resentment over what had happened to our client, Marsha, turned to compassion and a simple call for balance. The jury naturally followed what we were doing as it spoke to something very aligned with nature. Even the conservative judge was warm and open to considering theories that I assumed he would have a propensity to reject.

Coming from different political perspectives, I was surprised by the laughter and lightness in my dealings with Judge Baldock. The trial took on a strange atmosphere of more unity than divisiveness and over the ten days I grew stronger rather than depleted. Even opposing counsel took to hanging out with us on breaks more than with her client. Balance is contagious.

I argued the case to the jury on the one-year anniversary of the 9/11 attacks. It was powerful day on which to speak to the jurors about American values of hard work, free speech, and equality. Judge Baldock invited us to a prayer ceremony before court on the steps of the Federal courthouse. We all held hands and prayed for peace. I felt I had dropped into an alternate reality. Court employees, the judge, the opposing counsel, my client, even a few jurors, all paused to remember our common humanity on that day. It was an exhilarating start to an amazing day, as the jurors came back after several hours with a $4.4 million verdict.

The practice of using the elements brought a new sense of joy and meaning to my work life. It not only assured that my clients were strengthened through the litigation process, but it also assisted in my personal growth; I achieved greater balance in my life and rekindled my passion for practicing law. I was discovering that as I practiced from a point of balance, these principles become fundamental aspects of my life. By touching people in such a human way, and seeing the world through the dance of the Five Elements, the spirit and nobility of lawyering returned to me and I saw how it could help heal the planet as a whole.

A New Language

Whether it's ubuntu or the Chinese Five Elements it had become clear that in order to thrive as a profession and as human beings we need a new language to change the way we frame conflict. Andre Gregory speaks to this new language in the brilliant film *My Dinner with Andre*:

> I keep thinking that we need a new language, a language of the heart, a language ... where language [isn't] needed—some kind of language between people that is a new kind of poetry, that is the poetry of the dancing bee, that tells us where the honey is. And I think that in order to create that language we're going to have to learn how you can go through a looking-glass into another kind of perception, in which you have that sense of being united to all things, and suddenly you understand everything.

In South Africa I saw strength, compassion, and understanding woven out of the evils of apartheid. Philmer Bluehouse affirmed for me that we can "rediscover being non-adversarial." By repatterning a new tomorrow for the parties in dispute and for our world, we travel far beyond the courtroom by modeling a path that rejects the warring nature of the prior centuries. I was heading through the looking-glass.

Marx was wrong when he declared that you have to "forcibly overthrow all existing social conditions." What must be overthrown is not a particular market system or government, but a way of thinking and living that has isolated us from our true nature. As Gandhi, Havel, and King found, it is only through a universal awakening of consciousness and the creation of institutions that respect our mutuality that we can overcome institutionalized systems of injustice. It is not about the proletariat versus the bourgeoise, us versus them, or even the 99 percent versus the one percent, but about opening our minds and hearts to our interconnectedness: then everything shifts.

As I took my practice deeper, conflict became an opportunity for growth and transformation for not only my client but for myself. New principles were driving my ship, a type of *legal wellness* that can build relationships and:

- Expand the human potential for communication and understanding;
- Help the law reflect that we are an interconnected, interdependent life system;
- Encourage lawyers to express themselves creatively through the practice of law;
- Help clients experience more peace rather than guilt or blame;
- Respond with love rather than fear;
- Release the outcome;
- Remember that the means are inseparable from the end result;
- Cultivate empathy and engage in real dialogue between the parties;
- Empower clients to shape their destiny;
- Respect the integrity and worth of each individual.

Living and working with such ubuntu-based objectives not only enhanced my cases and relationships, but was healing an ancient part of my heart. Henry David Thoreau wrote, "Things do not change. We change." I'd wanted to change the world, but it took a major opening inside me to take the leap. Now that my practice was becoming more reflective of principles of peacemaking and heart, I felt a new sense of dignity and peace. Ubuntu is a way of life that makes us all peacemakers, weaving, as Machado might say, "new honey combs" for our future.

▾ ▾ ▾

But as the twin towers fell and we marched to war, it became clear that the twenty-first century would not be launched with consciousness and the spirit of transformation. In a nation thirsty for revenge, I was being dragged back into battle, clutching to my new-found peace in a flood of tears and tear gas as the mob chanted, "USA, USA, USA."

▾ ▾ ▾

PART V

The Challenge

. . . when the rain falls down
You know the flower's gonna bloom
and when the hard times come
You know the teacher's in the room
and when the sun comes up
You know that I'll be there for you
Don't let it go, oh no. . . .
–Michael Franti

CHAPTER 24
Taking Sides

Of course the mind can rationalize fighting back... but the heart,
the heart would never understand. Then you would be divided in
yourself, the heart and the mind, and the war would be inside you.
–The Dalai Lama

Lake Champlain, Vermont, USA—September 11, 2001

Shady's fever grew intense. My wife is rarely sick. Days before, on September 9, 2001, we taught a workshop called "Holding a Healing Space for Lawyers" at the Holistic Lawyers Conference. It was a transformative and hopeful time. Overnight her headache, like the events unfolding, came out of nowhere, and with a vengeance. I assumed she was simply worn out by the trip. As she slips into the bathtub to ease the pain and find her balance, the first plane hits the tower.

We had scheduled two days rest before flying home from Vermont, choosing a quiet retreat on Lake Champlain. Adirondack chairs dot the huge lawn at lakeside, crying out for relaxation. Stepping outside, the cleaning woman from the room next door tells me a plane hit the World Trade Center and it's live on the news. Like most, I figure it must be some wayward small prop plane—an accident or suicide. Poor pilot.

I turn on the television and the tranquil peacefulness of the lake resort is broken by an eerie, piercing silence. Smoke is coming from the tower and the commentator is trying to make sense of the scene. Just then I watch as a second plane hits the other tower. "Holy shit," I shout, telling Shady, "You gotta see this. Two planes just hit the World Trade Center in New York. One right after another." She pulls the washcloth over her face and sinks deeper in the tub.

People are falling or leaping out of the towers and the buildings collapse in plumes of smoke and ash. Moments later a building nearby mysteriously implodes. The strike at the Pentagon comes moments later. A new millennium would begin not with heightened wisdom or a culture of peace, but with our pounding another nation into the stone age. The skies clear, as all planes are grounded, and Shady and I find separate flights home over the next week. As I arrive on my doorstop I feel relieved to have arrived safely at home, but as the media continues to broadcast the falling towers again and again, I can feel a war brewing.

Days before the world came crashing down, Dhyani Ywahoo, a spiritual leader, peacemaker, and author of *Voices of our Ancestors*, spoke to a gathering of nearly a hundred holistic lawyers. Dhyani is a Native American chief who had been trained in sacred knowledge since early childhood under the direction of her grandparents and elders. She reminded me why I've become a peacebuilder: "Conceptualize, visualize, and energize your dream for the benefit of all. For you are an ancestor of those yet to be born."

It was not just her message to "plant seeds of kindness" or that "we all have within us what is holy" that moves me, but it's her presence and example. "Make the movement of your feet and your speech on the earth a prayer," she said to the transfixed group of lawyers searching for meaning in their practices. Like Archbishop Tutu years before, she modeled the power behind taking a moment to connect to others. She made a point of making eye contact and speaking directly into each person as she made her way around the circle, as if we were sharing a one-on-one intimate conversation

"Lawyers play a special part," she said, "like a musician seeking to bring what appears as discord to a place of harmony." I've been watching my new way of working based on ubuntu unfold, and Dhyani made my legal cup feel filled with "loving-kindness." I left on such a high, but days later it felt as if my cup had been shattered.

Tears in the Street

After 9/11, a long-simmering anger was released and America became increasingly fractured. I was called to defend protesters, even a group chained to gas pumps, as they proclaimed "No Blood for Oil." A mass demonstration in Albuquerque resulted in key activists being singled out and charged with inciting a riot when police arrested them for stirring up a crowd by insidiously "chanting slogans." It took several trials before the court finally acquitted them. But it felt again like I was holding a finger in a dam that was about to blow. And a machine gun in my face would shake my patience and my role as a peacemaker to the core.

Route 66, Albuquerque, New Mexico—March 20, 2003

March twentieth is the United Nations International Day of Happiness, but to me it's always a stark reminder of the day the war began in Iraq and the soul of my city fell victim to rubber bullets, pepper spray, and angry divisiveness. Early that morning as the bombing began, I negotiated a deal with the police on behalf of demonstrators to orderly arrest those protesting who want to make a statement. We'd been in the streets every day for weeks, and it was clear that this action would bring out a crowd. I swap cell phone numbers with Captain Gonzales of the Albuquerque Police and the Deputy Police Chief Ray Shultz so that if any problems arose we could talk and ensure that the demonstrators' first amendment rights were respected.. It felt like democracy was working.

But the lines between "us and them" were being drawn. A battle was brewing in the street and the police, some sporting new American flag decals on their riot gear and dark patches over their badges, had come for a fight. When I arrive the crowd is close to a thousand people. They walk, holding up their hands in peace signs, while getting struck in the back by police with billy clubs.

As the rain falls lightly, the police line begin to don their gas masks before a group that now was dancing, drumming, and chanting peace slogans. It's clear that the officers are preparing for something other than orderly arrests. I call Captain Gonzales. It rings and rings, but he is not picking up the phone. I leave message after message with him.

"Please Captain. We are here to help. We can have an orderly arrest process. These people are peaceful. Please do not march on the crowd." Still no answer.

I ask officers where is Captain Gonzales and they ignore me. One officer points his machine gun in my face and says:

"Get out of the street!"

"I'm not in the street I'm on the sidewalk." I shout back.

"I don't care," he says. "Go home."

They don't want us to speak up; to be heard. They appear more concerned with silencing the message than with clearing the streets. President Bush had effectively stated that those of us opposing this war were "with the terrorists." We've become the enemy in the eyes of the police.

As the rain increases in ferocity so does the police response. They march in with dogs, horses, guns, they shoot rubber bullets, tear gas, and pepper spray. Later on video I saw Captain Gonzales on one of the police lines spraying the demonstrators randomly with pepper spray, an action clearly meant only to harm, as pepper spray causes you to fall to your knees and become demobilized. It's not a great way to clear a street or make "orderly arrests." Small children and seniors clutch their faces and cry. I too am weeping inside and out from both the tear gas and the hard-heartedness. But even more, I'm royally pissed.

As the fog settles we follow the arrested to jail and a few lawyers spend most of the night meeting in jail cells and helping people get released. I cannot remember ever being so angry. All my lessons in peacemaking, tolerance, and forgiveness seem to be slipping away. This could have been so easily avoided. In the early morning I fall into bed and after dreaming of dark clouds and strange demons, the phone abruptly awakens me.

"Eric?" the voice said. "I heard what happened. The mayor wants to meet with you." The caller is City Attorney Bob White.

"He's upset about what happened," Bob tells me, "and wants to see that it doesn't happen again."

"It didn't have to happen at all," I tell him, my anger coming back. "Gonzales wouldn't pick up the fucking phone. We were there. We had a deal."

"Just come in. Ten o'clock. Just you."

"I'll come, but not just me. I want Larry Cronin and Bob Anderson with me."

Larry was a courageous new lawyer in town who'd also been out in the street and helped broker the failed arrest deal with the city. And Bob, a well-known activist and former Green Party gubernatorial candidate, had also been in the street that night.

Attorney White reluctantly agrees.

The meeting is stacked with every city official imaginable. Mayor Chavez meets me at the door and thanks us for coming. Gonzales is seated between the chief of police and the head of public safety, Nick Backus. Mayor Chavez looks worried. He should be. I tell him, "This police riot could have been avoided." I see Gonzales tighten up at the notion that the police could start a riot, but I'd seen it happen many times when they smelled battle and were critical of the people who took to the street.

Gonzales doesn't deny that I had called several times, nor does he explain why he ignored my pleas. It was clearly a calculated action meant to disperse and diminish dissent. Mayor Chavez talks about his "early days" as a protestor during the Vietnam era and says that people should have a right to use the streets to protest. He says what had happened should not have occurred and that it's not what he wants in response to protests, especially when more demonstrations were likely to occur. I switch to finding a more common-ground way to make it a win-win scenario, and after we reach an understanding on how future speech will be protected, the mayor exits. As the three of us are being escorted toward the back door, I suggest to his chief of staff that we should do a joint news conference to tell the public that we were working together, express regret for what happened, and calm the fears of the people. She smiled sheepishly and said, "Well, he's having a press conference on it now."

Of course they were ready to escort us out, but I decided to claim my power.

"Great,'" I say, reversing course and heading into the conference room filled with reporters and television cameras. "Let's do it together."

I go to the front where the chief and mayor are standing and I get a glance from them as if I'm a wedding crasher ordering at the bar. The mayor makes his statement, but unlike in our meeting he does an about face and declares for the cameras, "I fully support everything the police did last night."

I was livid and felt betrayed. He was taking sides and falling right into the black and white, us versus them scenario, rather than using this opportunity for healing and standing up for American values. There are plenty of ways to say you generally support the police without agreeing with everything they did. I was not given a chance to make a full statement, but did answer a few questions. The press clearly wanted to play up the protestors' refusal to leave the street rather than examine the police reaction and how it could have been avoided. I tell them it could have been avoided, but the media seems uninterested. I try to steer it to common ground and the chance to come together for the community, but the mayor quickly ends the conference and waltzes out. And the police, feeling vindicated, return to the streets to flex their muscles and attempt to keep dissent, or in their eyes, the "terrorists," contained.

Later that day the police close a twelve-square-block section of the city to traffic as we march along the police-chosen route that mostly looped through residential areas. Convenient, but when protesting, people want to go where they will actually be seen. When the march ended, I got an emergency call from some demonstrators. Three blocks away there's a standoff on historic Route 66, where a group of eight demonstrators with signs have wandered off down the sidewalk in search of cars and people. More than forty police and sheriff's officers are flanking the demonstrators on three sides with their weapons pulled and pointed at the demonstrators.

I sprint to the scene and see Gonzales through the crowd and ring his phone, and lo and behold, he answers. "It's not the agreed upon route," he barks.

"Can we talk?" I ask.

"Not till you move them away from that gas station," he says, getting very serious. "We don't want any sabotage or explosions."

I glance over at the ragtag group of protesters: two elderly grandmothers, two young students, and several members of that subversive group, the Sierra Club. Has the world gone mad? I ask the demonstrators to move back across Central Avenue and they willingly comply, again reiterating that they just want to go where there were cars so people could see their signs.

Gonzales signals me to pass through the line of police who are now lined up ready to act. I move past their suspicious eyes, pointed weapons, and angry scowls and arrive at the captain.

"You got your march and they can't be here," he says as I approach. "They should go back to the university by the bookstore."

"This is the sidewalk and they have a right to go where they please. We can't control everyone," I tell him, thinking about the First Amendment and how in wartime the Constitution can become so paper-thin.

"Well you'd better get your people under control," he growls, looking around nervously.

"I suspect some of them may want to cross your line here and sit down and be arrested to make a point about freedom of expression."

He leans in and says, "There is a mix of sheriffs and others, as well as my own men here," as I wonder who the "others" were that are pointing guns at us. "If they cross that line I cannot guarantee their safety."

I'm shocked. "Serve and Protect" was the motto, but they were still itching for a fight, and the mayor's public support had emboldened them rather than curbed their enthusiasm.

I go back and talk to the group. Dorrie, one of the oldest, tells me, "We just want to be seen. We don't want to be arrested. We'll gladly go back by the bookstore if they will open up traffic down Central."

I called Gonzales with the offer, rather than pass again through the gauntlet, just as he is getting off the phone with someone else. He agrees, and as we move, traffic and democracy begin to flow.

That night I tell the city attorney we would be going the next day into Federal court for an injunction to uphold the right of citizens to walk down the street and express themselves without being held at gunpoint by the police. The pressure works. The mayor backs the police off and declares the next day that sidewalks, parks, and public areas are free-speech zones that will be protected and honored. By the third night the police were escorting us along a new parade route with only half the street closed to traffic. Trust was slowly being built, and fear reduced. We wrote and passed a new City ordinance that allows rallies without permits in public places and requires the police to assist rather than attack demonstrators.

We are All America

It was in this environment that I first met Salah and Kalief, political refugees who'd fled Iraq after the Gulf War. They had refused to participate in Saddam's invasion of Kuwait, and after surviving seven years under extreme conditions in refugee camps they were chosen to go the United States. After the 9/11 attacks, they secluded themselves in their apartments for more than a week, afraid, as Arab Muslims, to show their faces.

Midnight Rodeo Dance Club, Albuquerque, New Mexico— September 27, 2001

Like the rest of us, Salah and Khalif felt traumatized by the events of September 11. On September 27, they decided to get their minds off the terrible images and go to a club—the Midnight Rodeo—for some dancing. They knew little about American culture, so they failed to anticipate the volatile combination of liquor, anger, and cowboys. They just wanted to dance.

Americans were thirsty for blood and needed someone to blame for the unspeakable horrors. At first Salah and Khalif ignored the stares and angry faces, but when Salah entered the restroom he was confronted by a burly, irate "patriot," more aptly pegged an angry bigot, who called him a "terrorist," bellowing with an obvious drunken swagger that he should "go home or we'll kill you." A crowd gathered. Salah is a gentle soul. He tried to explain that they were home and that they too were angry about what happened, but as security arrived the cowboy spit into Salah's face and a scuffle ensued.

As if it were a wild west saloon, security grabbed the belligerent drunk cowboy and dumped him out the back door. Salah, wiping the spit and embarrassment off his face in the sink, was told he'd also have to leave. He found Khalif, who was now talking to some girls and had little interest in fleeing. "We just got here," he protested. But the urgency on his friend's face told him it was time.

Unknown to them, Salah's assailant was in the parking lot stirring up an angry mob and as the two walked to their car a shout went up, "They're from the Middle East. Get them."

Salah and Khalif were thrown to the ground and savagely beaten and kicked. They cried for help but the sound was lost in the crowd's fervor.

"Go home," one shouted.

"You do not belong here," a woman said, kicking Salah repeatedly in his kidneys.

"We will kill you, " the original assailant threatened.

But the refrain they remembered the most was the crowd chanting as the blows were landing, "USA, USA ,USA."

Club security arrived, and instead of calling the police they simply told all the assailants: "Go home." All descriptions of the assailants were conveniently lost in the security team's mind that evening by the time police and paramedics arrived, summoned by a frantic call from Salah. His 911 tape was haunting. We sued the club, as someone should be held accountable for the cover-up and their passive-aggressive maintenance of an unsafe environment. The case became a chance to speak to the public at large and remind the world of our common humanity. No Iraqis had been involved in the September 11 attacks. It took nearly three years to come to trial—ironically months after we as a nation began bombing and invading Iraq, taking out our anger in drunken cowboy fashion.

Bernalillo County District Court, Albuquerque, New Mexico— January 2004

Such a trile in the post-9/11 climate presented both a challenge and an opportunity. We faced great prejudice and fear of those from the Middle East. Yet it called upon the best of what I'd been learning about finding common ground, creating empathy, and reminding people of our ubuntu nature. Clearly I would face people frozen in fear, a water imbalance, and what had happened was an affront to everything we valued—metal all the way. Metal breaks the ice and fire forges the metal, so a mix of values: fathering, passion, and connection became the foundation of my closing.

Closing arguments are an opportunity to speak to the hearts of juries and remind them that "we the People" is not just a slogan; that they have the power to administer justice. I began discussing "shattered American dreams," their journey from the refugee camps to freedom, and their ensuing nightmares. I shared my journey to the Statute of Liberty and the plaque there that reads, "Give me your tired, your poor, your huddled masses yearning to breathe free." Leaning on the jury box I say, "It is the lamp, the torch of liberty, that she lifts in the Harbor. It is that lamp of liberty . . . of justice . . . that she passes to you as a jury in our legal system."

I always want a jury, after sitting quiet for so many days or weeks, to feel their power: "You carry on that noble tradition upon which our country was built. You stand as the ultimate symbol of America. Jurors become the pinnacle of democracy—the ability to send a message across your community, across the country, and around the world. That you reject violence That you respect human dignity."

With the media present, our message went not just to the courtroom but around the world: "those who come seeking freedom, as our forefathers did, may do so without being labeled terrorists."

"How ironic," I add, "that Salah and Khalif fled the violence of Iraq only to find violence on the streets of Albuquerque." Violence is violence, regardless of ideology—it's never black and white.

Lawyers are barred from telling jurors to put themselves in the shoes of your client. This is called the Golden Rule, and all law students learn early in their career that such statements are grounds for a mistrial. Yet this is what we try to get jurors to do on a regular basis, to dig into their natural feelings and know that if it had happened to them that they would expect justice. So instead I used myself as a silent proxy: "Walking today with the cold against my face, I thought of Khalif coming across the desert in winter. It made me think about how much we take for granted. Like safety. True freedom is to not be afraid of simply walking down the street."

My goal is also to validate my clients in the eyes of the jury and humanize their story. Most on the jury have not experienced such deprivations and struggle. "I've been proud to represent them," I say, putting my arms on the back of each of them. Touch, like when Archbishop Tutu took my hand, expresses something intimately human and defeats the stereotypes that divide us. "They should be proud of where they've come from—their journey, their home, their heritage," I say. "No one should be able to rob you of that through a hate crime."

To me, they were representative of all immigrants. I thought of my grandparents arriving in 1912 with their two children, speaking no English and facing backlash and an uncertain future. My eyes tear up as I say: "They want to feel whole again—to be accepted not just on paper, nor just on the list at the refugee camp, but as a member of our community."

It was in the end about healing: "Today you can acknowledge his dignity that was shattered when an angry bigoted man's spit was running down his face and when a mob of people told him he was less than human."

No jurors are perfect. They all come with their own imbalances and baggage. My goal is to move anyone sitting on the fence or confronting their own bias to have no choice but to rule for my client. Whenever possible I get them to believe it is the most patriotic thing they could do.

"This is not the America I know," I begin. "This is not the America I believe in. Tell the owners of this club that this is not the America you believe in."

Unlike an average case, I had to work hard to demonstrate that my clients were not at all aligned with terrorism, but just the opposite: "Khalif and Salah were men of peace. They left Iraq because they believed in peace. They did not resort to violence, threats, or terror. They turned to you."

"This week is about the justice and fair process that they were seeking. They came from a world of threats, intimidation, and violence in Iraq. But today represents why they trucked across the desert, why they stayed for years in refugee camps, and why they still can say that they love America. Because we handle things differently. Justice comes not from a fist but from the heart. The cloud of confusion that was landed with fists and feet can be lifted. You can validate the greatness of democracy."

I am gritting my teeth a little but I summon up the power of the presidency: "President Bush has said that 'Our Nation is chosen by God and commissioned by history to be a model for the world.' Few times do we get to make a difference, to help heal a fractured heart, to make a statement to the world that safety is the essence of liberty. Now is your time to step up and remind them why they came to America."

Could the jury act like America should have acted after September 11 and, rather than engage in violence, go after the criminals through a civilized process? I give them a chance to put a different face on America.

The jury had the courage to listen, rule against the club, and award more than $30,000 in damages to Salah and Khalif because the club had been negligent in handling violent situations at the bar. A small victory, but also bittersweet, as the perpetrators were never identified or held accountable.

The case helped close down the bar, as we dug up a history of violent incidents in the parking lot—shootings, stabbings, and fights on a regular basis. I told the media at our press conference: "Midnight Rodeo could not have stopped the bigoted, sad comments, and humiliation in the bathroom. However, they had a chance to do the right thing. To protect patrons, to remove the assailant safely from the property. They did not have the manpower or the willpower to do it. The jury acknowledged that hate crimes should be taken seriously and will not be tolerated."

The 9/11 tragedy did not have to be a time of taking sides. It could have been a rallying point for the world to come together. Rallies around the world, even in far off places like Tehran, Iran demonstrated our human unity. Around the world we saw the words of solidarity, "We are America." Instead our government led the chant "USA, USA, USA" and marched to war. We then got dehumanizing incidents like Midnight Rodeo, the Abu Ghraib scandal, lack of due process at Guantanamo Bay, targeted assassinations, and an endless war.

America can aspire to be much more—a moral superpower. "The most important human endeavor is the striving for morality in our actions," Einstein wrote. "Our inner balance and even our very existence depend on it. Only morality in our actions can give beauty and dignity to life." While the world appeared more divisive than ever, I made the conscious choice to not get dragged into the muck, nor the battle, but to rise above it. Lawyers can be part of restoring dignity.

But I'd witnessed the ugly head of hate wrapped in our flag, and felt how easy it is to give in to anger and blame when people react with violence. Could I hold onto the forgiveness, compassion, and ubuntu I'd learned in my spiritual and holistic journey and apply it outside the courtroom to the community and our world at large? It was not simply a commitment or awareness, but would require imagination, creativity, and a little rhythmic grace to remind me to keep my heart open to new possibilities. I did not, though, expect to be saved by a poem.

▾ ▾ ▾

CHAPTER 25
Committing Poetry

The situation is bigger than you and me
Blindness is the curse we share
and my empowerment is not a threat to you
unless you let it
as you continue to fail to see
So stop judging me
I don't have to hate you to be free.
–Adan Baca

On the day the bombs first fell in Iraq in March 2003, Bill Nevins, the coach of Rio Rancho High School's poetry team, had a pink slip dropped on him by the school administration. He had questioned the request from his principal to weed out controversial poems from the team's public performances after one of his student poets had read a poem with antiwar themes as part of stunt news over the school video intercom.

The poem graphically told of an America filled with homeless children, disrespected and fearful teachers, and imperialism as a motivation for the current wars. It also challenge the "American illusion of perfection." It was aptly title "Revolution X." Meanwhile, the school's military liaison, Brigadier General Lawrence Morrell of the state's private militia force, threatened to inflame the wrath of the conservative community by circulating an email calling for whoever authorized the poem to "be horsewhipped."

The nervous principal didn't pull out his horsewhip, but suspended and fired Nevins. This included trumped-up charges of unauthorized field trips by the poetry team—not to bars or hotels for illicit activity, but to Barnes and Noble to read poetry. No teacher came forward to sponsor the performance poetry team, and as a result it was disbanded. Kelli, a young, articulate, and vocal student poet admitted, "After that we just kept our work to ourselves. We were too afraid."

Despite all the lessons of peacemaking and equanimity, when Bill Nevins came to me for help, weeks after we'd been attacked by the police in the streets, my blood was boiling. But was I surprised? When you're told from the White House that "either you're with us or against us," it percolates down to all levels of America—workplaces, schools, and the streets. In Rio Rancho, New Mexico, the headlines read "Poetry Team Gets Slammed," and the echo following the silence was huge.

To the Inuit people. "to breathe" also means "to make poetry." Our ability to express ourselves, whether through poetry or our life's work, distinguishes us as humans and helps us find life's lessons in the most unusual experiences. In law, as in any profession or job, when we take the creativity and poetry out of it, it loses its luster and power to feed the soul. When Bill Nevins came into my office I knew the time was ripe to wax poetically for justice. Perhaps creativity was the missing link for fully returning joy and meaning to my practice of law.

▾ ▾ ▾

As the war began, a cloud hung over our entire nation. Peace became a dirty word. The police had attacked demonstrators with tear gas and rubber bullets not only in Albuquerque but in Oakland and Portland, and free-speech zones were keeping dissent isolated and on the run. After Bill approached me to be his lawyer I knew we had to do something to empower people and break through the blanket of fear. In the past I would have tried to get all the bad press I could against the school district and make them pay, but I remembered Philmer Bluehouse's reminder that the peacemaker "helps people take responsibility back as part of the healing process." Drawing upon my old mentor Ernie Goodman's advice, to organize a community as much as bring a case, I told Bill I would represent him but we needed to hold an event to raise some funds and some consciousness in support of Bill and the student poets.

We called the event "Poetic Justice: Committing Poetry in Times of War." We quickly assembled musicians and poets and did not know who would come, but as I entered the theatre it was packed with more than three hundred people. The poetic and artistic communities were here to say they would not be intimidated. It was electric.

One after another, poets took to the stage and spoke their minds to the world, demonstrating the power when we mix poetry with social justice. "I don't have to hate you to be free," poet Adan Baca said, while Demetria Martinez, who herself had been prosecuted based on her poetry in the sanctuary trials of the 1980s, said "America, I can't sleep with you anymore." I took to the stage for my talk "Poetic Dreams," grateful that a lawyer had been granted some poetic license. I began:

> Albert Einstein said:
> "Small is the number
> of them that see with their own eyes
> and feel with their own hearts."
> This lawsuit, this poetry gathering,
> this movement,
> is about educators feeling free
> to allow the hearts and minds of our children to open.
> Students in the Slam Poetry club were expressing what
> they saw all around them . . . we need more teachers
> with the courage, strength, hope and willingness to tap
> into the sheltered soul within every child.

We went on to hold these Poetic Justice gatherings in Santa Fe, New York, New Orleans, San Francisco, and Vermont. The lawsuit proceeded and eventually settled, but Bill never got his job back. I used all my attorney fees from the case, and more, to co-write and produce a free speech film, *Committing Poetry in Times of War*, that told the story of the Slam Poetry Team, the attack by the police in the streets and the danger of trying to put free speech in a box. It won some awards and went to more than twenty film festivals before settling into Hulu, iTunes, and in boxes piled high in my closet.

I never recouped what I put into the film, but what I got out of the representation of this brave "Word! Warrior" and the preservation of this important story was immeasurable. The impact of firing one person can ripple so broadly into our collective consciousness. My highlight came not from the stage, rallies, or press coverage, but surprisingly from my encounter with the State Militia's Brigadier General Morrell, the school's military liaison, the "enemy," at his court-mandated deposition.

The General

US Federal District Court Deposition—April 2005
It would have been easy to press down on General Morrell and get into a battle with him. Those who recruit and manipulate young minds into serving in an illegal war make me angry, not peaceful. Morrell had been so hostile toward my client and the student's poem, but nearly two years had passed since the war had begun. General Morrell's deposition was a chance to put into practice the principles of nonviolent advocacy and holistic lawyering that had become part of my life. I look into his eyes from across the table and suddenly feel a rush of compassion through me, as if seeing him as a human being for the first time.

I ask him, "Has your position on the war in Iraq changed at all?"

The question appears to take him by surprise. He looks down for the first time.

"I have known many young men who have gone over there, some not coming back," He pauses, glancing up and out the window. "And really," he says, looking back at me, "no one has yet to explain to me why."

Even the General's cold heart had thawed and America was waking up to the fraud and deceit that led to the loss of so many lives in Iraq. Rather than fight him, though, a turf he knew all too well, I wanted to find common ground with him, what Fidel said about "finding a little beachfront in the soul of someone."

I knew the strongest common ground would be reminding him why he loved America and what he was protecting. I show him a copy of the student's poem, Generation X, and ask him to read it. I'm not sure if he really "listened" when he reacted with such anger during the march up to the war. I did not know what it would bring out in him and I watch him read it again line by line. Then I ask him the only question I have prepared: "Should a student have the right to read that publicly at a public high school in America?"

He looks me deep in the eye and sighs, as if having been given a second chance: "In retrospect, yes, a student has that right," he says with some degree of genuine remorse. Honest reflection can often arise as a result of creating a heart space within the battle of litigation.

These moments have taught me that a legal case is not about winning. It is about contributing to healing the fracture created by a conflict. While the school administration refused to acknowledge their actions or accept ultimate responsibility, in the end they paid nearly a quarter of a million dollars and Bill Nevins went on to teach in other jobs around the state. Sadly, the poetry team was never reinstated at Rio Rancho High School.

But with each case I look for a growth or transformative point, and in *Nevins v. Rio Rancho Public Schools* it came from the most surprising place—the "evil" General who had sought to "horsewhip" dissenters. It reminded me that everyone can change, and perhaps this case was brought as much for Bill Nevins as for that moment. The treasure in conflict is often buried deep and takes effort, patience, and tolerance to open to its gifts.

Preserving the Magic

Artists challenge us, as poet Langston Hughes said, to "dare to dream of something greater." Eclectic author Tom Robbins pointed out to a gathering of us in a small Albuquerque bookstore, "If you take any activity, any art, any discipline, any skill, take it and push it as far as it will go, push it beyond where it has ever been before, push it to the wildest edge of edges, then you force it into the realm of magic." At times, in the cold stark world of litigation and windowless courtrooms, artists and poets help me remember that we create our lives and the conditions in which we operate and that we are all connected to something greater: On another. Nowhere had that been more clear than in my magical moment pushing the envelope in the streets of Havana.

Havana, Cuba—April 2000

My lecture was usurped by a million smiles. I was to present a paper called the "The Myth of Aggression" to stir the pot at the International Association of Democratic Lawyers (IADL) Congress in Havana. But a march had been planned that day outside the US Interest Section (our makeshift embassy in Havana) to call upon the US government to release the boy Elian Gonzales from his relatives in Miami to his father in Cuba. It was not only a march of politics, but one of the heart. I went to the rally with every intention to return for my lecture, but fate intervened.

The crowd was amazing, more than a million, spread out along the seaside Malecon and moving forward in waves. I felt a need to reach out and connect. "We need a sign," I told my small group of truant conference attendees. We found a cardboard box and tore out the side. But we had no pen. I thought of how resourceful the Cubans have been, holding their economy together at times with bailing wire and hope, and looking up at Debbie's smile it came to me. "Lipstick," I said. "Of course. Do you have lipstick?" She laughed and produced a tube of Red Delight. Spreading the cardboard over the ground I wrote "Somos de los Estados Unidos—Embargo No, Fidel Si," which loosely translates as "We are from the United States. No to the Embargo, Yes to Fidel."

Now, how to be seen by the crowd? Looking up, we saw the answer. A spiral statue with a small gate surrounding it. A few Cubanos had already secured the bird's-eye-view of the gathering, and we charged it like peasants storming the Bastille. From the top ledge I thrust the sign out to the waves of people passing by in a sea of small Cuban flags. Instantly there were cheers from the crowds that ran straight through my body. I made eye contact with tens of thousands of Cubans as they passed. People smiled and leapt in response to our message: There are peace-loving Americans who want an end to the madness and our policy of separation. Who want relationship over ideology. Who refuse to demonize. On that day we were one.

I was living what Václav Havel told the US Congress: "The salvation of this human world lies nowhere else than in the human heart . . . in human responsibility." I chose to connect with hundreds of thousands of people who saw our message of peace, rather than go and lecture to a breakout group of lawyers. We stood on that monument for hours and my heart felt as if it had doubled in size and capacity. My cheeks ached from the smiles I shared on that day. The world felt smaller and I felt more alive—the product of living ubuntu, of being an active witness who shares hope and speaks with the power of truth into the hearts of others—who proclaimed "Not in my name."

We can all play a part to change the trajectory of nations and help reframe conflicts and relationships. I felt the isolation and separation of a nation yield to our innate connection to one another and understood that we could change our world if we seized the moment, and the monument, with a new message for our fractured world. It was poetry in motion.

It takes risk to stand on that corner with that sign; to step up to the microphone and speak a poem; to choose to be a healer, rather than a destroyer. It takes risk to stand for peace deep in your heart in a time fraught with war or conflict; to buck how we're supposed to live or work and commit to creating the world we want to live in. A poem, a kind word, an expression of heart, or an act of courage can shift the trajectory of our world.

Some people think me foolish, naive, or a relentless optimist. But I subscribe to Howard Zinn's view of history and hope:

> To be hopeful in bad times is not foolishly romantic. It is based on the fact that human history is a history not only of cruelty, but also of compassion, sacrifice, courage, kindness. What we choose to emphasize in this complex world will determine our lives. If we only see the worst, it destroys our capacity to do something.

How we choose to walk in this world makes all the difference and I was about to walk, creative peace-building tools in hand, into a minefield of challenges as I crossed the DMZ to North Korea.

▾ ▾ ▾

PART VI

Shifting the Axis

If it were all so simple,
If only there were evil people somewhere
insidiously committing evil deeds,
and it were necessary only to separate them
from the rest of us and destroy them.
But the line dividing good and evil
cuts through the heart of every human being
And who is willing to destroy a piece of his own heart?
–Alexander Solzhenitsyn

CHAPTER 26

We are All Korean

*If the future of humankind is not to be jeopardized by conflicting
spheres of civilization and culture, We have no other alternative,
but to shift the ray of our attention from that which separates
us to that which unites us.*
–Václav Havel

The stadium shook with the thunderous voices of 150,000 North Koreans shouting "Kim Jong-il. Kim Jong-il" as the reclusive "Dear Leader" emerged through the tunnel below us. The hair on my neck stood,
like the soldiers surrounding his entourage, as Kim glanced back in
my direction and smiled wryly. Like Dorothy in the land of Oz, I knew
I was not in Kansas anymore.

Days before, I'd stood next to a North Korean officer in a building that straddles the demilitarized zone (DMZ) with my left foot in
South Korea and my right in North Korea, known as the Democratic People's Republic of Korea (DPRK). It felt like we were all part of
some cosmic joke, but no one was laughing. Why didn't everyone see
the absurdity? A Talking Heads lyric danced in my head: "How did I
get here?" But I would discover the chorus more closely reflected the
legacy of tears: "Same as it ever was, same as it ever was, same as . . . ."

From Good to Evil

Pyongyang, DPRK—2003
The new millennium felt so hopeful. A summit on June 15 brought
the South Korean President north to Pyongyang and a Joint Declaration set the path for gradual reunification and peace. Later that summer, North and South Korea marched into the Olympic Stadium in

Sydney under one flag. The top military man in North Korea, General Jo Myong Rok, sat with Bill Clinton in the Oval Office and negotiated a written pledge that "neither government would have hostile intent toward the other." US Secretary of State Madeline Albright visited the North and paved the way for a visit by outgoing President Bill Clinton in which a treaty was likely, including a deal wherein the US would purchase their long- and mid-range missiles.

But the contested presidential election of 2000 dragged on, leaving Clinton's year-end trip hanging like a dimpled ballot chad in Broward County, and suddenly a new president with a different plan for the Middle East and Asia dashed hopes for peace, riding into the White House like a gunslinger seeking a fight. The Bush administration's neocon blueprint, their "Project for a New American Century," saw the world as a clash between "the West and the Rest." September 11 changed the face of America and George W. Bush introduced us to his infamous "axis of evil" and preemptive war.

Within weeks of 9/11, the DPRK was identified in White House directives as a target for a US preemptive strike and a war plan was leaked that included the option to use nuclear weapons against the DPRK, Iran, and several other nations. Our promise of "no hostile intent" from a year prior appeared empty and worthless. President Bush called Kim Jong-il, the leader in North Korea, "a pygmy," and told reporter Bob Woodward "I loathe Kim Jong-il"; not great words and actions for building relationships.

When I was asked to join a small delegation of lawyers going to North Korea, I jumped at the chance. Could we help usher in a new story for this fifty-year-old tragedy? I knew it was not as black and white as we were being told. The words of Alexander Solzhenitsyn, who had been a prisoner of conscience for years in the Soviet gulag prison system, ran through my head: "the line dividing good and evil cuts through the heart of every human being." As my government was bombing and launching the invasion of Iraq, I found myself on an old Soviet plane from Bejing to the "axis of evil."

Under the Skin

I felt nervous about the trip—so many unknowns—and weeks before my departure a headline caught my eye: "Noah's Ark Found in North Korea . . . but Kim Jong won't let the world near it." Apparently, a recent defector has seen the ark and the article says that this "powerful symbol to Christians" is the trump card of "a man whose sanity is very much in doubt." It ends with a plea that "The US must move quickly to save this priceless treasure." I read this, admittedly, in a supermarket tabloid, but in 2003 it was not a far cry from stories in the mainstream press and the attitude of the man on the street toward the "hermit kingdom." All I'd known about Korea was that we had fought there and what I'd seen on *M.A.S.H* reruns. But something was pulling me to "go a little deeper."

The world was not focused on North Korea like it had been on South Africa with its strong international anti-apartheid movement. The "forgotten war" had become the "forgotten peace." It felt like entering a mysterious swirling abyss. I packed my back-up glasses, fearing that if I were detained or imprisoned I would be left with shriveled contacts and dry eyes. I wrote a will, gave a long and teary hug to my wife and children, and wondered, "What am I doing?"

My experiences in South Africa had taught me that when we look through the eyes of an alleged enemy we build understanding and relationship, discover more creative solutions, and reduce conflict. When we actively listen to the feelings and experiences of the "other side," we deepen our connection and put into practice the essence of human relations—compassion.

Listening and solutions were in short supply in Korea. The Korean War ended with the 1953 Armistice Agreement that called for the removal of all foreign troops, a peace treaty, and a ban on introducing new weapons onto the peninsula. Yet as I landed in North Korea, the US still had thirty-six thousand troops on the ground, along with nearly 100 permanent bases and posts. We had over the years introduced more than 700 nuclear weapons into Korea, and continued to help fuel a painful and dangerous division. The focus was more on the personalities than the peace, on demonization rather than dialogue.

My travels around the world have reinforced that people everywhere all want the same things: to feel safe, to feed their families, to be acknowledged and respected. Something told me that harnessing this commonality of purpose, and restoring respect to our relationship with the DPRK, held the key to peace, but first I had to listen.

As a trial lawyer I'd spent my life trying to understand the motives underlying the actions of others, and when they were malicious or in bad faith to push for punitive damages. But my holistic rumblings taught me to listen with more empathy and heart. It's easy to raise human rights and nonproliferation, but why might the DPRK be compelled to crack down so hard on dissent, seek nuclear weapons, or mistrust us? If, at our core, we all crave the same things, Korea seemed like the perfect palette with which to paint some peace and understanding.

Panmunjom, North Korea, DMZ—April 2003

Five rivers that traverse the lush landscape and beautiful hills of the DMZ, making it more suited as an eco-park than a war staging ground. At the "joint use" village of Panmunjom, where the 1953 Armistice was signed after negotiators from both sides met more than a hundred times during the war, I watch the surreal standoff as soldiers from each side stare each other down across an imaginary line. Actually the showmanship seems stronger on the South side as the North Koreans face each other rather than look at their counterparts who stand just feet away.

When we arrive, US and South Korean soldiers, reportedly chosen for their size, watch us through field glasses as we approach the borderline—a two-foot-wide and six-inch-high segment of concrete running between three powder-blue single-story bunker-like buildings.

It's our turn to go into the unit that straddles the border—a small room with a table in the middle. The five of us stand in different parts of the room, silent, knowing that it represents something much greater than its stark and simple appearance. A place without borders. Without division. A *situs* of unity. A repository of sadness.

Moving further down the border, we're met by North Korean Major Kim Myong Hwan, the officer in charge of negotiations between the North and South military in the DMZ. Major Kim smiles and soon is sharing his dream of having wanted to be a writer or journalist, then describing in more somber tones the story that led him and his five brothers to "walk the line in the DMZ" as soldiers. "I want to share my story with you not just as Americans," he says, "but as lawyers because lawyers bear trust and justice in their hearts."

Assuring us that their struggle is clearly "with the American Government, not the American people," he describes being "lonely for his family, lost at Sinchon" during the war—his grandfather was strung up a pole and tortured, while his grandmother lay dying from a bayonet in her belly. I'd later travel to Sinchon and it would become etched in my heart.

As he describes his grief, I recall the testimony in South Africa, the burnt bodies and the hands floating in the bloody sea at Crossroads. Pain knows no borders when it comes to war. Tears well up in his eyes as he describes his father being orphaned at the age of six, and his inability as a young child to defend his family. Through years of trials I've come to recognize crocodile tears, and I could tell he spoke from his heart. "So we have to do it," he said, as we moved farther along the divide.

A few miles away we meet Colonel Kim, who sets up field glasses so we can look across the divide. A loudspeaker continuously blares propaganda in Korean and music from its speakers, and I'm surprised to see it's coming from the South Koreans. "The irritating noise," Kim tells us placing his hands over his ears, "goes on for twenty-two hours a day."

The Colonel urges us to help people see what is really going on in the DPRK, instead of basing their opinions on misinformation. I listen with a grain of salt, as I know both sides have their viewpoints to sell, but I'm surprised at the sprinkling of ubuntu he shares when he says, "We know that like us here in the DPRK the peace-loving people in America have children, parents, and families." I tell him of our mission to carry back to America a message of peace and that we hope to return someday and "walk with him together freely in these beautiful hills." He pauses, looking out over the lush valley, and says, "I too believe it is possible." It feels like he has been waiting there a long time.

This somber and reflective visit to the DMZ from the North stands in sharp contrast to its marketing in the South. In my hotel night-stand in Seoul I found tourist brochures promoting bus trips to the DMZ and Panmunjom, as if the alleged "most dangerous place on earth" were really a Disney theme park. Photos of tourists at the fence topped by razor wire complete the sales pitch. If I take the "Monorail enhanced DMZ tour," Good Morning Tours will give me five percent off! I can only laugh at the absurdity. It's as if no one is looking at the impact on real people or confronting the pain of the separation. If we got serious about peace, the savings would be far greater.

Pyongyang, DPR—2003–2005

Watching kids playing hacky sack, walk curbs like balance beams, paint in the park, or compete in after-school programs, reminds me of our shared humanity. When you step away from the politics, the people of the DPRK are not so different from us. They play, laugh, celebrate, feel proud about their nation, and raise families, often with few resources. When our driver beeps at some kids running in the road they, like kids everywhere, all turn and yell back at the driver. It didn't sound like "sorry."

On the Metro in Pyongyang I share a laugh with a couple who were trying to get their baby to pose for my camera. A smile between lovers catches my eye as I glance at people smoking, visiting, or sharing a laugh.

On a cold November day we pass a group of young army men clad in uniforms and woolen caps on the scrubby winter lawn at the zoo. Most are sitting in a circle and several have stood up and were enthusiastically singing songs and dancing. They clap their hands, stomp feet, and take turns singing. They are so genuinely enjoying one another's company and performing that merely witnessing it gives us all a glow. A far cry from the high-stepping soldiers I and the world see crossing Kim-il Sung Square in military parades.

Many North Koreans have the same demonic stereotypes of Americans, so I want to leave a different message. I tell soldiers along the DMZ and groups of people in parks or at gatherings that there are millions of peace-loving Americans who support coexistence with the DPRK. I watch the Koreans we meet drop their guard, smile, and express their hope that our trip can play a part in healing this conflict. You can see in their eyes that they pray deeply for peace. It's similar to what Americans do when they learn that I'm trying to bring some peace to this dangerous lingering tension—a deep breath and a heartfelt expression of appreciation.

The DPRK remains insular, but not as isolated as we assume. It has formal diplomatic relations with over 160 countries. I've met people around the world working in the DPRK: a Canadian providing aid to North Korean farmers; a Swede who was going to help farmers learn how to handle cows; diplomats; British journalists; a Russian establishing art exchanges; a teacher from Liverpool providing training on international stock exchanges; a Norwegian Red Cross nurse touring rural clinics; and Canadian teachers of English in Pyongyang. Along the way I encounter busloads of Chinese tourists, and even meet a few South Koreans.

I never know for certain that I'm making a difference by reaching across borders, but I've come to believe it's up to each of us to help achieve what the Dalai Lama meant when he said war can "become obsolete." When President Kim Yong Nam, the head of the National Assembly in the DPRK and right-hand man to both Kim Jong-il and now Kim Jong-un, came to me we clasped hands. A translator leans in to us both as I tell him "I want you to know that there are millions of peace-loving American's who want an end to the war and for there to be peace between our nations." He squeezes my hand tighter and a smile comes to his face, "It is our greatest aspiration," he tells me. Perhaps at an important time he will remember my smile when thinking about America, rather than the insults and threats posed by the Bush administration in Washington. We hold our handshake for several seconds, as if lingering in the hope for a different world.

▾ ▾ ▾

Pyongyang, DPRK—2005

Beautiful voices and musicianship resound in the DPRK. Music, like beauty itself, transcends borders. As I watch the North Koreans perform I turn to the young Australian next to me and say: "Who could think of bombing and stealing such voices?"

Some of the performances are jaw-dropping. The mass gymnastics included 100,000 performers and I watched as 150,000 in the stadium went wild when Kim Jong-il came in below us. The gymnastic performance is a type of opera, told through movement, dance, song, and shifting card images in the crowd. You see thousands of performers dressed in blue moving in ways that transform the floor into a wild sea that dancers struggle across, and acrobats fall from the sky of the stadium. Tens of thousands perform at once.

Our 2005 delegation ended with the first ever US/DPRK Ping Pong Table Tennis tournament where I offered myself up to Mr. Bong (often pronounced "Pong"—which should have given me a clue about what to expect) and despite my best efforts, lost three straight games to his deep-court play. I should have known I was in trouble when he dropped his pants to reveal a table tennis outfit underneath his suit.

What was more important than the score was the joy on his face as our "roles" as lawyers and members of enemy nations dissolved and we became friends playing a game.

Laughter can be such a great connector and healer. During one trip I visited Kim-il Sung University and rather than make a speech I joined the students in games and dancing. Though no Dennis Rodman, I sank a basketball on a driving layup as our team, dubbed *Solidarity*, took on one called *Friendship*. We danced in long lines and wove through each other—Macarena, North Korean style. I was living the story of the World War I soldiers from Germany and England who danced and socialize during a Christmas Eve truce before returning to their separate trenches and the bloody task at hand.

After a week of fiery speeches, military parades. and rockets, it was such a relief to simply play, as I watch an elderly European woman race across the floor keeping a balloon pushed to the head of her young DPRK partner. My friend Fred Donaldson, who teaches what he calls "original play," sees such connection as innate in us all. It breaks down fear and exists beyond our learned win/lose competitive mindset.

Perhaps the next round of bilateral talks would be well served by starting with thirty minutes of play. Shake us out of our habits and addiction to this conflict. For it's in these magic moments outside the box that we remember our common humanity. As we approach yet another anniversary of the Armistice Agreement, my thoughts go out to President Obama and Secretary of State Kerry: "Be yourself courageous for peace . . . and bring your balloons."

Human Rights

There is great beauty and tenderness in North Korea. Yet prison camps, starvation, and public executions are often all you hear about. Like many countries around the world, the DPRK must do better to guarantee human rights, and any such offenses should be condemned. The obsession with control, fear of dissent, and broad crimes against society, however, are not knee-jerk reactions of an evil dictator, but must be viewed in a political and international context. The fear and mistrust generated by an ever present state of war must not be underestimated. We cannot reach in and change the government, but we can take responsibility for the role of our threats and militaristic solutions in Korea in fueling such crackdowns. Peace, stability, and more exchanges are the path to the change we seek.

But those of us standing for peace in Korea have allowed the human rights issue to be co-opted by those calling for regime change or expanding our military intervention. We should stand tall for human rights, but must not forget that true human rights can arise only through peace. Peace in itself is a human right, and UN Resolution 39/11: *The Right of Peoples to Peace*, says that all nations must actively work for peace and not make threats or engage in threatening behavior and as citizens of the planet we all have a right to peace.

A nation cannot simply sit back and lob judgment from afar. The Resolution says all countries must "do their utmost to assist in implementing the right of peoples to peace through the adoption of appropriate measures at both the national and the international level." Thus we must get in and be a player, be in relationship. Only from that point can we address human rights, non-proliferation, and peace. Sadly, President Obama appears to have forgotten what he said in Prague at the start of his administration: "If we fail to seek peace. It stays forever beyond our grasp."

The US and the DPRK should be having mutual discussions on human rights, nuclear weapons, militarism and peace, but they must be shoulder-to-shoulder among equals. We cannot simply point the finger and not expect to get "the finger" back. Is the US willing to talk about any real or perceived human rights violations in our own country? Why would we not allow such discussion if there is nothing to hide? Perhaps we could reflect upon why our country in 2008 cast the only vote in the United Nations, 186-1, against making the *right to food* a human right. We, too, should be called to task about such issues. We need to approach peacemaking and politics not from a point of force but a point of equality.

In the end what country lacks an underbelly? Spend a night in a squatter camp in India, or under a bridge in most urban cities in America, and we can see that the good and evil scenario breaks down. But only from mutual respect as human beings can such talks take place, and they must be talks covering nuclear weapons and human rights on both sides of the table.

In an article I published after my first trip to Korea, I looked at our own failings in healthcare, workplace rights, and prisons. I wanted to demonstrate that the situation was not black and white, good and evil, or us versus them. The article was also published in the DPRK in Korean, and I met people who had even memorized parts of it to recite to others. I felt proud that my words of peace had reached so far.

But the point of the piece was that we cannot control everything that happens in the DPRK, and we cannot simply hurl rocks of judgment when we have many challenges at home. The common ground between nations is more than arts and culture; it is in our domestic struggles as well. There is strength in vulnerability in all relationships, something most men and nations forget. As Winston Churchill so wisely said after World War II devastated Europe, "It's better to talk, talk talk, than to fight, fight fight." If crazy Dennis Rodman, with his red hair and piercings, can go and sit with Kim Jong-un and share basketball enthusiasm, can't our leaders do the same and strike up a relationship? Let the movement for human rights in Korea begin with peace.

Heartbreak Knows No Borders

Today there are up to one million separated families forgotten in the political shuffle, whose members are dying without ever seeing their loved ones again. In Chicago in 2013, ten years into Korea peacemaking, I'm reminded of the pain inherent in this grand separation.

"Thank you for what you are doing for the Korean people," the elderly minister said as he sat next to me at breakfast. He had a soft grin and sad eyes. "I am originally from North Korea and I came to the South with my father during the war. I want to share with you my story."

"Of course," I tell him.

"My four sisters stayed in North Korea with my mother. I have been there twice now and seen three of my sisters. One was gone before I got back."

"And your mother," I ask. "Did you ever see her again?"

"No. I never saw her again," he says, looking down.

I lean in and take his hand and his eyes meet mine. I tell him, "I'm sure she would have been very proud of you."

Tears well up in his eyes as he nods, feeling the loss and also opening to our compassionate connection. It's so important that people listen to what real people have suffered. For him the war is never forgotten.

It's no surprise that in the US it's called the "Forgotten War." It is painful to face what happened in Korea. It was one of the most barbaric and brutal wars in the history of the world, a testing ground on many levels: a "police action" launched without Congressional approval; it utilized seventeen million pounds of napalm, chemical and biological weapons, and demonstrated how far the American people would go in fighting a war to roll back communism.

US planes carpet-bombed urban areas, in violation of international law, obliterating virtually everything until, according to the American military, "nothing worthy of a name" was left standing. North Koreans carry with them this unacknowledged devastation when they approach us. This is why, when I travel there, I seek to put a more compassionate and peaceful human face on America.

But in any war, heartache knows no border. More than 53,000 US soldiers died, and more than 100,000 were wounded, let alone the thousands of vets returning with their souls in their hands, silenced by deep psychological scars and "battle fatigue."

If we truly opened up to the pain in Korea we could all weep together. In the North there were more than 3.5 million victims of the war. One in ten Koreans were wounded or killed. Perhaps our entire nation's march through Vietnam, the Cold War, and the wars in the Middle East demonstrate a collective trauma in need of healing. The symptoms of PTSD are characterized by psychic and emotional numbing, anger, cynicism, and distrust, along with memory loss and alienation—all part of our national story. But I'm slowly forgiving my country, for it's a natural reaction to suppress the horrors we've seen, to separate and distrust the tools of our heart: compassion, empathy and love. Naming it and accepting we need help is the first step toward healing.

The Shame of Sinchon

In the DPRK the war is anything but forgotten. I've watched as young children, soldiers, and others are regularly taken through the displays and museums in an effort to educate people on the horrors of the war, but also to prepare them to stand up for their country if attacked again. Pointing to displays of chemical and biological warfare and mass graves, they are told that this is what can be expected if the US military returns to the DPRK. I feel embarrassed, but also know that the loss of life on all sides in another full-out Korean war would be horrific.

I find myself in Sinchon, nestled in the province of Hwang Hoe, where many of these atrocities were documented by the South Korean Truth and Reconciliation Commission. Thirty-five thousand people died during the brief occupation of this province by South Korean and US troops. The shame is beyond words.

We now know that there was a South Korean policy to hunt down and kill Communist party members and their families. I stroll breathlessly past rows of photographs and depictions of attacks on civilians and of charred and decapitated bodies. I freeze by the graphic photographs of over five hundred people who'd been forced into a ditch, doused with gasoline, set on fire, and left to burn to death. I'm in an air raid shelter with walls blackened by burnt flesh, where over nine hundred people, including women and children, huddled during the onslaught, and where US soldiers allegedly poured gasoline down the air vents of the "shelter" and set it on fire. The North Koreans say murders were allegedly conducted and ordered by a US officer named Harrison, who is said to have dropped lit dynamite down the air shaft of another shelter as well. While the details of who ordered what are in dispute, similar atrocities have been corroborated by the South Korean Truth and Reconciliation Commission.[1]

In the blackened air raid shelter my body begins to shake. Sickened, I hurry up the stairs to the exit. Emerging from the shelter I see hundreds of North Korean soldiers being told the heartfelt story of a woman whose family had died at Sinchon. Her voice shakes with emotion, and the soldiers watch us carefully as we move forward to place some flowers at the monument and mass grave site of Sinchon. Shame does not even begin to describe the painful feelings I experienced at Sinchon.

Such tragedies leave us with a choice. In days gone by I would have been angry and bitter. I would have joined the voices around me in the DPRK crying out about US imperialism. But there is another route, which the South Africans taught me: "We can forgive but not forget." Sinchon bolsters my commitment to work for peace and demonstrate that war is "obsolete" and can never be an option. I share this story each year on dozens of college campuses and communities

---

1. Dong Choon Kim, "Forgotten war, forgotten massacres—the Korean War (1950–1953 as licensed mass killings," *Journal of Genocide Research*, December 2004, vol. 6, no. 4, pp. 523-544.

around the United States in an effort to reach the hearts and minds of others. This cannot happen again and I swear to never forget.

Returning to Sinchon two years later as part of a large international delegation, I'm asked to speak to the crowd of more than a thousand North Koreans gathered to commemorate those who died there. Gazing out at the crowd so silent and neatly lined up, I pause and look back at the bunkers for a moment, whispering a prayer for peace. Tears well up in my eyes before I've said a word. I use no notes because I want to look into the eyes of those gathered. I want to bridge the gap between what separates us and what unites us. I begin:

"I'm a lawyer, a father, and an American, but today I am speaking to you as simply a human being."

I share my feelings of horror and anger and tell them: "When I speak about Sinchon in schools, community centers, and towns in America they have the same reaction about Sinchon." I explain that Americans simply don't know about such horrors.

"But the truth," I say, pausing and glancing down the steps to a group of young children standing so still and in perfect lines, "must be told."

I speak about the importance of listening and then, as if I am proxy for an entire nation—one that is greater than its mistakes and nightmares—I say, "And on behalf of Americans I deeply apologize for what happened here."

A part of me wonders, "Who am I to speak for my country?" But I believe in the proclamation "We the People," and I've made the choice to not be silent when things are done in my name.

I close with the choice we all have, citing a Native American storyline:

> We can't change what happened here. In my country the Native Americas suffered greatly at the hands of US soldiers, and their wisdom is valuable here. An elderly grandfather was telling his grandson a story. He said there are two wolves doing battle within us. One is angry, vengeful, and violent. The other is peaceful, caring, and compassionate. The little boy looked up with big eyes and concern. "But grandpa," he said "which one will win?" The old man simply answered, "Whichever one I feed."

I repeat the line: "Whichever one I feed," and conclude, "We can choose anger and war, or we can choose peace and moving forward." I assure my Korean friends that I and millions of other Americans would do all we could to see that it didn't happen again.

I felt a release from the shame of Sinchon that had lingered since my first visit. There is something deeply healing about apologizing, taking responsibility and moving forward—of acknowledging the suffering of others. Yet, words and apologies are not enough. We need to back words with actions, and that will take time. Trust takes time to develop. My participation at the Sinchon cremony or in Korea as a whole has been just one step in that direction.

The tragedy of Sinchon is a powerful reminder of who really suffers when governments sound the drums of war. More Americans must visit Sinchon, lay wreathes of peace, and strongly say "no longer in our name."

Having made several trips to the DPRK, in late 2005 I knew that I would not return for some time. It was time to go to South Korea to see the occupation firsthand, and then to Washington to challenge my government to find the high road.

▾ ▾ ▾

CHAPTER 27
Building Bridges

When nations and peoples allow themselves to be defined by differences, the gulf between them widens. When we fail to pursue peace, then it stays forever beyond our grasp.
–President Barack Obama

Why had I chosen this work? Or had it chosen me? Was it guilt about my nation's role in the division of Korea in 1947 and feeling responsible for the reconnection? My spiritual side thought about past lives and sun scars—karma and unpaid debts. On a political level, the Korean standoff had it all: nuclear weapons, US occupation, broken promises, separated families, threats of war, military exercises, and human rights violations on both sides of the border.

But few I knew had it on their radar. It's been a challenge to overcome the media's demonization and rhetoric that blankets the dialogue, which infects even my most progressive friends. More and more for me it's becoming about the separation, and the need to foster ubuntu.

I told Congressman Dennis Kucinich, a member of the House Intelligence committee, that I was going to North Korea in 2004. It was the height of George Bush's axis of evil rhetoric and threats. Dennis was running for president. We were walking on the University of New Mexico campus and he took my hand and said, "You tell them that there is one candidate running for president who will not demonize them and truly wants peace. Please share that message with them." Years later he joined a group of us from the National Campaign to End the Korean War on the steps of the Capitol to call for a peace treaty and an end to the war. Few people who have graced the halls of Congress have ever been so courageous when it comes to peace.

Washington DC—October 2005

Congressman Kucinich organized a Congressional briefing and invited several of us to make presentations. Despite my years as a political activist I'm embarrassed to say that this visit in 2005 was my first effort to directly influence Congress with rationality and truth from anywhere other than the street or an occasional letter. I was surprised by how accessible key staffers from the Foreign Relations Committee on both side of the aisle and other members of Congress were to us.

The room is overflowing as the briefing begins. I focus on building understanding by asking: "What has the impact of fifty-plus years of being on the edge of war, and fearful that it could happen again anytime, especially after a hellacious unspeakably violent war, done to the psyche of a nation?" I speak on the need to formalize relations, acknowledge the great suffering in the Korean War, and end provocative annual war exercises. I tell them we should bring our troops home, and—in an effort to find common ground—reopen bases in their districts, rather than leave our military personnel in harm's way across the sea in a nation strong enough to defend itself. "If we can declare peace with Vietnam, certainly we can do so with Korea and begin to heal the wounds." I conclude by reminding them that peace gets us everything, and costs nothing.

Comprehensive presentations by Korean scholars follow and it's an historic briefing. The audience of mostly staffers politely listens, but translating ideas into courageous action is something else. Most of the comments were "Interesting" or "Good luck," and the questions usually focused only on the human rights issues. Little changes.

Nearly every year since on the anniversary of the Armistice Agreement I've returned to Congress with other activists to talk to staffers and share materials that can provide new language and approaches to this challenging problem. It's easy to get discouraged when even the staffers for highly progressive members focus on the worst rather than what's possible. A peaceful North and South Korea, China, and Japan would have a huge impact on world peace and unity.

But Korea isn't on their radar and they seem caught in cold war politics and age-old divisions between us and them. Sadly, all that extreme partisanship battling within the halls of Congress—like an extreme sport—carries over into their worldview. It will take great courage and leadership to shift the tide. But it takes us all to relentlessly remind them of their common humanity and their responsibility to find peace.

Exchanging Peace

Seoul, Republic of Korea—August 2005
It's hard in the "axis of evil" days to garner much support at home. South Korean President Roh travelled to Pyongyang and worked out an historic agreement in 2003 to build relations, but the process seems stalled. I bring two lawyers to a meeting, at the presidential Blue House in Seoul, with members of Roh's National Security Team. It's a chance to share our experiences in being north of the DMZ, but to also align them with US voices for peace, as Washington's rhetoric about the DPRK is increasingly caustic. They share with us their commitment to peace and reunification, but also intimate that Washington's attitude needs to change with the times.

In the US we rarely hear about peace efforts. While in Seoul a group of South Korean LPGA women golfers—and if you know golf you know how amazing they are—leave this week to play in the first ever Pyongyang Open in North Korea. This is not something you read about at home in *The New York Times*. We will gladly cover the rumor that Kim Jong-il claims to have made ten holes-in-one in a row, supporting the popular "mad man" theory, but not care about heartfelt and positive human exchanges that make peace possible.

South Korean peace groups have coined the term 40/60, reflecting the forty years of Japanese occupation followed by sixty years of US occupation. Mass protests have been held against US troops, US tainted food products , and increased militarization of their nation. Living in the bubble of the United States we forget that people carry resentments about our conduct around the world, even within so-called friendly nations. Breaking down those resentments is the essence of building a culture of peace.

In our first meeting after arriving in Seoul, I'm given a chance to practice my active listening when an elder chairman of a reunification NGO casts his eyes down and says, "It is hard to meet with you. I feel such anger toward America."

"I know," I reply. "We too are angry. So much is done in the name of our nation round the world that we find unjust and unjustified. I understand your anger well."

His honesty helped clear the way for my acknowledgment of his pain. This compassion has always opened doors for me. As we share our peace work and our hopes for a new relationship in Korea, we find our common ground. By the end of the meeting we're nodding together and a small smile appears at the edge of his lips as we pose together for a picture.

The next morning in Seoul we meet in a small corner office with a group of older gentlemen who each had been imprisoned in South Korea for expressing their opinions or trying to build peace. This is not ancient history. Shortly after I arrived in South Korea, a professor was being investigated by prosecutors under the National Security Act because he told his class that the Korean War "was a war for unification"—a view that happens to be shared by North Koreans and most credible historians. South Koreans cannot, without express government approval, attend meetings with North Koreans or publicly side with the DPRK on an issue.

The U.N. Human Rights Committee has termed the South Korean National Security Act, which authorizes prosecution for such violations or opinions, "a major obstacle to the full realization of the rights enshrined in the International Covenant on Civil and Political Rights." This failure to have an open democratic dialogue about history, aggression, and North/South relations still stand, a figurative Berlin Wall blocking transformation.

A seventy-one-year-old peacemaker in another NGO glows when I tell him about our peace efforts and support for reunification efforts without interference from Washington. Smiling, he begins clapping his hands together, saying "Yes, yes, yes." He had been to prison five times. He takes my hands in his with warmth and joy, saying, "Thank you, thank you." He, and other Korean peacemakers, had been waiting for years for America to hear them, to listen, to join shoulder-to-shoulder with them on a road to peace.

The Pink Elephant

Lushan, China—August 2005
During a break between trips to North and South Korea, I visit the

World Peace Park in Lushan, China, where life-sized statutes of world leaders form a ring of peace. A powerful silence surrounds the gathering of stone leaders in the Peace Park, though the symbolism of being the only visitor is not lost on me. China remains the pink elephant in the room with regard to why the US might not vigorously work for peace in Korea. A unified and peaceful Korea, with a combined population of seventy-seven million people, coupled with the growing economic power of China and increased trade with Japan, makes Asia an increasing threat to the economic interests of the United States. Already China is the largest manufacturing country in the world and has had an unparalleled growth rate for over twenty years. By maintaining instability in Asia, the US can justify its massive military presence and keep China at bay in its relations with South and North Korea and Japan. But isn't it time that we question whether this is in our national interest, and whether it reflects the world we want to see?

The groundwork for an inevitable arms race is being fostered with the construction of the massive Jeju Island Naval Station. The base is part of President Obama's strategy to shift military resources from Europe to Asia. We know all too well how an economic military battle can deplete the resources of any nation. Add to this the fact that South Korea has often been the largest importer of conventional weapons from the United States, and one can see living proof of Eisenhower's maxim that "we must guard against the acquisition of unwarranted influence, whether sought or unsought, by the military industrial complex." Sadly, it appears that economic fears may be trumping peace in the region.

Seoul, South Korea—2010

Horrific photos of unearthed remains and executions line their conference room walls, reminding the workers at the South Korean Truth and Reconciliation Commission of the heartache and importance of their mission. I'm in Seoul providing input into the TRC investigatory process. Between 1948 and the early days of the war in South Korea, according to the commission, more than 100,000 people were summarily executed and placed in mass graves by the South Korean government, often with US knowledge or participation. The photos and other evidence I've seen depicting acts of extreme barbarism, carpet-bombing of civilians, and torture have never been the subject of US inquiries or international condemnation. Instead we've survived by tucking it away as the "Forgotten War."

Seoul is bracing for the funeral of former President Roh, who had leapt to his death in response to sectarian politics, and police are blocking demonstrations in the streets. At the same time, ironically, the TRC Communications Officer is taking me south by train to venture deep into a mine shaft where bodies from mass executions by South Korean and US soldiers were dumped. There is evidence of more than two thousand such mass graves, but there's been time to excavate only a few dozen sites. The government has been anxious to cut off their funding, deciding they'd had enough truth. Like the South African perpetrator outside the hearing in full police uniform, the inquiry here is starting to knock at higher places.

I have to bend nearly in half to make it through the tunnel as I descend into a story of unspeakable horror. Holding the bones that still contain the stories and cries of the victim, my fingers slide into the bullet holes in the unearthed skulls. I glance skyward to the opening where the bodies were thrown from and the cries of the victims feel as if they've lingered for decades waiting to be heard. My chest is aching.

I meet Mr. Lee, who lost his entire family in the killings when he was a small boy. His sad eyes reveal a life of struggling for the truth and he describes how hard it was for the government to even acknowledge what happened. He and other family members led the movement for the formation of the Truth Commission, often holding fasts and sit-ins in an effort to be heard. Together they'd begun on their own to unearth remains, publicly presenting the bones until such raw images could not be ignored.

In a small office near the gravesite an elderly woman holds my hand and strokes it, describing how she lost her young husband to the massacres. I listen intently as she describes living the past half-century without him and existing in the shadow of the dark, mistrusting eyes of the government and community. The stain is borne by all families of the victims, for they were portrayed by the community as "them"—communists or the enemy.

I feel helpless. Inside I know there is little I can do, as statutes of limitations on civil actions have long expired and few forums exist to deal with forgotten war crimes. But I listen and tell her, "I understand. It must have been heart-breaking. I can only tell you that I will do all I can to work for peace so that he did not die in vain." As we get up to leave she is still holding my hand, as if I am the lifeline to her thread of hope—to her sense of justice. I almost have to pry myself free and I leave knowing I will never see her again—feeling impotent and saddened by the heartache borne by the battle between us and them that continues long after the guns go silent.

Saving Our Soul

Trying to heal the separation tragedy of Korea has been an amazing journey. We each play a role in creating a safer and more peaceful world. It took years, but I'm beginning to understand my role in this Korean work. The Koreans I meet here and abroad appreciate that a non-Korean American is willing to work for peace in their country. Their sense of valuing what I am doing hits me deeply. Yet for me it is not merely about helping others. I have come to see that I'm engaged in a deeply patriotic action for my own nation. For by achieving peace and reunification in Korea, and the removal of US forces, we actually look to save the soul of America. America must learn to apply its principles of equality and justice to its relationships around the world. But I also believe that we have the capacity to be the most compassionate and caring nation on earth and that such an approach will be the greatest antidote to division and terrorism.

This symbol of separation in Korea, like many others, must be broken for us to be whole again—to find our true selves. Korea is a metaphor for our fractured world and the struggle within us all. Inside we all seek unity, to break down the barriers that separate us, but too often are told that there is only us and them. How many of us compulsively walk our own internal demilitarized zone, armed and ready for battle? Can we lay down that part of ourselves and embrace peace?

The mirror in Korea provides us yet another opportunity to finally get it right. America has the opportunity to look in that mirror to see our own reflection and evaluate our actions. We can rediscover the nobleness of peacemaking and benefit from the reunification of our national heart and soul. We can meet the challenge posed by the South African grandmother before the TRC, of deciding "who we will be tomorrow."

▾ ▾ ▾

CHAPTER 28

No Ordinary American

True patriotism hates injustice in its
own land more than anywhere else.
–Clarence Darrow, Esq.

Miles from Nowhere

Ashland, Oregon—2008
"I'm with the FBI, ma'am. I'm looking for Eric Sirotkin."

I was curled up with a hot cup of South American Yerba Mate in my favorite coffee shop, Evos, a bohemian Ashland hangout, when I get the call.

"Eric. There's a man here looking for you. He says he's with the FBI," Shady says over the phone. "Is he in any trouble?" she asks, holding the phone where I could hear him.

"No. If he was in trouble there would be a lot more of us," he tells her with a smile.

What should I do? I've always advised people never talk to the FBI. You are not required to talk with them and your words can get turned back against you. Lying to a Federal agent about some innocent fact can be a felony. They sometimes get people they want to cause trouble for with a lie, instead of their original underlying reason for inquiry.

"Send him over," I tell her. This could be fun. "Tell him I'm wearing a blue shirt and a green coat."

But as she starts to describe me he stops her and says "I know what he looks like."

I thought of my first and only known FBI visit in 1957 when my mom held me in her arms and slammed the door on an agent who had come to our house seeking names and letting my parents know they were on their radar. I smiled, imagining them opening a subversive baby file on me after that visit.

When the agent arrives I can see from his ruffled collar that he must have taken one look at the hippie coffee house and removed his tie. He comes in and waves at me that he's going to the counter for a drink. I wave back and begin to wonder if I'm making a mistake. But I'm just too curious.

When he sits down he introduces himself and shakes my hand "I'm Miles," he says. "I'm with the Portland field office." I look around me, more worried about giving the wrong impression with my community than what faces me in my first FBI interview. I ask him for a card, something people often forget to do, so I can identify him later.

He slides it across the table starts in quickly, "You attended a conference in Lima, Peru sometime back, that included some North Koreans, is that right?"

"I did attend a 'peace conference' there."

"Do you remember the names of the people who were there?" Now he's bothering me.

"I'm sure I do, but I'm not about to talk about them with you." He perks up.

"Really? Why not?" Perhaps he thinks he has stumbled onto some grand conspiracy.

"Because I believe in the First Amendments right to freedom of association and I strongly believe that people should be able to attend a peace conference without ending up on an FBI list." I thought of my parents' stories of the FBI taking down license plate numbers at some of their gatherings in the 1950s.

He continues to push for some names and I tell him, "It's really not right to question ordinary Americans about their peace activity."

"But you're not an ordinary American." Glancing down at his list he says, "You've travelled to more than a dozen countries in the past three years. Not too ordinary."

I can see his notes. South Africa heads the list.

"Sorry, I'm not giving you any names. It's just not right," I tell him, still wondering who it was he was concerned about at the conference, which seemed like a ragtag, harmless event. Perhaps they are still chasing Latin America communists.

"Who pays for your trips?" he asks, hoping to find some link to a subversive or foreign agent.

I can't help but laugh. He seems puzzled.

"My wife wishes someone paid for my trips. I pay for them."

I didn't have to answer the question but I am trying to help him see that we are very committed people doing peace work, not subversives.

"Have you been in any email communication since then with any North Koreans?"

I hear a voice in my head saying, Eric, time to shut up.

"If you knew about North Korea you'd know that they don't have email outside of their country. I wish they had email because it's damn hard to get ahold of them to make travel arrangements."

A part of me wants to stand up and walk out, make some noise, call him some names, and let him know I am not on his "side." Instead I ask about his coffee and then decide to move on to give him some food for thought and show some understanding. I say, "Look. I know you guys have a tough job these days—especially since 9/11. It's such a delicate balance to try and avoid such things and protect civil liberties. You must be under a lot of pressure. But you have to maintain that balance. You have to remember what you are fighting to protect, what America values most: our freedoms. When you go and question, people please do it with an appreciation for the very rights you have sworn to protect."

He is looking down now. By finding the common ground—preserving American values—and using it as a teaching moment, I have shifted the energy and given him an insight into who I am rather than his initial impression that on paper I am some "unordinary" terrorist or anti-American peacenik. I call this approach "putting a human face on our us versus them biases."

The energy shifts. Instead of plowing forward he asks about what type of law I practice—as if they didn't know.

"Employment law primarily," I tell him.

He perks up again. "Really? Can I ask you a question?"

"Sure," I say, amused at his shifting attitude.

"My sister had a contract at work with this noncompete clause and she wants to get an idea if it's valid. She doesn't think it's fair." I smile. I give him some free legal advice and he thanks me profusely and leaves.

I glance around to see if anyone in the coffee shop has any idea what just happened at the little table by the window. Everything looks the same. All except me. I didn't draw a line in the sand, declare him the enemy, and tell him to go fuck himself. I stayed with it, ended up helping him with some legal advice, and explained to the FBI, which works for us as taxpayers, about balancing their job with the First Amendment. And I put a human face on a peacemaker.

A few years later I requested my FBI files under the Privacy Act. After many months and threats of litigation the file arrived and was most notable for the strange sketch of me by some police artist, and its heavily whited-out sections, page after page. It's more than two inches thick. I could go into court over the white-outs, but I have more important things to do than chase them into battle and argue over national insecurity. I'm determined to look forward, not back, and search for higher ground.

▾ ▾ ▾

CHAPTER 29

Reaching Higher

Man's proneness to engage in war is still a fact. But wisdom
born of experience should tell us that war is obsolete.
–Martin Luther King Jr.

Pyongyang, DPRK—April 15, 2012
My heart is aching after attending the grandiose parade with its flood of weaponry through Kim-il Sung Square. Waves of people hold plastic flowers above their heads. They pack the square, stretching for blocks back to the river's edge. More than ten thousand high-stepping soldiers pass before me and the crowd roars as a squadron of fighter planes loops in formation above us. Waves of tanks and truckloads of weapons appear to grow larger with each vehicle. The DPRK is clearly sending a message that it is ready to defend itself, but at what cost to its heart and soul? The international press is in a frenzy with this "defiant" parade of force, beaming the images across the planet.

The crowd cheers the armaments as if they'd just won the World Cup. Kim Jong-un looks right at me, clasping his hands together in a display of unity. Déjà vu from my first encounter with his father—a sensation the world experiences with the Kim dynasty in North Korea. But despite his warm smile I'm silent, unable to celebrate or praise military power as the answer to this conflict.

"How did you like it?" asks Mr. Bong, the vice president of the Democratic Lawyers Association of the DPRK, beaming with pride.

I cannot hide my feelings. "It deeply hurts me to see how we cheer weapons whose only real purpose or end-product is to kill women, children, and grandparents."

Mr. Bong's eyes grow larger, shocked by my reply. They are used to dealing with "comrades" whose politics offer unabashed support.

"Oh, no, no, no," he quickly adds. "Defensive only. Defensive. We must be able to defend ourselves."

Non-proliferation of nuclear weapons has been my passion, but climbing into their skin I understand their fear and why they feel they need such a bomb. A US Presidential Directive in September 2002 listed the DPRK as a target for "nuclear preemption." The Department of Defense had stated goals to effect "regime change," with strategies that include surprise military exercises designed "to force North Koreans to head for bunkers, and deplete valuable stores of food, water and other resources." Increasingly large war simulations with live ammunition have been undertaken along the border with more than 200,000 soldiers, naval vessels, and fighter jets, some of which are nuclear-capable. This doesn't make you want to invite someone to tea.

After the US invaded Iraq, the DPRK, issued a statement: "The Iraqi War teaches a lesson that in order to prevent a war and defend the security of a country and sovereignty of a nation it is necessary to have a powerful physical deterrent force." Considering the facts of the Iraq War—the mounting casualties, the use of torture, and even white phosphorous bombs that do dreadful damage to internal organs—it is far too simple to dismiss the DPRK's increased effort to develop a nuclear deterrent as the musings of a madman.

What's mad is that both sides still use militarization as a solution to conflict. After the parade in Pyongyang I express my sadness to the former deputy prime minister of Uganda, who had experienced a protracted military struggle in his homeland. He looks into my eyes and says, "We humans can be so cruel and senseless. Even lions only kill when they need to eat." It made me wonder about our self-designation as the "higher species."

I am invited by North Korean lawyers to speak on creative peacemaking at a 2012 conference in Pyongyang, during the centenary celebrations of the birth of their founder, Kim Il-sung. I jump at the chance to step up with a vision for another way of relating—to reach for our higher selves on a global level and integrate ubuntu. So far my time with North Koreans had been focused on building trust. Having integrated my ubuntu view of humanity with my legal work, I now turn to using it with my international activism.

Birthday Bash

I am invited to Kim Il-sung's one hundredth birthday party. A few years earlier I had visited the palace to formally pay respects to him— the "Eternal President" of North Korea. Like Mao or Ho Chi Minh, Kim's body has been preserved for viewing and as a reminder to his people that the revolution continues.

It was a solemn visit, and we were told to dress in our finest clothes. We had to pass many guards and metal detectors. No cameras were allowed. Mr. Pak, our translator and ever-smiling patent lawyer, and Mr. Bong, the KDLA Vice Chairman, accompaied us. When we entered the chamber we went through an air tunnel that blew all the dust and loose hairs off us. I think of how Mr. Pak, who was becoming quite bald, must have gone through many times. I was fully dusted and cleaner than I'd been in ages.

There Kim Il-sung lay, a few feet from us. We went to each side and bowed together on cue from Mr. Pak. I couldn't help but wonder what Kim's spirit thinks—if it's looking down on all this body worship.

On this commemorative birthday in Pyongyang, we gather in anticipation as a statue of the late Kim Jong-il is revealed from behind a giant drape next to his father's likeness. As with most things in the DPRK, it is huge and embarrassing in its grandiosity. To the sound of blaring, teeth-grating marching music, the drapes drop from the four-story statues to reveal father and son cast in bronze, smiling and soaring above the city. The crowd, numbering in the tens of thousands applauds and cheers. Across town, where a statue of Kim Il-sung rides a horse, Kim Jong-il now rides beside him. People have dual pins on their lapels with the faces of the late leaders. The images of Kim Jong-il appear taller, more lean, and warmer than his public persona. He rarely gave talks or appeared at public gatherings, perhaps daunted by his father's warm relationship with people.

Before me is the young new leader, Kim Jong-un. I'm struck by his resemblance to his grandfather. He's standing next to the giant bronze shoes of his father and grandfather's soaring statues, and the irony is not lost: he clearly has big shoes to fill. He smiles and waves at the crowd and heads to the podium to give, in somber tones, his first ever public address.

The pressures on this young twenty-eight-year-old must be overwhelming. He makes all the "right" statements of strength and military might, and the international press reports on his references to weapons and defending themselves. But some statements are overlooked: his calls to "walk hand-in-hand" with others who want peace with the DPRK, and his assertion that peace "is the ultimate and highest goal of any nation." People follow his every move and cheer with great passion.

Time will tell if he can rise above the division, us and them, and truly lead his nation to peace. It will take bold action. And the waiting-game strategy of the US, regime collapse, like peace, doesn't seem close. Some of the adoration for the Kim family is rooted in their traditional Confucian beliefs and its reverence for leadership, and it was Confucius who said, "He who learns but does not think, is lost. He who thinks but does not learn is in great danger." Same as it ever was.

Addiction

Taking a theme from the Alcoholics Anonymous playbook, I prepare my *Roadmap for Peace* as a formal twelve-step model. When an addict lives in denial, or says one thing and does another, we know there must be some intervention. Barack Obama spoke about breaking the cycle of isolation politics when he ran for president:

> When the world was on the brink of nuclear holocaust, Kennedy talked to Khrushchev and he got those missiles out of Cuba. Why shouldn't we have the same courage and the confidence to talk to our enemies? That's what strong countries do, that's what strong presidents do, that's what I'll do when I'm president.

While Obama's overtures to Iran and Cuba have changed the dynamic and opened doors, North Korea remains an enigma. Ending the Age of Separation's "enemy" mentality and accepting that on various levels we are all in this dance together, will help us survive and thrive as a planet.

More than forty years ago, while in jail during the Montgomery bus boycott, Dr. King asked: "Why should we love our enemies?" He said, "The first reason is fairly obvious. Returning hate for hate multiplies hate, adding deeper darkness to a night already devoid of stars. Darkness cannot drive out darkness; only light can do that. Hate cannot drive out hate; only love can do that." But then, critiquing our "get tough" approach to our "enemies," he said: "Hate multiplies hate, violence multiplies violence, and toughness multiplies toughness in a descending spiral of destruction." It's not that we have to kiss and embrace Fidel or Kim Jong-un, but isn't it time we at least showed up at the dance? Whether in law or international relations, it's not merely theoretical, but a moral imperative, to break through the denial of our true connected nature.

Today we are told that the "enemy" is the terrorist and we have no choice but to "get tough." We've moved from exploding cigars and poison to secret prisons, drone attacks, waterboarding, and other forms of torture while spawning a generation in Afghanistan, Libya, and Iraq who have lost families and friends to our war on terror. With the resulting "descending spiral of destruction" and martyrdom, it's clear the US has failed miserably to heed Dr. King's wise warning. We keep compulsively repeating our mistakes like an enemy junkie, addicted to divisiveness and to winning the next battle, denying the problems flowing from such behavior and feeling disconnected from one another and from the rest of the world.

As people of the United States of America, we need some truth and reconciliation with that part of ourselves that remembers our ubuntu nature and help our nation release its obsession with battling the enemy. It's never too late to break through the denial and reach out to those we've demonized, form a new alliance, a G-12 for peace, and stand and state "My name is America . . . and I'm an addict."

The Twelve-Step Model for Peace

Pyongyang, DPRK—April 2012
Nearly a decade after my first visit to North Korea I'm sitting in a round UN-style meeting room at a Pyongyang International Peace Conference. My name plate is the only one that reads *United States of America*. I'm speaking from my heart, echoing Mandela, Havel, and Tutu. I remind the gathering that "We are beings of unlimited potential and we have the power and creativity to break through this paralyzed state of war and conflict. But we have to be willing to let go of much that has defined our relationships for decades. We need a change in consciousness."

I outline the *Roadmap to Peace*, first to this Pyongyang audience and later provide it to the President of the Presidium, Kim Jong Nam. A few months later I take it to the US Congress and the State Department. The conflict in Korea continues to anchor the obsolete Age of Separation with its senseless cycle of militarism and gamesmanship, and prevents us achieving the world we can all imagine. But these twelve steps are also a new ubuntu-based perspective on international relations that can change the trajectory of the planet and our nation's relationship to the whole of humanity. It's the culmination of my long walk to ubuntu and it instills hope and opens the possibility that we all can join the new story.

STEP 1: LISTEN DEEPLY
Albert Einstein said, "Peace can never be achieved by force. It can only come through understanding." Step 1, Listen Deeply, has two elements: 1) dialogue with deep listening, and 2) talk without preconditions. I tell the conference that it's easy to "voice angst and anger, but what we need is to remember how to listen." I talk about the power of *empathetic listening* in international relations, wherein conflict can become a creative, rather than a destructive, force.

In Washington I share the same message and ask our leaders to climb into the shoes of the North Koreans to build understanding, saying that "Through my trips to the DPRK, I can say that we will never have peace until we listen to the trail of broken promises, accept that for them the war has not officially ended, and understand the role self-reliance, independence, and saving face holds in their culture."

STEP 2: FOCUS ON WHAT UNITES US
With Step 2, we acknowledge our common ground and share concerns. I draw from Václav Havel, the late poet, playwright, and president of the Czech Republic, who bravely reminded the US Congress that if we are to survive as a civilization, "We have no alternative but to shift the ray of our attention from that which separates us to that which unites us." Too often, we focus on what divides us and we miss the chance to move closer to peace and unity. And we are more alike than we know. In Pyongyang I told the peace gathering: "We raise our children with some of the same values: Truthfulness, fairness,

responsibility, and respect for life. We must bring these same values to the negotiating table, regardless of our political viewpoints."

STEP 3: BUILD HARMONY
Step 3 builds harmony through the power of creative exchanges in art, sports, and culture, and I stress the power of *experiencing beauty and playing together*. In Pyongyang in 2012 I met members of a Baptist men's choir from south of Atlanta who, on a Friendship Tour, lent their voices to peace, just as the New York Philharmonic had done. "We're all just people," one member told me. "We're here simply to sing."

Such exchanges have the power to heal, to remind us of our common humanity, and to represent the beauty that exists in harmony. It's no surprise that Tutu called ubuntu a communal "harmony" and the Navajos goal is hozho, "to achieve harmony." In this step we try to achieve what Dhyani Ywahoo described as the role of lawyers, comparing them to "musicians seeking to bring what appears as discord to a place of harmony."

STEP 4: RESPECT THE OTHER SIDE
This step requires us to demonstrate respect. In Washington I push hard on diplomatic relations and the failed policy of using it as a carrot or a stick. I ask State Department officials: "How do we have discussions about troop levels, nuclear weapons, missile launches, human rights, or other concerns if we don't have a sufficient relationship or show enough respect to say 'You are an independent nation'?" We should be on the ground everywhere, relating to our neighbors all over the world and showing them our respect. Even with countries such as China, Rumania, Saudi Arabia, Burma, Somalia and the Sudan, we abhor their human rights records but have diplomats and embassies to continue building relationship and providing the opportunity to model something greater.

STEP 5: PRACTICE NONRESISTANCE
In Step 5 we practice nonresistance, what the Buddhists call wu wei, in order to transcend hostility and break cycles of tit for tat. For too long we have allowed reactivity and anger to dictate our relationship with nations such as North Korea. Martin Luther King Jr. said,

"Violence begets violence . . . and its aftermath is tragic bitterness." Certainly with unspeakable violence and loss of life in the Korean War, and millions of separated families, much bitterness has been spawned. But the challenge is to take a higher road and break the chain of pain.

By disengaging from cycles of hostility, we tap into a deeper wisdom that allows them to wind down. An Aikido master, for example, does not respond to his opponent with anger or aggression, but uses his opponent's energy to guide him to a place where he can do no harm.

STEP 6: GROW UP

Name-calling and demonizing, even in private, does little except aggravate and further isolate the two sides of a conflict. Despite this, it has become the norm in our dealing with North Korea. Step 6 tells us to grow up: to release demonization and paternalism and move beyond good versus evil. President George W. Bush's reference to Kim Jong-il as that "Pygmy dictator" in the "axis of evil," or President Obama's infantilizing statement, "You don't get to bang your spoon on the table and somehow get your way" didn't change anything about North Korea's policies or bring us closer to peace. In mediation we call this type of language "you messages" that rarely lead to open dialogue and resolution. It's time to approach international relations with maturity and wisdom, rather than school yard taunts.

STEP 7: MOVE FROM REACTION TO RELATIONSHIP

In Step 7 we move from reaction to relationship so that we that we can reduce the tension that arises when a relationship is based upon conflict or domination. This is ubuntu. Peace is not the opposite of war, or simply a treaty obligation. It is a state of being and how we relate to one another. Without good relationships, it's quite challenging to have peace. As Archbishop Desmond Tutu once told me, "What I do to you I do to myself. Our humanity is all about relationship."

North and South Korea, for example, have unification ministers in their cabinets, a common language, 1,300 years of shared history, and written agreements to work toward peace and reunification. We can choose to foster these relationships rather than give in to reacting with war exercises, sanctions or troop deployments.

STEP 8: CHANGE TO A LANGUAGE OF PEACE

Both sides must think about what we value as human beings and cease making violent threats. In Pyongyang, where the policy is "Military First," and great pride is taken in armaments, I would remind officials: We all too often see war and the military as something glamorous and heroic. We talk of our weapons as a marvelous accomplishment or achievement in human ingenuity, ignoring that their end product is to kill and maim living beings. It's time to stop and change what we value. Nuclear weapons will not make us stronger or greater. Only peace can do that. Come to the table as the peacemaker.

The American government also needs to be called on its obsession with weaponry. "Smart" bombs and drone flights into Pakistan are seen as technological wonders and risk-free, but the corpses of children tell us otherwise. Putting a human face on such violence, and exercising compassion, is a step toward changing to a language of peace, and provides hope that some light will get in.

STEP 9: FORGIVE THE PAST AND MOVE FORWARD

In South Africa, Dullah Omar used to tell us that the true road to peace and reconciliation was to "forgive but not forget." The DPRK can learn much from the South African experience by forgiving the past and moving forward. I have seen how the North Koreans immerse themselves in the atrocities and tragedies of the past and seem unable to forgive, let go and move forward. While in the US we ignore the truth and dub the war "forgotten."

In search for common ground I tell them both that while we can't change history, we can all honor the dead and acknowledge the pain to the families left behind on all sides. When peace calls it is not the time to point fingers but to rebuild trust. Forgiving means accepting that it's time to move on. I challenge both sides of any and all conflicts to discover the path forward.

STEP 10: REDEFINE THE STORY

British philosopher Bertrand Russell once wrote, "What is demanded is a change in our imaginative picture of the world." Step 10 calls us to redefine our story by reaching for a higher level by basing international relations on relationship. The fragile and too-often painful state of the world is not what any caring person would wish for others. By being stuck in old conflicts we miss out on the chance to collaborate on a healthier planet. Instead of teaching our citizens to mistrust or hate we can help them rediscover a higher purpose to their lives and relationships. But to do so requires releasing a very old and entrenched story that has defined our generation.

It would be a major change for the United States to move from the militarism and power-over model to a new role of engagement and a shared planetary stewardship, or power-with. Korea provides the perfect template to redefine our story and lead with both our head and our heart. It's what all people crave deeply.

STEP 11: DEVELOP A CONVERSION STRATEGY

The Armistice Agreement signed in 1953 by the United States promised that negotiations would take place so that all foreign troops would leave Korea. The Chinese left in 1958 and the Soviets years before. The US has never left. A peaceful Korean peninsula allows the US to bring its troops home.

The challenge for the US is to not only declare our commitment to peace, but to transform our nation's identity from the most powerful military to the most caring, respectful, and humanitarian country on the planet. It takes thinking outside the box wherein a conversion strategy emerges. Around the world we maintain more than 800 military bases. Perhaps food distribution centers would bolster our national security more than military instillations.

The Korean Demilitarized Zone, now filled with land mines and troops poised to fight, could become a park for peace, ecology, history, and culture. Its unique ecosystem can offer up to the world a prime example of what is possible when we choose the path of peace. It's never too late to change direction. I challenged the US Congress to remember the words of Thomas Paine during the American Revolution in 1776, to make this an opportunity "to start the world over again."

STEP 12: LET GO OF THE ROPE

The final step on this pathway to peace calls to mind the game tug-of-war, in which the two sides pull on a rope in opposite directions. If one side uses its force to pull the other over the line they win. But we forget that if a nation lets go of the rope, the war also ends. In both Washington and Pyongyang I implored them to embrace the courage it takes to unilaterally let go, declare peace and end the state of war.

Such actions are not only helpful, but mandatory as the UN General Assembly passed a resolution in 1984 making it a "sacred duty" for all nations to "eliminate even the threat of war." We think of the right to live in peace as something that governments negotiate, but it is a way of life, a right belonging to the people of the world.

But when the United States, for example, runs provocative war games, fails to recognize a nation's right to exist, occupies another country with tens of thousands of troops, and gives up working proactively to negotiate an end to this state of war, it is not complying with its legal duty under the resolution to "remove the threats to the peace." We have been tightly clasping the rope and pulling with all our might.

John Lennon and Yoko Ono sang: "War is over. If you want it." I didn't fully grasp his meaning or why he put it on billboards around the world in the 1970s. But now I know that is incumbent upon the people of the United States to demand of their leaders their right to peace, and for the DPRK it is time to unilaterally declare the war over. This does not mean surrender or weakness; it will be a demonstration of great courage and strength of the higher ground we all seek.

If we follow the principles underlying these twelve steps, we can break the addictive cycle and create a durable peace—reshaping our world, our work and our relationships into something we all desire. Korea, like the legal profession, have been sustained by obsolete ideas of war, separation and aggression. I was likely the first person in North Korea to quote William Jennings Bryan, a late nineteenth-century American politician, when I shared with the peace conference attendees his words: "Destiny is not a matter of chance; it is a matter of choice; it is not a thing to be waited for, it is a thing to be achieved."

▾ ▾ ▾

When I finish my presentation of these twelve steps at the conference, I'm surrounded by North Koreans and others from around the world thanking me for "finally truly including peace in the discussion." But it was the young North Koreans' appreciation that struck me deeply; it appeared to spark some hope in their hearts and they, like their young leader, are the future.

Gandhi once said that the "goal of reconciliation is not to bring adversaries to their knees, but to their senses." The world is waiting for us to assume the responsibility that goes hand-in-hand with power—to model a new way to relate in the twenty-first century—to institute Ben Franklin's vision that "America's destiny is not power, but light."

▾ ▾ ▾

Principles of compassion and connection are inner paths to guide individual behavior, but when reflected outwardly they have the power to heal the planet. Without the space and safety to speak one's truth, there can be no reconciliation. But human beings have an innate desire and capacity to forgive and it's this deep knowing that keeps hope alive in my heart that even the US and North Korea can forgive the past and forge a new relationship—*if we can awaken humanity in the hearts of our leaders and citizens.* This is where the people must become active witnesses and lead, and then the leaders will follow.

▾ ▾ ▾

On my last evening in Pyongyang I'm listening to a beautiful classical performance of string instruments. Leaning against a column in the dining room, I am overcome with emotion at the thought that we would consider bombing a nation and killing such beauty. I thought of the children killed at Sinchon, or the 500,000 children UNICEF says died owing to the US economic embargo in Iraq, and wondered about the beauty lost, the great voices likely silenced. Ubuntu consciousness opens a heart awareness to "all our children" and it becomes only natural to actively stand for peace.

Freedom is not simply a question of free elections or democracy, but building bridges across the great divides between people. The Age of Separation has kept us as human beings from truly tasting freedom. The antidote lies in living with ubuntu. Archbishop Tutu once told me that "separation" is a human "contradiction." When we understand that our success is intrinsically linked to yours, all boats rise. But first, as both individuals and nations we must remove the chains we have placed across our hearts and minds.

▾ ▾ ▾

CHAPTER 30
Home

It is from numberless diverse acts of courage and belief that human history is shaped. Each time a man stands up for an ideal, or acts to improve the lot of others, or strikes out against injustice, he sends forth a tiny ripple of hope, and crossing each other from a million different centers of energy and daring those ripples build a current which can sweep down the mightiest walls of oppression and resistance.
–Robert F. Kennedy, Cape Town, South Africa, 1966

Living as we think human beings should live, in defiance of all that is bad around us, is itself a marvelous victory.
–Howard Zinn

Hiroshima

The bullet train reaches 200 miles per hour as I'm heading south to the city of Hiroshima—forever etched in our vocabulary as place of great injury and heartache. It is now a bustling city, rebuilt from the ashes, but at ground zero they have left the lone shell of the round tower that remained after the bombing. The site has been converted to a peace park dedicated to non-aggression. In the museum they confront both Japanese imperial aggression as well as the American bomb.

I walk through the park in silence. It is a place all Americans should visit. I remember how it moved Judge Madrid to open her courtroom to truth in the Kirtland case years before. For me it is a peace pilgrimage, an acknowledgement of the insanity of violence. There are thousands of paper cranes—symbols of peace from school children around the world. But it's not lost on me that these symbols of peace are, like our fragile state, paper thin.

My body shakes visibly as I move through the park. A strong pulse strikes me to the core as the wind rises up, sweeping my face. But then the cries. It's people screaming. I shake my head and look around but see no one. The energy remains—imprints of people screaming, children crying. The three-year-old still clinging to his tricycle as the firestorm raged or the shadows on the steps where the man sat waiting for the bank to open that morning, his body outline scorched forever into the concrete. What could warrant incinerating people in this fashion? What message did it send? Was not a part of our humanity lost in that firestorm on August 6, 1945? Hiroshima does not sleep until we really learn that "an injury to one is an injury to all."

Grasping the rope firmly, I send a log crashing against the Hiroshima Bell of Peace with a force aimed at reaching across time. The sound cuts right through me as I soak in its lingering vibration. As I leave the bell dome the cries subside, as if my hopeful ringing out for peace has stilled their restless spirits, who long simply to finally be heard.

Hanoi

Hanoi feels alive and bustling with pride. Strolling around the lake in central Hanoi, I'm swept away by so many lovers embracing on park benches, rows of elderly women doing Tai Chi on the lawn, or the bride posing for photos in an ancient arch. So many smiles. They had been our enemy. We once sought to kill them as they sought to kill us as invaders, but now we have normalized relations and extensive trade ties. It's a powerful symbol that we can replace war with peace.

Outside of the city in Ha Ta Province I visit Friendship Village U.S.A., home of more than a hundred victims of Agent Orange, a dioxin-contaminated herbicide America used as part of our chemical warfare to destroy forests and deprive the enemy of food and shelter during the war in Vietnam. The project, which provides education, healthcare, and vocational skills, was started by George Mizo, a Vietnam war veteran, to help heal the wounds of war. George says, "The horrible experiences during the war and the suffering of everybody on all sides inspired me to do something that would be a living symbol of peace, reconciliation, and hope."

I'm struck by the feeling of love when I look at the smiles of the children born with deformations from the toxins we sprayed into their DNA. We play games and help them with art projects. There is much laughter and some tears. The young people do not see the world as us versus them, and their welcome is nonjudgmental and caring. These children are our children, and it's once again ubuntu.

Moving out into the sunshine and heat of summer, I wander through a vine-covered arch into their organic herb and vegetable garden. Friendship Village exudes the very peace they seek to build. Thich Nhat Hanh, a Vietnamese Buddhist monk and one of my heroes for bringing peace home, comes to mind. Martin Luther King, Jr. nominated Nhat Hanh for the Nobel Peace Prize in 1967, and he had the distinct honor of being banned by both sides of the conflict in Vietnam as he spoke out for peace and against the violence sweeping the country. His mindfulness retreats have helped thousands of individuals seek peace in their hearts, and in their world.

Thich Nhat Hanh sees peace as part of our everyday lives: "Every day we do things, we are things that have to do with peace. If we are aware of our life . . . our way of looking at things, we will know how to make peace right in the moment, we are alive." My efforts in South Africa, Korea, and Cuba have felt like a natural step toward peace and ubuntu, as they were countries caught in the politics of separation. But for most of us it's in everyday life that peace plays out. As a lawyer, I've come to work hard to find the healing space for the client and help them find peace within, while diminishing the battle outside. Each person I meet, whether the judge, opposing lawyers, or witnesses, gives me an opportunity to celebrate and remember ubuntu. Doing so makes me feel alive, connected, and part of a greater human family.

Before leaving Vietnam I traverse rice paddies and reeds along the Yen Vi river. I see only a few fisherman and the tips of pointed country hats peeking out above the fields. Closing my eyes, I can hear the sound of gunfire and feel empathy for the fear and confusion that soldiers felt as they too came downstream in search of the hidden enemy.

I descend deeply into the cave to a huge Perfume Pagoda where people come to make peace offerings . . . or prayers to help in landing a husband. The cave was a sanctuary, protecting thousands during the US bombing campaign. As I light incense along the wall, a ray of sunshine streams down the entrance and I bask in a magical light. Much of my lifetime has been a quest for light and clarity. I've challenged war, multinational corporations, and governmental abuse, but in the end saw that there were no demons to conquer, only the hate or fear in my heart.

My journey from warrior to peacemaker has taught me that every human life is sacred, and reaching across the world, the congressional aisle, or our street to connect with another human being provides a palette with which to paint the essence of being human. We are, after all, spiritual beings having a human experience where we can choose to awaken and move beyond the age of separation, and live in the new story of ubuntu.

For every atom belonging to me as good belongs to you.
–Walt Whitman

▾ ▾ ▾

Gratitude

To my parents, still rocking at 90, who gave me the compassion gene and a belief that the world deserved peace and justice.

To my boys Khlari and Sasha, whose love, creativity, and musical talent brought me to that deep place between the notes.

To my sister Jeanne, a skilled and passionate writer who in the late 1960's floated to San Francisco, but kept her baby brother's long winded letters for over 45 years. And to my brother Allan, whose chocolate, maple syrup, and courage never ceases to amaze.

To my Relentless Optimists crew, Bill, Jeff, Will, Jack, Bill and John, who cheered me on, let me safely break open my heart, and helped guide me to a new dawn and life.

To Shady, who taught me to trust my inner voice and supported me thinking and living out of the box. Who loved me even as my love faded and despite the painful choices that ensued, was always willing to love.

To Viviette, who found me after so many years, restored my faith in myself and love and was miraculously there to welcome my heart when I landed.

To those who gave me manuscript feedback and deep encouragement over the years, from Garry, Shoshana, Natania, Will, Jeff, and, of course, my publishers Steve and Stephen.

To all my Relations. Who gave me the stories and signposts within Witness, and helped me understand the essence of being human.

To the people of South Africa and the Korean Peninsula, who welcomed me in their homes and hearts, who dared to dream of something greater, and who still struggle today to find their way from painful separation to Ubuntu.

To the planet that reminds us that we as powerful as a mountain and as insignificant as a drop in the ocean. But always reminding us that collectively we are powerful and can sweep down the mightiest walls of resistance and oppression.

About the Author

ERIC SIROTKIN helps people and nations navigate conflict in a way that enhances their well-being and health. He trains lawyers to integrate wellness principles into their practices to benefit both themselves and their clients wherein the conflict becomes an opportunity for transformation and growth.

Since 1981 he has engaged in complex litigation in many cases against major multi-billion dollar corporations, universities, and governmental entities that have addressed constitutional violations, free speech rights, discrimination, fraud, and more. He served as an adjunct professor of law at the University of New Mexico School of Law and regularly guest lectures on campuses.

Around the world he has spoken about ubuntu, peace and justice, and engaged in peacebuilding activities in India, Peru, Cuba, South Africa, Japan, Vietnam, North and South Korea, France, Canada, the Netherlands, and China. In 1991 he assisted with the new Constitution in South Africa, was a UN-sponsored election observer at President Mandela's election, and coordinated the International Monitoring Project of the South African Truth and Reconciliation Commission. It was through this experience that he learned about the wisdom of ubuntu and interjected a new more holistic method to his efforts to resolve conflict and into his life.

Eric helped found the New Mexico Human Rights Coalition, the Ashland Culture of Peace Commission, the Ubuntuworks Education Project, the NLG Korean Peace Project and is the Executive Producer of the award-winning film *Committing Poetry in Times of War*. He was the recipient of the City of Albuquerque Human Rights Award.

Eric received his Juris Doctorate from the University of Detroit School of Law. He maintains an active law practice in Albuquerque, New Mexico and is the CEO of Interactive Entertainment Company, whose patented processes are impacting the convergence of television, the internet and reality. His boys also let him tag along as their business manager in their music careers and he has built homes of adobe, straw bale, and other ecological materials in New Mexico, Oregon, and Mexico.

To contact Eric write him at eric@ericsirotkin.com or visit www.ericsirotkin.com.